SARA HOLBROOK & MICHAEL SALINGER
with STEPHANIE HARVEY

From Striving to Thriving WRITERS

Strategies That Jump-Start Writing

D1592949

SCHOLASTIC

This book is dedicated with love to our dear friend,
Bonnie Campbell Hill, who introduced us to the
world, and to another lifelong friend, Janet Allen,
who introduced us to Bonnie.

Photos ©: 33–35, 50: Courtesy of Stephanie Harvey; 80 bottom: quietbits/Shutterstock; 88: Potapov Alexander/Shutterstock. Photos © Shutterstock (by slide): 1 (Prath), 3 (Potapov Alexander), 6 (quietbits), 7 (Maxger), 8 (lukmanhakim), 20 (Yganko). All other images courtesy of Michael Salinger.

Credits: Pages 41 and 44: "Angry Me" by Sara Holbrook from *Nothing's the End of the World*. Copyright © 1995 by Sara Holbrook. Originally published by Boyds Mills Press. Used by permission of the author. Page 50: "The Library" by Sara Holbrook from *The Poetry Friday Anthology®*. Copyright © 2012 by Sara Holbrook. Originally published by Pomelo Books. Used by permission of the author. Page 59: "Happy Moves" by Sara Holbrook. Copyright © 2018 by Sara Holbrook. Published by Scholastic Inc.; "Happy Glow" by Sara Holbrook. Copyright © 2018 by Sara Holbrook. Published by Scholastic Inc.; "Jubilant" by Michael Salinger from *Well Defined: Vocabulary in Rhyme*. Copyright © 2009 by Michael Salinger. Originally published by Boyds Mills Press. Used by permission of the author. Pages 95 and 97: "If I Were a Gear" by Michael Salinger from *The Poetry Friday Anthology® for Science*. Copyright © 2014 by Michael Salinger. Originally published as "Gears" by Pomelo Books. Used by permission of the author. Pages 103 and 105: "Brave" by Sara Holbrook. Copyright © 2018 by Sara Holbrook. Used by permission of the author. Page 111: "Luck" by Sara Holbrook from *By Definition: Poems of Feelings*. Copyright © 2003 by Sara Holbrook. Originally published by Boyds Mills Press. Used by permission of the author. Page 130: "Then & Now" by Michael Salinger. Copyright © 2018 by Michael Salinger. Published by Scholastic Inc. Page 131: "I Used to Be" by Elizabeth Thomas. Copyright © 2018 by Elizabeth Thomas. Published by Scholastic Inc. by arrangement with the author. Page 133: "The American Bison" by Sara Holbrook from *High-Impact Writing Clinics*. Copyright © 2013 by Sara Holbrook. Originally published by Corwin, a division of SAGE Publications Ltd. Used by permission of the author. Page 139: "Where Does the Sky Begin" by Michael Salinger from *The Poetry Friday Anthology® for Science*. Copyright © 2014 by Michael Salinger. Originally published by Pomelo Books. Used by permission of the author. Page 163: "To Be" by Sara Holbrook. Copyright © 2018 by Sara Holbrook. Published by Scholastic Inc. Page 178: "Mountain Bike Soufflé" by Michael Salinger. Copyright © 2018 by Michael Salinger. Published by Scholastic Inc. Pages 178 and 180: "Recipe for a Tall Tale" by Sara Holbrook. Copyright © 2018 by Sara Holbrook. Published by Scholastic Inc. Page 186: "Found Poem" by Michael Salinger. Copyright © 2018 by Michael Salinger. Published by Scholastic Inc.; excerpt from *The Enemy: Detroit, 1954* by Sara Holbrook. Copyright © 2017 by Sara Holbrook. Published by Calkins Creek, an imprint of Highlights for Children, Inc. Used by permission. Page 187: Excerpt from *Twelve Days in May: Freedom Ride 1961* by Larry Dane Brimner. Copyright © 2017 by Larry Dane Brimner. Published by Calkins Creek, an imprint of Highlights for Children, Inc. Used by permission. Page 196: "My Official List" by Sara Holbrook. Copyright © 2018 by Sara Holbrook. Published by Scholastic Inc. Page 221: "When I Ride My Bike" by Michael Salinger. Copyright © 2018 by Michael Salinger. Published by Scholastic Inc. Page 224: "Nocturnal" by Sara Holbrook and Michael Salinger. Copyright © 2018 by Sara Holbrook and Michael Salinger. Published by Scholastic Inc. Page 230: "My Brother" by Sara Holbrook. Copyright © 2018 by Sara Holbrook. Published by Scholastic Inc.; "Disappointment" by Sara Holbrook. Copyright © 2018 by Sara Holbrook. Published by Scholastic Inc. Pages 230 and 231: "911" by Michael Salinger. Copyright © 2018 by Michael Salinger. Published by Scholastic Inc. Pages 249 and 251: "100% Me!" by Sara Holbrook. Copyright © 2018 by Sara Holbrook. Published by Scholastic Inc. Page 252: "100% Firefighter" by Michael Salinger. Copyright © 2018 by Michael Salinger. Published by Scholastic Inc. Page 264: "Use Your Voice" by Sara Holbrook and Michael Salinger. Copyright © 2018 by Sara Holbrook and Michael Salinger. Published by Scholastic Inc.
All rights reserved.

Publisher/Content Editor: Lois Bridges
Editorial Director: Sarah Longhi
Development Editor: Raymond Coutu
Production Editor: Danny Miller
Senior Editor: Shelley Griffin
Assistant Editor: Molly Bradley
Art Director: Brian LaRossa
Interior Designer: Maria Lilja

ISBN-13: 978-1-338-32168-5
ISBN-10: 1-338-32168-4

1 2 3 4 5 6 7 8 9 10   14   27 26 25 24 23 22 21 20 19 18

Text pages printed on 30% PCW recycled paper.

SPECTRUM OF THRIVING WRITER BEHAVIORS, ATTITUDES, AND UNDERSTANDINGS

A sampling you might monitor, document, and analyze

Knowledge of Genre, Format, and Text Type

- Writes regularly in a variety of genres and text types and, as a result, becomes confident and skilled in those genres and text types
- Recognizes and replicates various text formats, such as essays, stories, reports, and poetry, as well as text types, such as persuasive, procedural, narrative, and expository
- Attends to text structures when crafting fiction and nonfiction
- Understands the importance of using verifiable citations
- Considers audience and purpose when choosing a genre, format, and/or text type
- Studies mentor texts and uses knowledge gained from them in personal writing
- Incorporates both the graphic and text features in all genres

Knowledge Acquisition

- Activates and builds background knowledge
- Writes to both inform and learn
- Reads, writes, speaks, listens, and thinks across content areas
- Researches questions, follows a line of inquiry
- Engages in, cares for, and takes action through writing
- Exercises good digital citizenship when researching on the Web and writing on a device

Writing Process

- Thinks dynamically to construct meaning from personal writing and the writing of others
- Conveys the literal and implied meaning of text
- Uses a variety of text elements to construct meaning
- Reflects understanding through retelling
- Uses and evidences comprehension strategies when constructing text
  » Explores connections
  » Asks questions
  » Leaks information onto the page, nudging the reader to infer
  » Shows, not tells, allowing readers to visualize
  » Focuses on important information
  » Summarizes and synthesizes
- Monitors writing to ensure it expresses meaning
- Expresses understanding concisely and precisely
- Revises to clarify meaning

Vocabulary Development

- Chooses words carefully
- Puts academic words into action through voluminous writing
- Uses an expanding content-rich vocabulary to express understanding
- Collaborates to figure out words to expand understanding
- Recognizes and uses figurative language to enrich text
- Crafts strong sentences by using words in a variety of ways
- Understands the difference between objective and subjective terms in their own writing and others'
- Chooses appropriate vocabulary and genre to reach the chosen audience

Spectrum of Writing Behaviors

Language

- Uses the entire linguistic repertoire for making meaning
- Collaborates with others to ensure the writing makes sense
- Experiments with language, crafting versions that grow in sophistication
- Considers organization and structure and their impact on the reader
- Works toward logical development of ideas
- Uses written and spoken language to synthesize information across content areas
- Recognizes multilingualism as an asset
- Communicates well through writing and speaking
- Expresses voice as a writer

Fluency

- Reads personal writing and the writing of others with expression
- Practices PIPES (projection, inflection, pacing, eye contact, and stance) when reading and speaking publicly

Conventions

- Demonstrates developing control of punctuation: periods, capital letters, commas, exclamation marks for a variety of purposes, apostrophes for contractions, apostrophes for possessives, etc.
- Demonstrates developing control of conventional spelling
- Demonstrates developing control of conventional grammar
- Uses conventions to enhance meaning

Volume

- Writes extensively in all content areas
- Is comfortable using written language to express ideas
- Builds empathy through writing from multiple points of view
- Enjoys discussing writing with others and refining it

Focus Skills by Framework

Framework	Grades	Persuasive	Descriptive	Narrative	Procedural	Research	Vocabulary	Figurative Language
Picture This, p. 48	K and up	x						x
Refrain Again, p. 101	K and up	x	x					x
Scaffolding Into Sharing, p. 255	K and up	x			x			
Inside Outside, p. 161	1–4		x			x		
My Official List, p. 194	1–5							
Simile of Me, p. 219	1–6		x	x		x		x
Then and Now, p. 128	1–8			x		x		
Feelings Made Visual, p. 39	1 and up		x	x			x	x
In My Opinion, p. 210	1 and up	x	x				x	x
100% Me, p. 247	1 and up		x			x	x	x
Harnessing Rhyme, p. 109	2 and up		x	x		x	x	x
Point of View, p. 93	3 and up		x	x		x		x
Mentoring Metaphor, p. 227	3 and up		x	x		x	x	x
Compare/Contrast, p. 168	4–8	x	x	x		x	x	x
Pinpointing Vocabulary, p. 57	4 and up		x	x		x	x	x
Personification, p. 67	4 and up		x	x			x	x
Virtual Haiku Hike, p. 86	4 and up		x			x	x	x
Wonder of Wonders, p. 137	4 and up			x		x		
What's the Story? p. 152	4 and up			x		x		
Recipes for Success, p. 176	4 and up		x	x	x	x		x
Found Poem, p. 184.	4 and up		x	x		x	x	x
Memoir, p. 200	4 and up		x	x				x
The Academic Essay, p. 144	5–8	x	x	x		x	x	x
Sentence Variety Pack, p. 30	5 and up	x	x	x		x	x	
Prepositionally Speaking, p. 77	5 and up		x	x		x	x	
Informercial, p. 118	5 and up	x	x	x		x	x	
Extended Metaphor, p. 235	6 and up		x	x		x	x	x

CONTENTS

The Purpose of Writing With Purpose

Language, both oral and written, is relatively easy to learn when we have a real purpose for using it (Halliday, 2004). This book is about helping our students harness the power of language to accomplish their own purposes for writing: to tell a story, to investigate an issue, to prioritize information, to persuade a reader, and to generally inform. Building on real reasons to write, writing frameworks jump-start writing and other communication skills—and in this way, help *all* students become thriving writers.

Steph: We need to explain what we mean by writing frameworks.

Michael: Writing frameworks are dynamic, flexible scaffolds that help kids create a repertoire of strategies for communicating ideas.

Sara: Writing frameworks engage kids in writing to deepen content understanding as they zero in on specific writing strategies, elements, and components that may be woven together to create more complex text.

Steph: The writing frameworks in this book help to build skillful, confident writers. Although we often talk about teaching kids "the skills," you can't actually teach a skill. A skill is something we have or we aspire to. We want to be skillful soccer players, skillful musicians, skillful readers, and skillful writers. Strategies are deliberate, whereas skills, once you've acquired them, are automatic (Afflerbach, Pearson, & Paris, 2008). We explicitly teach crafting strategies so our kids develop into skillful writers. Frameworks teach crafting strategies that lead to skillful writing.

Michael: The frameworks themselves are kind of like training wheels that we are going to toss to the side as students begin to get their balance and ultimately become skillful cyclists.

We aim to get kids writing in every discipline, build their confidence and capabilities, and familiarize them with the elements of strong writing, from engaging leads to effective comparisons to memorable conclusions. Steph and her co-author Annie Ward showed educators everywhere how to support striving readers in their book, *From Striving to Thriving: How to Grow Confident, Capable Readers* (2017). Writing frameworks grow confident, capable writers.

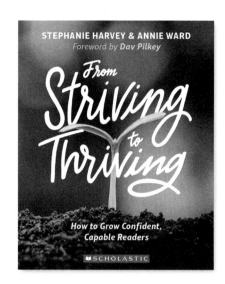

Too often in our classroom visits, we hear students proclaim, "I am not a writer." Echoing Steph and Annie (citing Johnston, 2004, and Dweck, 2014), we respond with a single word: *yet. You are not a writer yet*. We want to see all our students become knowledgeable, eager, and effective communicators.

Why are so many students so bummed out about writing? Striving writers, like striving readers, often have had negative experiences. Perhaps they haven't had enough scaffolded writing support to become familiar with the process, or they have been expected to write in isolation and felt put on the spot, unable to toss ideas around with peers. Students may be writing in journals or responding to prompts, filling in worksheets, or attempting to emulate mentor text. But without an authentic purpose to write, explicit instruction, and lots of practice, many of those efforts don't result in improved writing and, therefore, communication skills.

Children learn to write by writing—a lot—for a real purpose about things that matter to them. We know that striving readers thrive when they find books that engage and delight them and begin to read voluminously. In a similar way, we want our students to practice voluminous writing!

As professional writers, we can tell you that (fortunately) there is no one correct way to compose text, nor one reason to compose it, for that matter. But there is always that driving force, a desire to reach an audience, a sense of purpose. This is why we most often pair our writing lessons with content area learning, affording students the opportunity to deepen and evidence their understanding about topics that they care about. And kids recognize this. They can see that writing about igneous rocks or reptiles helps them learn. We give them an authentic reason to write and step-by-step instruction on how to make that happen.

Michael: Ever been a witness to a kid's sporting event where one team is playing above its league? The results are predictably disastrous, leaving the losers feeling like, well, losers.

Sara: We see this happening with student writers all the time. Being asked to replicate complex text without explicit instruction is like asking kids to play above their level, a quick road to disengagement. They just give up.

When it comes to mentor text, immersion without instruction may lead to floundering. This is why we always co-construct short text with students before turning them loose to discuss and write in pairs. We show them exactly how the process works and how to be writers before they venture out on their own. We want students to head into the writing experience with "energy, action, and confidence rather than dread" (Harvey & Ward, 2017).

We create a culture of conversation throughout the writing process. Students discuss the craft and content of their writing, practice reading the mentor text aloud, and read their own writing aloud throughout the composition process. A culture of conversation is essential for all students, but especially so for strivers and students who are just finding their way into English (Echevarria & Goldenberg, 2017).

Marshaling the full force of literate communication means reading, writing, speaking, and listening. But too often speaking and listening fall by the wayside because they're difficult to evaluate and, let's face it, they're not on the test. Still, what skill is more important than expressing oneself clearly and confidently? This is why we provide more than one speaking/listening opportunity in every framework. Again, we are building a culture of conversation. As Richard Allington (2012) asserts, "If we wish to help children and adolescents become thoughtfully literate, classroom talk around texts is critical."

Why Writing Frameworks?

There are many benefits to writing frameworks. In this section, we explain some of them.

Writing frameworks stimulate thinking and offer students multiple ways to organize their thoughts. They help students expand, synthesize, articulate, and share their literacy and content area knowledge. More importantly, our framework process emphasizes reading, discussion, partner research, composition, rereading, revision, and sharing, building both content knowledge and communication skills. This culture of conversation—student-to-student interaction and oral language support—is especially important for English learners and for "children who have not been exposed at home to the kind of language found in written text" (Dickinson & Smith, 1994).

Furthermore, Sal Kahn, of the Kahn Academy, points out that too often we teach concepts within arbitrary time constraints, allotting a few hours or days to teach a concept, and then we test. Students show 70, 85, or 95 percent understanding of the subject, and we move on. The problem is that at some point students will hit a wall because there are gaps in background knowledge. And when that happens, they disengage. Our goal is to keep every student engaged, thinking, and writing about their learning.

Writing frameworks generate student work that can grow into essays, fiction and nonfiction pieces, speeches, and poems—and provide you with material for formative assessments. Our frameworks can help scaffold learning in any genre of any text type. They zero in on practical writing strategies and creative elements and can "plug into" any existing writing resource or program.

Writing frameworks are doable. We give students a graphic organizer called a GO Sheet to manage their raw material before they begin to write. (See the next page for details.) Striving writers find success while they practice the craft of writing. Their confidence grows as they think through and organize their thoughts into fluent text. Our thriving writers benefit because the frameworks help them focus their knowledge and creative ideas. And ultimately, our frameworks go a long way in turning striving writers into thriving writers, which is our goal.

Fifth-grade students in Elyria, Ohio, share the contents of their GO Sheets before transitioning to their Chromebooks to write.

GO SHEETS

The optional graphic organizer that accompanies most frameworks, which we call a GO Sheet, is *not* a worksheet. A worksheet is finished when all the blanks are filled in. A GO Sheet is a way to organize thoughts, facts, and details *before* the writing begins. If you choose, your students can work in their notebooks instead. But the GO Sheets provide a scaffold, of sorts, that helps students hit the ground running. As a prewrite, it functions as an outline that students can use as a reference, guiding and enriching their compositions. Ready. Set. Go, go, go!

A Few Questions Answered

In this section we answer a few questions we've been asked about our approach—and you may be asking yourself.

Won't frameworks kill creativity in my students?

Assigned topics and structured prewrites do not preclude creative writing. In fact, too much choice can be overwhelming to striving writers. Instead, we suggest topics inspired by content area lessons, using writing frameworks to simultaneously build content area and literacy know-how as well as writing skill. In this way, we help all students become "agents of text," rather than victims of it. As a result, their confidence and capabilities grow because they're using writing to serve their own purposes for writing (Harste, 2018).

Writers gather and examine facts before applying their creative talents. Writing frameworks help students do that and more. They provide students with a variety of ways to organize their thinking—a bulging pencil case of implements to use to express their ideas and understanding, as well as time to think and practice.

Sometimes creativity is perceived as merely a by-product of self-reflection,

A victim of too many choices.

separate from the business of learning. No fewer than a dozen books on creative writing contain the phrase "writing from the inside out" in their titles. All of them promise that self-examination of our innermost selves, our most heartfelt thoughts and feelings, unlock the creative writer within. This sentiment is so pervasive that it is almost embarrassing for us to raise our hands and say, "Yeah, but…"

Yeah, but we are creative writers by profession, and while *inside out* is a romantic depiction of the writer's existence, it is rarely the way we write. We believe it is rarely the way most people write. Instead, we write for a particular audience to communicate ideas. We write to evoke a response from that audience, *Okay, got it! Gross! Wonderful! Horrifying!* Writers want to move their readers to experience what they are talking about, not merely express the writer's feelings or opinions. Creativity is so much more than diary-keeping. It is finding accurate and surprising ways to reach others in a world battered by decibel damage. Writing with purpose has as a central requirement: creativity!

Steph: Yes—consider the daily texts you push out to families, or the class newsletters you lovingly craft with your students.

Sara: Exactly—the day-to-day correspondences, a memo to your staff, e-mail to a colleague, a lesson plan to share.

Michael: The district manager looking for details on an order or the appellate judge reading your motion aren't all that concerned about what is plucking your heartstrings. Precise and concise communication skills are in demand across all walks of life, however.

By focusing on specific elements of writing, frameworks help *every* writer—the striver, the thriver, and every writer in between—whether he or she is a future computer engineer, doctor, welder, poet, or novelist. We want purposeful creativity to be an active player in the game of learning, not be sidelined as an occasional indulgence. Writing frameworks provide countless opportunities for creativity—after we get the facts straight.

Shouldn't students be able to choose their writing topics?

Yes, of course they should! We agree with Ralph Fletcher (2017) who writes, "Giving young writers genuine choice is the best way I know to create an environment where they can flourish." But writing instruction shouldn't stop there. It's also okay to focus writing practice on suggested topics. It is important that students see how they can use writing as a way of organizing complex thinking and communicating knowledge to others. Writing frameworks afford students the opportunity to prewrite and draft, incorporate facts and ideas, to make mistakes, and improve their communication capabilities by reading their work aloud.

Sara: Professional writers work on assigned topics more than not: speeches, blog posts, press releases, and so forth.

Michael: Some of the pieces I am most proud of as a writer started as assignments for which I was given the topic: themed anthologies, a commission for a wedding, work instructions for the emergency generators at the Cleveland Clinic.

Sara: Creativity is the ability to make something that wasn't there before. In my career, whether I was composing a poem or a novel, or ghostwriting an op-ed on mergers and acquisitions for the *Wall Street Journal*, they all required creative thinking as well as knowledge of the craft of writing. Learning to write on assigned topics is a requirement for writers.

Steph: My son Alex is a theatre/film director; much of his work is driven by commissions.

Ever wandered around a sculpture garden and marveled at the mastery of sculptors who envision and cast larger-than-life bronze figures? How do they do that? Where did their ideas come from? Ever wonder if you might be able to replicate one of those sculptures by, you know, using their work as a mentor text?

Lynn Dorfman, the Co-Director of Pennsylvania Writing and Literature Project, defines mentor texts as "pieces of literature that you—both teacher and student—can return to and reread for many different purposes. They are texts to be studied and imitated…Mentor texts help students to take risks, try out new strategies and formats, and to be different writers tomorrow than they are today.…And a mentor text might be a poem, a newspaper article, song lyrics, comic strips, manuals, essays, almost anything" (2013)—including a metal sculpture!

Before filling journals with ideas about creating metal sculptures, it might be good to remember that, prior to creating those masterpieces, the sculptors had to learn a bit of metallurgy and the intricacies of metal shaping. They had to understand clay, how it reacts to the knife, in order to transport their vision to a foundry. As Walter Isaacson (2017) insisted in his biography of Leonardo da Vinci, artists make multiple versions of their work, as well as a few colossal mistakes. They need practical skills to put their ideas into form.

Any profession taken to its highest level becomes an art form. The plastic surgeon who reconstructs a shattered cheekbone, the engineer who designs a bridge, the film editor, the mechanic, the negotiator, the educator are all eventually called upon to invent something that wasn't there before. It is the same for writers; we need to practice seeing how words work together in order to communicate our ideas artfully (Holbrook, 1997).

It's fine for students to write like authors, but why not also write like engineers, financial managers, sergeants, and scientists, by gathering facts and using logic? Creativity must not be confined solely to literary pursuits. If it is, we are all doomed. Our world requires ingenuity at all levels, in all professions.

Can writing frameworks help students with diverse interests and abilities?

All students will not grow up to become authors. Thankfully, some will be accountants, musicians, programmers, builders, plumbers, and middle managers who will be required to communicate ideas in writing.

145,900
Number of writers/authors according to the Bureau of Labor and Statistics (2015)

321,400,000
Population of the USA

.04%
Odds of a student becoming a professional author

As educator Susan Ohanian points out so eloquently in her article "Against Obedience," "We need artists, bakers, lumberjacks, manicurists, welders, and yurt builders, as well as people who study math and science in college. Let's respect the variety of skills needed in our communities—and make sure everyone receives a decent wage" (2012). In the wildflower bouquet of skills needed to make society function, creativity is the velvet heart of every blossom.

One size fits all doesn't work any better in education than it does in pajamas.

Creativity, yes! But asking all students to aspire to be authors is, frankly, silly.

Besides, do you have any idea how hard it is to support yourself as an author? (BTW, thanks for buying this book.)

Sara and Michael were business writers before they were teachers, and Steph was an educator before she was an author. Before they studied the methods of writing instruction formally, Sara and Michael were working as writers in the corporate world and doing creative writing as an avocation. Steph was managing a class of 35 fifth graders.

Sara: I worked in the fields of drug prevention, law, and public housing, and as a public relations executive for about 12 years. I hired and supervised other writers, ghostwrote speeches and articles, and did my share of framework writing, from press releases to annual reports.

Michael: I worked as a machinist and then an engineer for 23 years. As a quality engineer in the automotive field, I was a full-time problem solver. It was my job to figure out why one or two parts per million were off and to communicate to the client why it would never happen again. I also wrote work instructions and myriads of reports. All had to be precise, concise, procedural, and most importantly, readable.

Steph: And as a special education teacher, I wrote my share of Individualized Education Plans (IEPs), which are legal documents and demand sensitive and precise language.

This is key: In our previous jobs, unless we were writing an email to a colleague, we never wrote alone. Legal briefs, political speeches, work instructions, brochures, reports of scientific findings, and financial statements—business writing is typically a collaborative effort. And so, too, is the writing of an IEP, which is always developed in concert with each student's family and school colleagues. While it is important that students learn to express themselves as individuals, it is equally important, if not more important, for them to learn to collaborate in the writing process. Not because it is easier, but because it is necessary. As Nell Duke (2018) writes: "A powerful purpose for students' collaboration, together with thoughtfully designed instructional support, propels effective collaboration."

All three of us came into our own as creative writers as on-the-job communicators. As we transitioned into the fields of professional writing (Steph) and creative writing (Sara and Michael), we learned that informational writing and aesthetic writing go hand in hand, nourishing one another. Although we've traveled different paths, we've all wound up in the same place, knowing that a solid understanding of craft comes first. Our journeys have given us a practical perspective, one that enables us to guide students of all abilities toward success in purposeful written communication.

Why a framework? Can't we just work from mentor texts?

Using a mentor text can be a good starting place, but students still benefit from instruction on how to craft and use elements of good writing. We know reading and rereading will build fluency. We also know that reading and rereading using comprehension strategies works better. It's the same in writing. Writing with mentor text can improve writing—but writing with mentor texts and strategies for writing elements works better.

Asking striving writers to read a mentor text and then come up with a topic to write about on their own, however, can be a real showstopper. Not the kind of showstopper where the chorus line breaks into high kicks, bringing the audience to its feet. No, we're talking about when the lights go out, the curtain falls, the show comes to a screaming halt, and audience members ask for a refund. We have been told by teachers that the writing program their school has adopted suggests that kids stare at the ceiling to come up with ideas after reading their mentor text. But we all know what can happen—a significant number of students just see, well, ceiling tiles. It's like showing kids a wedding cake and then handing them a bag of flour, some eggs and sugar, and telling them to go for it (Holbrook, 2016). Why not guide those kids to a specified topic, such as simple machines, transportation, or glaciers?

Sara: True story: My seventh-grade English teacher introduced us to poetry by reciting "Paul Revere's Ride" while galloping around the room. "That, children, is a poem," she breathlessly proclaimed. "Your homework is to write a poem." Wedding cake pedagogy at work. She showed me a model, but she did not follow up with a writing strategy that would help me find my own voice.

Believe me, I wanted to write like Longfellow, but it was so far out of reach, so dressed with pink roses and icing swirls, that instead of trying to copy his style, I copied a poem out of a book and turned it in. I got caught. What can I say? Desperate situations lead to bad choices (Holbrook, 2016).

Michael: We typically share one piece of mentor text and then co-construct a second piece, guiding students through the process. It's this co-constructing step that really helps our striving writers along as they see and help the work be created before their eyes. This text is not some seemingly divine text brought down from the mountaintop, but rather something they had a hand in creating.

Steph: And this scaffolded process aligns as well with the gradual release of responsibility (Pearson & Gallagher, 1983), which frames my work with comprehension strategies. The point of gradual release is to move kids toward independence and agency so they grow into writing and reading independently and confidently, and then apply what they have learned to new challenges.

How can I find time to implement writing frameworks? The curriculum is overcrowded already!

Best news of all! Writing frameworks don't require dedicated writing time that displaces inquiry or content area learning. You can use these frameworks tomorrow and won't have to give up engaging lessons about bugs and glaciers, cheetahs and volcanoes, the subjects that kids want to know about.

Steph: Never forget! It is the content that is seductive. Rich content sparks curiosity, and curiosity leads to the questions that drive learning and a quest for answers; cue reading and writing!

Michael: Kids are fascinated by the real world. Why don't we spend time writing about it?

Sara: Teaching writing in isolation, divorced from content area learning, results in an unhappy separation for both teachers and students.

Classrooms are chock full of writing topics! Guiding students to write about what they are learning using a framework will help them expand their content area understanding, as well as boost their abilities to communicate purposefully, especially in writing.

Okay, now that we've addressed some of your possible concerns, let's get into the nitty-gritty of our framework process.

Our Framework Process

We have honed this process by working with thousands of students around the globe. Over the past 15 years, we've visited an untold number of schools in the United States and nearly 50 countries on every continent except Antarctica, learning, growing, and adapting along the way. Just like you, we've had our share of missteps over the years and have learned from them. We promise to skip over those missteps and show you only what we have learned works in writing instruction.

We agree with Steph and Annie: Table the labels! All kids can write, and we have had success with a wide variety of students, using the following process.

One advantage to being writers-in-residence in classrooms around the globe is that we enter the classroom with no preconceived notions about the students. And fortunately, the students do not come with actual labels pinned to their shirts. We don't know which students have IEPs or which one is the classroom's "little author."

That's not to say that sometimes kids don't tell us. Upon entering one seventh-grade classroom, Michael was greeted by a student who proclaimed, "I have ADHD and I'm on the spectrum!" Michael replied, "Well, we all have something, kid—today you are a writer." And don't you know, he was!

THE FRAMEWORK PROCESS

1. **Discuss Lesson Goals**
2. **Analyze a Model Piece of Writing**
3. **Write Together to Model the Writing Process**
4. **Research and Discuss in Pairs**
5. **Compose Version 1**
6. **Revise Into Version 2**
7. **Share With One Another and the Class**
8. **Transfer: Combine Frameworks!**

1. Discuss Lesson Goals

Each writing framework lesson begins with *Here's what we're going to learn today*. So the lesson introduction might sound something like this: We are going to use a new writing framework (or one we've used before) to write about electric circuits (or seeds, force and motion, a piece of fiction). Most frameworks can be combined with a content area lesson.

By doing this, we make expectations visible, and students are aware of our goals up front. Striving writers are more likely to be successful when we demonstrate and clearly explain what we are hoping to accomplish.

Giving students a clear-cut destination with an end product encourages buy-in.

There's a benefit to us, too. The work students produce can be used for formative assessment, as a means to evaluate the lesson's impact and inform our instructional decision-making. Taking care to set clear goals up front also streamlines the assessment process.

2. Analyze a Model Piece of Writing

Every framework comes with a projection-ready mentor text. Just take a picture of it with your phone or tablet and turn it into a slide, or download it at scholastic.com/ThrivingWriterResources.

Master teacher and literature guru Paul Hankins reminds us: "Oh, teachers. Do you not understand? There's a kid in the room who's never heard the voice of a reader who reads well. You. Are. That. Reader." (tweet, September 29, 2017). Read the mentor text with wonder and emotion, modeling inflection. Then ask your students to read it aloud to develop their abilities to read expressively, fluently, with understanding. This kind of oral reading has been proven effective in helping striving readers in particular build word knowledge, print knowledge, fluency, and comprehension (Duke, 2016). There is no such thing as too much rereading!

This is the bulk of our "analysis": reading the mentor text aloud and asking what it is about. We might also point out a pattern or the break in a pattern, sensory terms, or other elements, but we don't dissect it. We want to leave it live on the table so we can poke it more a bit later.

Each framework provides you with some points for discussion, but make no mistake: A FRAMEWORK IS NOT A SCRIPT! Do not feel confined to these points. We offer them as guides. We trust that you know your kids and what they need.

3. Write Together to Model the Writing Process

When you co-construct with your students, you teach writing process, not new content. Do not skip this step! It's essential. This is where we begin to build confidence in the writer, particularly the striving writer.

We call it the apprenticeship step.

Michael: I worked for 23 years as a quality engineer in the auto industry. No one ever showed a new machinist an air-bag component and then gave him a rubric and asked him to re-create the part without giving instructions on the use of the equipment. Rather, an experienced machinist stands at the elbow of the novice and teaches. Once the fledgling machinist understands his equipment, he can be released to create any number of high-precision components because he understands the process.

Sara: The same is true for serving in a restaurant, becoming a checkout person at the grocery, or any number of jobs.

Steph: Educators know this well as the gradual release of responsibility!

Co-constructing can also be the scariest step for a teacher. We are asking you to write in real time with the whole class, on a whiteboard or projection system, so that all students can see. Model the writing process with input from students. Become a co-creator with kids. Go through the process, step by step—soliciting suggestions, assuming the duty of a scribe. Try to enjoy the ride.

Whiteboards are remarkable devices! As you co-construct, take several suggestions before committing any to the screen, solicit words and phrases, and combine ideas. Show the thinking that goes on before you lay down a line. Make mistakes! Remind everyone, including yourself, that nobody gets it 100 percent right out of the gate. Talk through the drafting process. Write things down and then erase. Don't stop to correct grammar or add conventions. And, please, do not polish the co-constructed text. Leave room for revision. Together, you and your students are testing out the framework, not honing a dissertation.

Title this text "Version 1."

Ask everyone to join you in reading your co-constructed Version 1 aloud together. Most likely, it won't be so bad but will need some help, which is normal. Reading it aloud celebrates its creation, yet still acknowledges that there is more work to do. We can't learn from our mistakes if we are afraid to make them. Too many writers self-censor, trying to work too many thoughts out before committing them to the page. Version 1 is where we let the ideas flow. The only type of writing that cannot be improved is that which is never written. Who knows, that phrase that isn't quite right might be the springboard for a great idea when revising.

CHOOSING A TOPIC FOR CO-CONSTRUCTION

If the goal is for students to write about seeds and soil, you might model using a topic such as soccer or the playground, which gives you an opportunity to talk freely about the framework before your students use it to write about their content area learning. If you use the topic under study, the students won't benefit from discovering the material on their own, and may just copy what you've co-created. Once they understand the framework, they can use it with any number of subjects. Let your mind go free! You will find possibilities to utilize these frameworks across disciplines, even combining them as students gain sophistication.

Sara: I have written hundreds of poems, as well as books and articles, and trust me; I never get it right the first time. I always have to make changes.

Michael: It is a relief to writers when they internalize that they do not have to get it perfect the first time.

Steph: Consider discussing with your students some "Version 1" drafts from geniuses across the ages, such as Leonardo da Vinci, Albert Einstein, and Steve Jobs. Drafting and revising are not punishment for mistakes made out of the gate, but rather the natural process of creating.

The students now have two pieces of mentor text before them: one that was shared with them that they have read aloud a few times, and one they have written together with you. Leave both of these texts visible as students begin writing on their own. This will create an "I can do that" mindset. Your students have gained experience with the framework, and now it's time to plug some new content into it.

VERSION 1

We always title our first draft Version 1, building in the expectation that there will always be changes. The good news is that this frees the writer to take risks and make mistakes. We often hear students remind each other in the writing process, "Oh, don't worry. Put it down. It's only Version 1."

Sara: Once a student drew a comparison between our Versions 1, 2, 3, etc. and the different updates received on video game software. "It's like that was V.1.0 and now I've updated to V.3.0."

Michael: Exactly! Updated to fix the bugs and offer new enhancements.

Teachers moan that kids don't like to revise. How true! That's why we don't wait until the end of the writing lesson to spring it on them. Writing is a process of constant revision. Just like computer games.

We like the term Version 1 rather than *draft* because it honors the first writing. We also like to preserve the versions if possible; they can become a touchstone later for longer or multiple works that evolve from the initial text created. Another plus to starting with Version 1 is that the number of versions that may follow is infinite.

When students are writing on a device such as a Chromebook, laptop, or tablet, we encourage them to copy/paste Version 1 and then work to create Version 2, preserving the first version in case they need to go back and retrieve all or part of it.

Michael: Kids even get competitive, bragging, "I'm on Version 3," answered by, "I'm on Version 6!"

No draft is final; it is merely the latest version.

Walt Whitman revised his seminal book of poems, *Leaves of Grass*, repeatedly, even after publication. We figure, if that strategy was good enough for Walt, it's good enough for us.

4. Research and Discuss in Pairs

Now it's time for students to team up to research and construct a Version 1 on their own. We like to put students in pairs when creating their Version 1. This stimulates discussion as students look over the content area material, prioritizing and selecting details to include, and provides support for strivers and English learners.

As Steph and Annie have so aptly noted, learning is a social act. Students benefit from continued conversation during the learning process. A study at the University of Colorado concluded, "Students who answered in-class questions were more likely to answer the question correctly after they'd had a chance to discuss it among themselves. . . . Of the students who answered the question incorrectly on the first try, 77 percent were able to answer the question correctly after discussion with peers" (2009).

Having research materials ready in advance will serve to direct the discussion. Students will engage with one another as they explore options. It is in this engagement that the real learning takes place. The piece of writing created is an artifact of the learning. As the students work together, they become the teachers. They sift through information collaboratively, identifying and prioritizing information they've researched.

Two children discussing writing together.

5. Compose Version 1

Students may be writing individually, in pairs, or in small groups, but in all cases they each need to write their own Version 1. This is important! As the writing progresses, they may choose to dissolve their writing partnership and go off on their own. So they will need their own Version 1, as well as the results of the research so they have source material for subsequent versions.

We like to give students a time limit for constructing their first versions: three to eight minutes. That said, you are in charge of the clock. If students need more time, by all means, stretch five minutes to 10. Circulate about the room as students work. Make research suggestions, reminding students to each make their own copy of Version 1. If your students are writing on Chromebooks, laptops, or tablets, instruct them to write in 20-point type. That way you don't have to squint as you do your drive-by assessments.

Many of the frameworks follow a step-by-step process. This provides you with frequent openings to ask for read-alouds, quick assessments that will provide you with opportunities to quickly gauge the students' progress.

Our writing workshops are noisy affairs. Frequently, we ask students to read their work aloud, everyone at the same time, urging them to listen for how the piece is working for them. Students often miss silly mistakes, as in they thought they wrote a word down, but didn't—or wrote "is" instead of "it." Writers can catch mistakes like those by reading aloud. Writing by ear helps develop voice and fluency.

6. Revise Into Version 2

Each framework provides ideas for revising Version 1 into Version 2, and sometimes Version 3 and beyond. Depending on the writer's experience and your instructional goals, you may wish to add challenges as the revisions progress. Suggestions such as, "If Version 1 had one resource, let's use three resources for Version 2." Or, "Add a quotation to Version 2, and watch your punctuation," or "Can you add one sensory reference to Version 3 to make the piece come alive?"

Our frameworks are designed to push you and your students forward, not to hold you back.

Set your revision goals to meet your classroom needs. If all you are looking for is a quick formative assessment on content area learning, you may want to stop at Version 1 or 2, once you have determined whether students can or cannot control, refine, and use the knowledge. In other instances, your students may have produced something that is worth developing into a longer essay, a blog post, or any number of other types of writing. This is your call. Our frameworks are designed to build content area knowledge and literacy capabilities in concert with one another, and students recognize this. We hear this from students during exit conversations when we ask, "What did you learn today?" Some students will mention the writing element ("We learned about point of view"), while others will mention the content area knowledge ("We learned about the role of pharaohs in Egypt").

Please *do not* feel compelled to grade every piece of writing or to refine it into something publishable. As every teacher knows, topics such as conventions and figurative language are not taught once and abandoned. Writing frameworks provide opportunities to reteach them and other crafting strategies, such as strong leads, narrative arcs, and literary devices. Later, students will be able to combine those strategies, gaining sophistication in their ability to think and communicate. The short pieces they create will also fit nicely into a portfolio for an inquiry unit. Because we know it is important to track students' growth, we have provided Assessment Checkpoints at the end of every framework—quick guidelines for determining how well students are progressing. We call these "checkpoints" because they are just stops along the way to better communication, not the final destination.

7. Share With One Another and the Class

Everyone shares his or her work aloud. No worries, we will help you scaffold into this. (See "Scaffolding Into Sharing," page 255.) Students will share aloud, everyone at the same time, like a seat symphony (Holbrook, 2000). Students will be called on to read single lines, to share with a partner, and finally share with the group. The process prepares students to use their voices, speaking with conviction—an important life skill.

Michael: That is worth repeating.

Sara: *Everyone* shares his or her work aloud.

Michael: This does not mean you need to plan for a long sharing time on each lesson. By fostering a culture of conversation, we build in the expectation that if called upon, each student should be prepared to share aloud.

Steph: Or as an alternative, build in time for "Pair and Share," where kids can share their writing with a partner, meaning everyone gets to share, not just the lucky few chosen for—or who volunteered for—the Author's Chair.

Sharing aloud is sharing the learning, helping to embed knowledge as students write and listen to one another's writing. We do not excuse students from reading because they are too shy. We don't say, "You don't have to learn to write if you don't want to." But we are in classrooms all the time where the culture is to only share if students want to, otherwise it's okay to hide behind your notebook.

Sara: On entering any given classroom, we are often greeted with one or more students pleading, "Will we have to read this out loud?"

Michael: Our intent is to change that culture into a sharing, conversation culture. All students must learn to speak for themselves.

Sara: We explain to reluctant communicators that a classroom is a safe space to get comfortable with the sound of their own voices. We know that no one else is going to stand in for them in a job or college interview, even if they are not thinking that far ahead yet. First impressions are made by the way people speak. Outside of the classroom, speaking is of equal if not more importance than reading and writing.

Michael: No one else will speak for them as they argue for a raise, against a traffic ticket, or in that all-important stay of execution.

Steph: Not to be too dramatic, but yes. Kids need to become comfortable with saying the words aloud—their lives and happiness may well depend on it.

Planning one big speaking event or unit a year tends to induce panic. Even waiting until the end of the writing lesson to share causes anxiety, which is why we have students do it all along, as part of the writing process.

Glossophobia is not fear of lip gloss. It is fear of public speaking, and it's real. It's the number-one fear of humankind, according to surveys (Chapman University Survey of American Fears, 2017). We confront this fear one day, one lesson at a time, by encouraging short bursts of speaking. By acknowledging that we are sharing a work in progress, we don't have to be embarrassed by oversights or missteps. It's all part of the process.

In *From Striving to Thriving*, Steph and Annie remind us of the value of risk-taking and mistake-making in learning—"We grow by trying something, working through it, and trying again." They also cite Sir Ken Robinson, who suggests that we should not "stigmatize" mistakes, but rather "value" the essential role they play in growth and creativity.

As conscientious teachers, we build that safe environment into our classrooms. If our kids don't learn to become outspoken with us, where will they?

8. Transfer: Combine Frameworks!

The ultimate goal of using writing frameworks is for students to become familiar enough with elements of composition that they will be able to combine those elements easily and automatically whenever they write or speak. For example, a strong lead, a narrative summary, sentence variety, prioritized facts and details, persuasive language, and convincing comparisons combine to make an impact.

Michael: Consider these frameworks to be akin to the elements of the periodic table.

Sara: Combine carbon and oxygen one way, you get carbon dioxide. Combine them differently, carbon monoxide. It helps to know what you're doing!

Michael: Same with writing, only much less volatile.

Sara: We always remind students that writing is not a chemical experiment or sky diving—you don't have to get it right the first time.

Steph: But kids need to have acquired the ability to use the elements of writing to suit their needs as 21st-century communicators. Ultimately, our goal as educators is to develop a classroom of thrivers—students who are confident, capable, independent readers, thinkers, talkers, and writers.

The instruction in this book generally follows the Gradual Release of Responsibility instructional approach, as does the reading instruction in *From Striving To Thriving: How to Grow Capable, Confident Readers*. The Gradual Release of Responsibility is a research-based instructional model developed by Pearson and Gallagher (1983). In this model, responsibility for learning and understanding shifts gradually over time from the teacher to the student.

There have been many adaptations to the Gradual Release model over the years, but it typically includes four basic steps:

- Model—*I do it*—The teacher models while the students watch.

- Guided Instruction—*We do it*—The teacher and the students work together.

- Collaborative Practice —*You do it together*—Students practice and work together while the teacher confers.

- Independent Practice and Application—*You do it alone*—Students practice independently and apply the strategy.

Following the lead of Adria Klein (2018), we now would like to suggest a step beyond independent practice and application: transference. You do on your own, even outside of school. As Klein explains, transferring means students apply knowledge or meaning from a familiar context to an unfamiliar context. At the point of independent transfer, children choose "to think" rather than simply choosing "to remember." In other words, children take what they've learned at school and transfer it to novel situations—often beyond their school life.

The writing frameworks then encourage students to ask themselves three key questions:

- What do I know?

- How do I know it?

- Where and how can I use what I know to express my ideas?

Don't be surprised if your students realize that combining the frameworks leads to new possibilities. See the example on page 27 from Laura Fishman's seventh-grade class in Shanghai. The student arrived at Version 6 first with the What's the Story framework, followed by Prepositionally Speaking.

So, with the information and, we hope, inspiration provided in this introduction, it's time to try some writing frameworks. Each framework features downloadable slides to project, suggested grade

Fifth-grade students in Elyria, Ohio, share their Version 3s with classmates. Everybody likes applause and we were happy to reward their great work with enthusiasm.

levels, sample writing stages, lesson extensions, and more. Choose the frameworks you think will work best, because no one knows your classroom needs better than you do. Experiment. Combine. Most of all, have fun as students engage in literacy and learning.

HOW WRITING FRAMEWORKS SUPPORT ENGLISH LEARNERS

Read. Write. Speak. Listen. All of these framework strategies fully integrate all four language processes, which makes them uniquely suited to support English learners. Sara, Michael, and Steph have worked extensively with teachers and kids in classrooms across the United States and taught American curriculum around the world. From Spanish to Swahili, students in American and international overseas schools are typically diverse and represent a wide spectrum of linguistic backgrounds. All students, wherever they call home, receive lifelong benefits from improved communication skills.

Students will find an authentic reason to converse, collaborate, and communicate in English as they write their way into meaning in science, social studies, and other content areas, encountering an ever-widening range of academic vocabulary. The frameworks provide extensive aural support via read-alouds, recitations, and collaborative conversation. Students are fully engaged as they read and write their way into meaning. Inviting invigorating inquiry, the frameworks provide the rich network of support via conversations, which helps students more easily absorb and assimilate the new words they learn (Duke, 2011).

Dr. Eugene Garcia (2010) recommends four goals that optimize support for English learners—all easily accomplished in classrooms that implement writing frameworks:

1. Provide students with a classroom environment that focuses on both language development and the acquisition of content-specific knowledge and vocabulary. Students will practice key writing elements while building content understanding. Constructing multiple versions encourages deliberate practice and affords opportunities for learning through mistakes and growth (Ericsson, 2009).

2. Make sure teachers have the instructional support needed to maximize student potential; the frameworks are highly scaffolded for both teachers and kids, and also provide formative assessments to guide future instruction.

3. Increase the opportunity English Learners have to interact with their teachers and peers and participate in learning activities. Frameworks promote engagement through daily conversations about all aspects of the writing and learning process.

4. Improve and expand how families contribute to the academic growth of their children (for more about this, don't miss the Family Literacy Workshop on page 269).

A culture of conversation in the classroom means students cooperate to meet classroom goals, reducing stress and encouraging understanding. When diversity is regarded and acted on as a resource for teaching and learning, all students thrive (Borrero & Bird, 2009). Writing frameworks help all students create meaning, communicate that meaning, and extend meaning in ways that engage their intellectual abilities and promote both academic and lifelong success.

We met teacher Laura Fishman at Shanghai American School, after which she moved to the American Community School of Abu Dhabi. While she was looking at UN Global Goals with her students, we asked her to remind us which frameworks we had used in her class the previous year. "You did 'What's the Story? The Five-Sentence Narrative,' using 'unfortunately,' 'fortunately,' 'finally' as the frame. You also did 'Prepositionally Speaking: Setting the Scene,'" she wrote to us in an email. And then she was kind enough to share this writing by a seventh-grade student—a beautiful progression that culminates in a piece that combines work from the two frameworks.

"WHAT'S THE STORY?" VERSION 1

Children are dying

Child labor rates are growing

Unfortunately, there are 153 million children in labor

Fortunately, the numbers are getting smaller

Finally, there will be equal rights and treatments to all children

"WHAT'S THE STORY?" VERSION 2

Child labor growing at the speed of an unknown virus

Children dying and used like tools

153 million

number decreasing

equal rights and treatments

"PREPOSITIONALLY SPEAKING"

Above pebbly and dusty ground stands children of young ages.

Between tiny hands are heavy shovels bigger than their body.

Despite sweat, blood, and fatigue, they are still working.

Toward the goal of financial success.

Without rights because of desire for money.

Through days, months, years, they have risked their lives.

Inside adults' point of view, these children are nothing but cheap tools.

Among these children, some die.

Like all of us who are fortunate, every child deserves equal rights, treatments, education, and love.

Until the end of inequality, poverty, they will not rest.

THE TWO FRAMEWORKS COMBINED

Above pebbly and dusty ground stands children of young ages.

Child labor growing at the speed of an unknown virus.

Between tiny hands are heavy shovels bigger than their body.

Despite sweat, blood, and fatigue, they are still working.

They will not rest.

153 million children involved in labor,

Toward the goal of financial success.

They will not rest.

Without rights because of desire for money.

Through days, months, years, they have risked their lives.

Children dying and used.

Inside adults' point of view, these children are nothing but cheap tools.

Among these children, some die.

They will not rest.

Like all of us who are fortunate, every child deserves equal rights, treatments, education, and love.

Until the end of inequality, poverty, they will not rest.

Off to success, the numbers are decreasing.

With banners of awareness and morality, children are being saved.

Part I: Learning About Language

We want students to understand language—
what it is and how it works—and how they can
use it to serve their own purposes. That means,
in part, understanding how texts are crafted and
the techniques and tools students have available
to write texts that engage and delight a real
audience, on the page and face to face.

scholastic.com/ThriveResources

Sentence Variety Pack: Crafting Engaging Text

TIME: about 45 minutes	**GRADE LEVEL:** 5 and up

MATERIALS:

- Slides 1–10*
- Sentence Variety Pack GO Sheet*
- One or more images for students to write about (we've provided some)
- Notebooks, computers, or tablets

*Available online at scholastic.com/ThrivingWriterResources

WHY TEACH THIS? To familiarize students with a variety of ways to begin a sentence other than with an article, noun, or pronoun, which leads to more lively and engaging writing.

CONTENT AREA CONNECTIONS: ELA

Persuasive	Descriptive	Narrative	Procedural	Research	Vocabulary	Figurative Language
X	X	X		X	X	

From Striving to Thriving Writers copyright © 2018 by Sara Holbrook, Michael Salinger, and Stephanie Harvey. Published by Scholastic Inc.

STEPH REFLECTS ON FRAMEWORK 1

Choice matters! Every child needs opportunities every day to choose what they want to read and write. But they don't need every choice under the sun every time. Dick Allington (2006) suggests "managed choice"—kids are invited to choose from a teacher-curated selection. In this framework, kids learn how to pump up their writing by choosing the most interesting words from a "sentence variety pack." And bonus: Kids enjoy galloping good fun with the parts of speech.

What is one thing most kids fear more than a zombie apocalypse?

Boredom!

A text in which every sentence is crafted *noun*, *verb*, *object* may be grammatically correct, but string several of those sentences in a row and, bam. Boring.

Happily, with a little experimentation, this tedious writing malady is easily cured. By examining an image and creating a sentence variety pack, writers will test out options, ultimately choosing the configuration that best suits their needs.

Let writers know that this writing framework will help them engage their readers with lively text and save them from being (gasp) boring.

1. Introduce the Framework

Project Slide 1, read it aloud, and explain to students that together you will be describing an image, using sentences beginning with different parts of speech.

Sentence Variety Pack:
Crafting Engaging Text

What are we going to learn today?
1. We will discuss how to make our writing more lively using varied sentence construction.
2. We will create a sentence variety pack.
3. We will write using varied sentences to describe an image.

Slide 1

PART I: LEARNING ABOUT LANGUAGE

2. Build Background Knowledge

- Project Slide 2 and explain that this image can be described in a simple sentence, beginning with the subject: *The dog ate the garbage.*

Slide 2

- Project Slide 3 and ask students to take turns reading the sentences that describe the same image (the dog) but begin in a variety of ways.

- Project Slide 4 and review the terms *article, adjective, adverb, preposition, infinitive,* and *participial phrase.* For further information on prepositions, see "Prepositionally Speaking," page 77.

But wait!

Could we say it another way?

Here is a variety pack of sentence beginnings.

Article: The dog ate the garbage.
Adjective: Hungry, the dog ate the garbage.
Adverb: Greedily, the dog ate the garbage.
Preposition: Without hesitation, the dog ate the garbage.
Infinitive: To satisfy his hunger, the dog ate the garbage.
Participial phrase: Tipping the can over, the dog ate the garbage.

Slide 3

Parts of speech:

A quick reminder

Article/Pronoun: *A, an, the* or *he, she, they.*
Adjective: A word that describes a noun.
Adverb: A word that describes a noun or a verb, usually ending in *-ly.*
Preposition: A word that explains where, when, or how something is happening.
Infinitive: A verb in its simplest form—"to run."
Participial phrase: A phrase beginning with an *-ing* verb that describes what it's next to.

Slide 4

3. Discuss the Mentor Image and Mentor Text

- Project Slide 5, read it aloud on your own, and then read it aloud with students, noting how the sentences begin differently.

Image Description:
The Happy Elephant

Sentences begin with variety:
Rolling in the water, the baby elephant blinked his big eyes.
Muddy and dripping, his ears flapped with delight.
With a splash, he fell to his knees and waved a happy trunk in our direction.

Slide 5

- Ask students to identify each sentence beginning and its part of speech: *Rolling* (participial phrase), *Muddy* (adjective), and *With a splash* (prepositional phrase).

- Project Slide 6 and discuss how the author experimented by creating a variety pack of sentences and then chose from those sentences to craft "The Happy Elephant."

- Project Slide 7, read it aloud, and ask: *What's wrong?* (Each sentence begins with an article or pronoun followed by its subject.) Boring!

Experiment!
Create a Sentence
Variety Pack

Article/Pronoun: The baby elephant rolled in the water.
Adjective: Muddy, he flapped his ears.
Adverb: Happily, he waved his trunk.
Preposition: With a splash, he fell on his knees.
Infinitive: To bathe in mud, he rolled in the water.
Participial phrase: Rolling in the water, the elephant blinked.

Slide 6

Boring Image Description:
The Happy Elephant

Each sentence begins with the subject:
The baby elephant rolled in the water as he blinked his big eyes. His ears were caked with brown mud and they waved with delight. He fell to his knees making a splash. He waved a happy trunk in our direction.

Slide 7

4. Co-construct Version 1

- Project Slide 8 and co-construct a sentence variety pack about the cheetah.

- Encourage students to experiment by offering several options that begin in a variety of ways.

- Keep the variety pack on display for reference as students write.

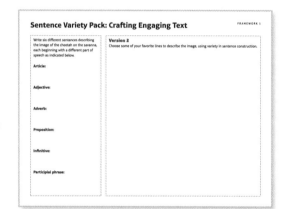

Co-construct a sentence variety pack to describe the cheetah, each sentence beginning differently:

Subject:
Adjective:
Adverb:
Preposition:
Infinitive:
Participial phrase:

Photo: Stephanie Harvey

Slide 8

5. Hand Out the GO Sheet

6. Have Students Write Their Version 1

- Ask students to pair up with a writing partner. Project Slide 9 of the elephant family on the savanna or ask students to find an image related to a topic they're studying.

Sentence Variety Pack: Crafting Engaging Text FRAMEWORK 1

Write six different sentences describing the image of the cheetah on the savanna, each beginning with a different part of speech as indicated below.

Article:

Adjective:

Adverb:

Preposition:

Infinitive:

Participial phrase:

Version 2
Choose some of your favorite lines to describe the image, using variety in sentence construction.

Sentence Variety Pack GO Sheet

- Have students complete their sentence variety packs and fill out the left side of their GO Sheets, encouraging discussion, as you circulate the room, providing assistance as needed.

- Ask partners to read their sentences aloud to one another to see how they are working. Ask a few students to share their favorites with the whole class. (See page 22 for the benefits of reading drafts simultaneously.)

Create a sentence variety pack about the elephants.

Photo: Stephanie Harvey

Slide 9

7. Co-construct Version 2

- Display your co-constructed Version 1 (generated from Step 4) and explain that together you will choose one sentence to begin your descriptive text. Invite students to suggest the best choice. Use Slide 10 as a prompt.

- Co-construct two sentences that describe the photo of the cheetah, not an entire paragraph.

Choose your favorite sentences from your variety pack and co-construct a description of the image.

Slide 10

8. Have Students Write Their Version 2

- Ask students to choose sentences from their Version 1 to create a description of their image, using a variety of beginnings. They may use the space on the right-hand side of the GO Sheet or transition to their writer's notebook, computer, or tablet.

- Let students know they can continue working with their partners or break out on their own.

- Invite periodic read-alouds, everyone at the same time. Also, periodically call on students to read out their favorite sentence to the whole class.

9. Share!

- Ask students to stand and share their work with a classmate.

- Encourage them to offer suggestions to one another on how to make the writing richer and the sentences more varied.

- Ask students to share with the whole class. If they have chosen different images, this will be more fun, of course. And if they have chosen images related to a topic they're studying, use share time to reinforce learning.

Lesson Extension Idea

Have students use their Version 2 as the basis for a longer text, challenging them to experiment with sentence construction while communicating information.

Sample Stages

Using this framework is a real eye-opener for students as they experiment saying the same thing in a variety of different ways, freeing themselves from the overused article-noun-verb sentence pattern. In all seriousness, eyes widen, and students sit straighter as they test out different construction strategies, clearly impressed with their own words. Writers are eager to share these varied sentences, reading them aloud to find their favorites. Shown below are samples from seventh- and ninth-grade students.

Seventh-grade teacher Libbie Royko of SOI, Willoughby/Eastlake School of Innovation in Ohio, began her lesson by pairing with a drama student in her class to read aloud the different sentence structures in the slides. "We were a great, expressive team!" she reported and went on to explain, "Then I asked for observations. Finally, I explained procedures for completing the framework, asking each student to research an image to write about. While I was feeling rather proud of our read-aloud, my kids far surpassed me! Humbling and amazing." A few weeks later she wrote to say that her students had used the strategies from this framework in a unit on business-letter writing as they wrote to government officials about proposed budget cuts in education. "They have learned more ways to express themselves now," she wrote in a follow-up email.

First, students wrote their sentences out by hand.

Article: Abraham Lincoln is chasing the vampire, Edward Cullen.

Adjective: Frightened, Edward Cullen runs away from the great Abe Lincoln.

Adverb: Hurriedly, Edward Cullen flees away from the hands of Abraham Lincoln and his lightsaber.

Prepositional phrase: In the dark shadows of the forest, Abraham Lincoln, on his pony, hunts down Edward while carrying a lightsaber.

Infinitive: To escape Lincoln, Cullen sprints through the depths of the forest.

Participial Phrase: Pondering his survival, Edward Cullen runs through the woods to reach his destination of freedom.

Well done, Zoey!

Then they transitioned to their Chromebooks. Zoey chose to write about an image from the movie based on one of her favorite novels: *Abraham Lincoln: Vampire Hunter.* This screen capture from her Google Doc shows Libbie's comments.

Lisa Levi's ninth-grade students at the American School of Chennai, India, used their varied sentences to begin to craft character descriptions for use in fictional writing. The writers were all working from a common image, but clearly each writer added his or her own creative twist as they began crafting their text utilizing diverse sentence constructions.

- Hands crooked at a certain angle, the mirror is faced towards the girl.
- Posing with her balance towards her back, she has an arrogant expression on her face.
- On her dress, she laid her arms that were covered with matching gloves.
- Fluffed, her dress looked like it was all made of feathers.

Hands crooked at a certain angle, the mirror is faced towards the girl. Posing with her balance towards her back, she has an arrogant expression on her face. Fluffed, her dress looked like it was all made of feathers. On her dress, she laid her arms that were covered with matching gloves. She was getting ready for her 10th birthday party. She was excited to join such a formal event in a formal and stylish gown.

- The crown sitting on top of her head, the girl stood confidently.
- Looking at herself in the mirror, she admired her stance.
- Proudly, she held her head high.
- With her dress swaying, she could not help herself think how beautiful she looked.

The little girl who loved dressing up, put on her red gown. The tiara sitting on top of her head, the girl stood with confidence. With her dress swaying, she could not help herself think how beautiful she appeared. She wanted to look older, prettier. Glancing at herself in the mirror, she admired her stance. Proudly, she held her head high.

- 1 absolute opener
- Eyes blinking, she stared at herself reflected on a spoon.
- 1 verbal opener:
- Wearing a red dress and a tiara, she felt like she became a princess and look better than anyone else.
- 1 prepositional phrase opener:
- On the spoon, her face seemed to be really small and pretty.
- 1 single adjective or adverb opener
- Slowly, putting down the spoon on the table, she went into her room to see the mirror so that she can make sure she's feeling the right thing.

A girl was getting ready for her birthday party, and went down to the kitchen when her mom called her to eat breakfast. Eyes blinking, she stared at herself reflected on a spoon. On the spoon, her face seemed to be really small and pretty. Wearing a red dress and a tiara, she felt like she became a princess and look better than anyone else. Slowly, putting down the spoon on the table, she went into her room to see the mirror so that she can make sure she's feeling the right thing.

From Striving to Thriving Writers copyright © 2018 by Sara Holbrook, Michael Salinger, and Stephanie Harvey. Published by Scholastic Inc.

Sentence Variety Pack: Assessment Checkpoint

SKILL	3	2	1
Structure and Organization	Demonstrates the ability to craft and recraft sentences using different beginnings to create lively text that engages readers.	Demonstrates to a degree the ability to craft and recraft sentences using different beginnings to create lively text that engages readers. Occasionally may not recognize repetitive writing styles.	Does not yet demonstrate the ability to craft and recraft sentences using different beginnings and continues to strive to create lively text that engages readers.
Grammar Conventions	Demonstrates an understanding of the terms *noun, subject, adjective, adverb, preposition, infinitive,* and *participial phrase.* Is able to recognize the terms and able to use them in a sentence.	Demonstrates to a degree an understanding of the terms *noun, subject, adjective, adverb, preposition, infinitive,* and *participial phrase.* May occasionally confuse these terms when attempting to use them in a sentence.	Does not yet demonstrate an understanding of the terms *noun, subject, adjective, adverb, preposition, infinitive,* and *participial phrase* and has not yet been able to identify or use them in a sentence.
Reading an Image	Exhibits an ability to translate the visual language of an image using a variety of sentence structures.	Partially exhibits an ability to translate the visual language of an image using a variety of sentence structures. May miss some important features of the image.	Does not yet exhibit an ability to translate the visual language of an image using a variety of sentence structures. Needs help focusing on important details.
Speaking Skills	Is willing to share aloud and consistently demonstrates effective presentation skills using good voice projection, inflection, pacing, eye contact, and stance.	Is often willing to share and partially demonstrates effective presentation skills using good voice projection, inflection, pacing, eye contact, and stance.	Is not yet willing to share and/or does not demonstrate effective presentation skills using good voice projection, inflection, pacing, eye contact, and stance.

Feelings Made Visual: Show, Don't Tell

TIME: about 30 minutes

GRADE LEVEL: 1 and up

MATERIALS:

- Slides 1–3*
- Feelings GO Sheet*
- Notebooks, computers, or tablets

*Available online at scholastic.com/ThrivingWriterResources

WHY TEACH THIS?

1. To encourage students to use visual language—to show, not tell.
2. To help students talk about their feelings and realize we all have ups and downs.

CONTENT AREA CONNECTIONS: ELA, Science (Health)

Persuasive	Descriptive	Narrative	Procedural	Research	Vocabulary	Figurative Language
	X				X	

STEPH REFLECTS ON FRAMEWORK 2

Kids need to share their feelings. So do we, for that matter! Strivers, in particular, often hide their feelings out of fear and embarrassment. When kids get the chance to talk about, act out, and write their feelings, they grow both their confidence and capabilities, and have fun doing so. Learning flourishes when kids are engaged, and *fun* offers the most direct route to engagement, and thus, learning.

Heart bumping. Hands holding. The best part is being in love.

You will love this and so will your students! It's true that kids say the darnedest things, but we're here to say they can make the craziest expressions when they try on emotions. Have a camera ready for this one! The pictures are a hoot to share in class and with parents.

While you are having a rollicking good time, emphasize that while we may act them out in different ways, we all have similar emotions and (thankfully) *NOTHING* lasts forever, despite what your grandmother may have told you about your wrinkled nose staying that way.

This writing framework is a great way to introduce the concept of *show, don't tell* by leading students to describe feelings through actions. It will also give you an opportunity to review nouns and verbs and to practice some patterned writing. During sharing, it is an ideal opportunity for students to practice reading with expression.

Think of this framework as a touchstone as you coach students in future writing. You can remind students how trying on feelings and translating their actions into words creates a picture in the mind of their reader.

1. Introduce the Framework

Project Slide 1, read it aloud, and let students know they are going to be acting out and writing about their feelings. If they look puzzled or worried, assure them they're going to have fun.

> **Feelings Made Visual:**
> Show, Don't Tell
>
> **What are we going to learn today?**
> 1. We will try on some feelings.
> 2. We will write about our feelings using nouns and *-ing* verbs to show how feelings look and act.
> 3. We will finish our writing with a strong conclusion.

Slide 1

2. Discuss Mentor Text, Version 1

- Project Slide 2, read the poem aloud on your own, then read it aloud again with students. Split the class in half and ask students to read the text again chorally: one half reads the nouns and the other reads the verbs. It may be fun for students to act out each line as they read it aloud.

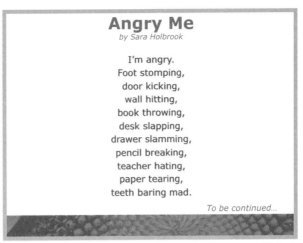

Angry Me
by Sara Holbrook

I'm angry.
Foot stomping,
door kicking,
wall hitting,
book throwing,
desk slapping,
drawer slamming,
pencil breaking,
teacher hating,
paper tearing,
teeth baring mad.

To be continued...

Slide 2

- Ask: *What is this poem about?* (being angry) *Do you see a pattern? What is it?* (noun-verb) Ask how the verbs act to describe anger.

- Ask students if they can picture the actions in their minds. We call this *imagery*—words that create a picture in the reader's mind.

3. Co-construct Version 1

- Divide your writing space into two sections with a vertical line.

- Brainstorm a dozen or so emotions (happy, frightened, surprised, etc.) and/or states of being (sleepy, hungry, silly, etc.) and list them in the left column.

The brainstorm of feeling words is on the left and Version 1 is on the right. To the far right we have brainstormed a variety of ways we might conclude our text. Here, a grade 2 student checks out a vocabulary word on the list: *devastated*.

- Vote on the top three emotions/states of being and then vote on the best one for the Version 1 co-construct. Write the winning emotion or state of being at the top of the shared writing space.

- Ask the students to stand and act out the winning emotion or state of being. While they are doing so, ask them to pay attention to parts of their bodies—their hands, legs, shoulders, etc.

- Take suggestions for your co-constructed text. Specifically, prompt students to think of body parts and supply verbs ending in -ing, such as eyes blinking, hands clenching, tummy grumbling.

- Transcribe six to eight of these combinations into the co-construct.

<u>Puzzled</u>
mouth twisting
head scratching
eyes widening
nose scrunching
hands bending
shoulders bouncing

4. Hand Out the GO Sheet

5. Have Students Write Their Version 1

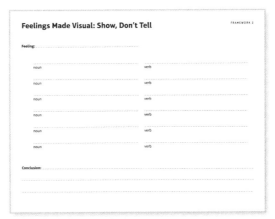

Feelings Made Visual GO Sheet

- Ask students to choose an emotion or state of being from your brainstormed list and write it at the top of their GO Sheet.

- Circulate and check that each student has made a good choice. If anyone is stuck, suggest an emotion or state of being for him or her. Remember, you are practicing a strategy. Don't let kids get overwhelmed.

- Instruct students to stand and act out their emotions or states of being. Delightful mayhem is about to ensue. Consider it a photo opportunity! Have them write nouns and verbs ending in *-ing* related to their actions on their GO Sheets.

- Invite the students to repeat their actions if they need more practice at describing exactly what they are doing with their hands, feet, face, and other body parts.

- Ask them to sit back down and begin composing their Version 1. Encourage discussion throughout this process; have students help one another reach for just-right nouns and verbs.

- Ask students to read their favorite noun-verb combination aloud to the class, and then read their entire text to a neighbor.

Although his conclusion is not visible yet in this photo, this grade 2 writer concluded that the best part about being sleepy is "I get so much energy when I sleep."

6. Discuss Mentor Text, Version 2

- Project Slide 3. Read it aloud once, and then invite students to read it aloud with you. What has changed? (It has an ending.)

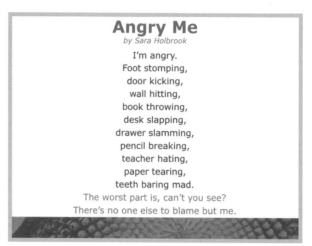

Angry Me
by Sara Holbrook

I'm angry.
Foot stomping,
door kicking,
wall hitting,
book throwing,
desk slapping,
drawer slamming,
pencil breaking,
teacher hating,
paper tearing,
teeth baring mad.
The worst part is, can't you see?
There's no one else to blame but me.

Slide 3

- Ask: *What does this new ending do to the piece? Why would anyone be mad at him- or herself?* (Maybe he or she forgot something? Got in the bath with socks on? Forgot to hit "save"?)

- Ask: *How might the text be different if it ended with "The best part is…" or "The funniest part is…"?*

7. Co-construct Version 2

- Project your co-constructed Version 1 and ask students to read it.

- Brainstorm and list six possible starters for a concluding line: ("The best part is…" "The funniest part is…" "The most interesting part is…" "The scariest part is…")

- Vote on a starter, plug it into your co-constructed Version 1, and finish it as a whole sentence. It doesn't need to be a rhyming couplet, like the mentor text's, but it could be. Don't let that challenge derail the lesson.

8. Have Students Write Their Version 2

- Ask students to relabel their GO Sheets "Version 2."

- Instruct them to select one of the brainstormed starters for a concluding line (or make up their own) and to finish their piece, as you did with the Version 2 co-construct.

- Ask students to read their Version 2 aloud at the same time. Ask them what they think of them. Does the text need more work?

9. Share!

- Ask students to share their work with one another. Get them up and moving around the room, reading and rereading the text.

- Ask a few volunteers to share with the whole class. This is a great video opportunity. Add what you capture to portfolios and share them with parents.

Lesson Extension Ideas

- Use this writing framework to have students describe a character in a story or book. You might also want to use it in a health lesson about feelings, appreciating that we all have a wide range of emotional responses.

- Combine two of the frameworks to create a text for two voices, comparing feelings (e.g., being scared and excited can both leave us shaking and breathless). Have students add illustrations.

- Use this valuable lesson in visual language as a touchstone in future writing. Ask: *How could you improve this character description by doing more than labeling him or her as* lazy *or* excited, *but actually showing how he or she looks and moves?*

Sample Stages

Sad… Brave… In Love… the range of human emotions comes to life as students describe feelings using visual language in this simple noun-verb framework. The collection of samples below bursts from the creative minds of primary students in various schools.

We always begin by acting out the emotion and noting what we do with our feet, faces, hands, and even inside our tummies. Note how the level of detail increases as students gain vocabulary skills.

Sad
Tears   driping
Arms   floping
Legs   curled
Eyes   crying
Heart   BraKing
Hands   flat
Mouth   frowning
feet   Hot
The   best   part is
that   you   Bounce
BacK!

A second grader shows what it means to be sad, but the best part is, *you bounce back.*

in love
hand's holding
eye   starring
head down
heart bumping
The best part is
when I get a
hug.

A first grader from Balikpapan, Indonesia: *The best part is when I get a hug.*

Vershon 1
Brave.
Mouth smiling
Spain stretining
Face glowing
Legs spreding
Body shining
Eyes wedirting
chicks grining.
But the
most luky
thing is that
braveis int
inside you.

A third grader shows first what *brave* looks like on the outside and then reminds us that: *The most lucky thing is that brave is inside you.*

Feelings Made Visual: Assessment Checkpoint

SKILL	3	2	1
Careful Reading	Demonstrates, through classroom discussion and writing, an understanding of the impact of word choice on conveying emotion.	Partially demonstrates, through classroom discussion and writing, an understanding of the impact of word choice on conveying emotion.	Does not yet demonstrate, through classroom discussion and writing, an understanding of the impact of word choice on conveying emotion.
Structure and Organization	Demonstrates the ability to recognize and re-create a writing structure, such as a strong conclusion.	Partially demonstrates the ability to recognize and re-create a writing structure, such as a strong conclusion.	Does not yet demonstrate the ability to recognize and re-create a writing structure, such as a strong conclusion.
Grammar Conventions	Demonstrates an understanding of how to use nouns and gerund verbs in an analysis and writing.	Partially demonstrates an understanding of how to use nouns and gerund verbs in an analysis and writing. May make a minor grammatical error.	Does not yet demonstrate an understanding of how to use nouns and gerund verbs in an analysis and writing.
Connotative Word Meaning	Demonstrates an understanding of connotative word meanings when using visual language to describe a feeling.	Occasionally demonstrates an understanding of the connotative word meanings when using visual language to describe a feeling. May make a comparison that does not seem logical.	Does not yet demonstrate an understanding of connotative word meanings when using visual language to describe a feeling.
Speaking Skills	Is willing to share aloud and consistently demonstrates effective presentation skills using good voice projection, inflection, pacing, eye contact, and stance.	Is often willing to share and partially demonstrates effective presentation skills using good voice projection, inflection, pacing, eye contact, and stance.	Is not yet willing to share and/or does not demonstrate effective presentation skills using good voice projection, inflection, pacing, eye contact, and stance.
Listening Skills	Actively participates in discussions about other students' work and is tuned in to student presentations.	Occasionally participates in discussions about other students' work and is tuned in to student presentations.	Does not participate in discussions about other students' work and is not yet tuned in to student presentations.

From *Striving to Thriving Writers* copyright © 2018 by Sara Holbrook, Michael Salinger, and Stephanie Harvey. Published by Scholastic Inc.

Picture This: Listing What We See

TIME: about 30–45 minutes	GRADE LEVEL: K and up

MATERIALS:

- Slides 1–3*
- Picture This GO Sheet*
- Several photos of areas that are familiar to students (e.g., the school foyer, a local park, a street scene)
- Tablets for students to take photos
- Paper, pencil, and a clipboard for each student (especially if tablets are not available)

*Available online at scholastic.com/ThrivingWriterResources

WHY TEACH THIS?

To read images for important details and craft sentences based on those details.

CONTENT AREA CONNECTIONS: Literature, Social Studies, Science, Art

Persuasive	Descriptive	Narrative	Procedural	Research	Vocabulary	Figurative Language
	X					X

STEPH REFLECTS ON FRAMEWORK 3

Striving readers and writers need a wide variety of entry points into literacy to become confident, capable readers and writers. A close examination of images offers a powerful entry point into meaning that goes beyond merely reading text—and it's a lifeline for strivers! There's no better way to engage kids than to let them have a go at taking their own photos, scrutinizing them closely, and curating them to sift out important details. As Frank Serafini notes (2017), "because communication no longer focuses solely on written language and includes visual images and other modalities, including visual literacy in traditional literacy curricula is essential."

In this writing framework, we will be writing from the outside in, examining an image and making a list of pertinent details. From this list of nouns, we will grow sentences and write a short text. But first, the essential list of facts. Lists keep us on track. From effective writing to doing any job efficiently, lists help us take note of and remember the important stuff.

Michael: Lists of tools, procedural lists, work instructions—the ability to make a good list is vital to success in manufacturing.

Sara: My Uncle Bill was a corporate pilot for over 40 years. He never took off before going through a written checklist. He never assumed.

Michael: The same is true for writers. Having a good list on hand will not only speed the drafting process, it will also keep the essential details from being forgotten.

Sara: A list is also a way of summarizing important ideas from a text, an experience, or an image.

We will venture out into the world and make detailed lists, show student writers that lists are useful, and assist them in building their observational skills. We will also help students prioritize information—one of the building blocks for comprehension. All of this will enhance their communication abilities as they see how gathering precise details enriches their writing.

The framework is written for primary and pre-primary students, but please know we have also used it with AP high school students who are looking to enrich their sense of setting.

We are going to be reading images we collect on our personal devices (which may be a writer's notebook) and then mining them for important details. We are focusing on facts, not opinions. We want, for example, students to describe a picture of the playground in terms of what we see, not simply say it is a *fun* place.

1. Introduce the Framework

- Project Slide 1 and read it aloud. Ask students to look closely at Nutmeg, the hedgehog in the picture, and come up with some details that describe him. *Pink nose, black dots for eyes, fits in a teacup, quills on his head.*

- Explain that this is the type of writing they will be doing: looking for details and putting them in a list.

Slide 1

2. Discuss Mentor Text, Version 1

- Project Slide 2 and read the poem aloud. Then read it aloud again, with students. Ask: *What is this about?*

- Project Slide 3 and explain that the poem evolved from a list of details about a library scene, similar to this one. Explain that writers often use word images—they make a mental picture in their readers' heads. This is called *imagery.*

The Library
by Sara Holbrook

Take the walk
to the open door,
this is where you
find out more
about the stars,
oceans, quakes,
dragons, cars,
cheetahs, snakes,
unicorns, and
jumping beans,
horses, bugs,
and time machines.

From killer whales,
and free tail bats,
to hammer heads
and kitty cats,
the library has got a book.
Come on in, take a look.
Learn how to cook
or write a poem.
Read it here
or take it home.
What do you want
to learn about?
It's free!
It's here!
Check it out!

Slide 2

Photo credit: Kimbra Power

Slide 3

Once upon a time, Sara and Michael were working at Shekou International School in China, a short ferry ride from Hong Kong. First Michael shared "The Library" with students, a poem by Sara that started as a list.

Then Michael projected this photo he took at a street market and asked students to examine it for details. Since the students were dual language learners (English and French), they made two lists, one in each language, as you can see in the following photo, turning and talking to come up with just the right words. We learn something in every lesson with students—for instance, the red bucket in the photo serves as a cash register. This is typical of an essential detail emerging through conversation.

After collecting a good list of details, the students and Michael co-constructed the following text. First, they prioritized the details, circling what they determined to be the most important ones, and then added some verbs to the nouns to turn the bullets into more complete ideas for their Version 1.

continued next page

Lady merchant selling, vegetables sleeping in boxes,
fruit being sold, tomatoes are red, the money bucket
is bored, mushrooms!

Was it perfect? Of course not! It was just Version 1.

Although this photo seems foreign to us, it wasn't to the students at SIS, who were not only well acquainted with outdoor vegetable merchants, but also their "stinky neighbors," the fish merchants.

Once you grow details into sentences and phrases, you and your students can craft them into a poem, or use them to flesh out a setting for a fictional story or nonfiction report. No matter where the writing takes you, it's best to begin with a solid list of observations.

- Ask: *Why do you think the writer selected these details?* (The person making the list considered them important.) Discuss how zeroing in on an image's most important details helps writers create images in their reader's mind.

- Ask: *Are there any details you might add to the mentor text?*

3. Co-construct Version 1

- Project several photos that you took before the lesson of areas that are familiar to students.

- Ask students to turn and talk about which is the best image, most likely the one that contains the most details. Choose one of the photos based on their input.

- Ask students to turn and talk about what they consider the most important or interesting details. Solicit their ideas, and list them in your co-construct writing space.

- Read the final list aloud with the students.

4. Hand Out the GO Sheet

5. Have Students Write Their Version 1

- Have students gather their details in one of two ways:

  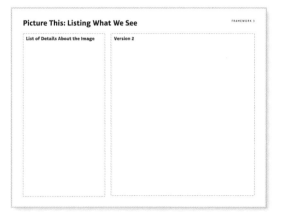

  Picture This GO Sheet

  1. Take a few pictures within the classroom, library, playground, or other easily accessed location. They will come back with dozens of photos. When they return with their collection of images, ask them to select their best image to write about. Ask them to jot down four or five of the most important details from that image in the left column on their GO Sheets. Set a time limit. For younger students working in the classroom, three minutes is plenty. If you go outside the classroom, make adjustments.

  2. On a piece of paper, list ideas about a place by stopping and noticing. Instruct the students to imagine they have taken a photograph with their mind's camera and to identify details in that photo. Then have them turn to another scene and repeat. Take three or four of these mind photographs. The students should end up with a bulleted list of three or four details on their GO Sheets.

- Once students have a list of details, ask them to read their lists aloud at the same time.

- Instruct students to read their lists to others in the class.

6. **Co-construct Version 2**

- Return to the list of important details of the Version 1 co-construct you created as a class.
- Turn each detail into a full sentence, perhaps using a prompt such as "_____ is important because…"
- Add a concluding sentence, one true statement.

7. **Have Students Discuss the Co-constructed Version 2 and Write Their Version 2**

- Instruct students to return to their own Version 1 and craft complete sentences, perhaps by only adding a verb, depending on their skills.
- Ask students to add one concluding sentence, a true statement about their observation.
- While students are working, occasionally call on volunteers to share one of their sentences with the class.

8. **Share!**

- Ask students to first share their writing with a neighbor.
- Call on individual students to share with the class.

Lesson Extension Ideas

- Have students use what they produce as a jumping off place for a persuasive newspaper editorial about improvements to a local park. Or have them add a character to the setting and turn the list into a piece of fiction.
- Rearrange and craft lists into a poem or song. Perhaps the writer might want to add a refrain line. (See "Refrain Again," page 101.)
- Have students use their lists for character analysis to help flesh out a piece of writing.
- Use this framework as a touchstone as students take on more complex writing assignments. Ask: _Have you made your list yet? Remember how making a list makes drafting easier?_

Content Area Extension Ideas

- With students in grades 5 and up, make multiple lists and combine the lists creatively. For example, make a list of words having to do with the circulatory system, and then make a list of words having to do with the cafeteria. Ask students to describe the cafeteria using circulatory words. (See "Extended Metaphor," page 235.)
- Share _Topography of the Library_ (on the next page). Ask students how many lists were involved in writing this piece. (Two: topographical terms and library observations) Discuss how the two lists are woven together. Ask students to think about how they might make their lists into a paragraph or even a poem.

Sample Stages

Lists are the most versatile of all types of writing. As you see here, we have used them to jump-start writing with students of all ages. In the samples below you can see how kindergartners use lists to practice sentence construction and how sixth graders use them to begin to talk about figurative language.

In this kindergarten class in Lusaka, Zambia, students made lists of three nouns about their homes, followed by one sentence naming a favorite thing about home for their Version 1. For Version 2, we added verbs to the nouns.

This kindergartner proudly displays her Version 2, complete with verbs and a strong sentence conclusion.

Kindergarten students work on their whiteboards, engaged in conversation as they make their lists about home. Using whiteboards helped students feel free to experiment with words.

Here, Sara is working at Jakarta Intercultural School on a co-constructed text (Version 1) combining two lists: a list of observations about the library, and one of topographical terms. Following this, the sixth graders chose nonfiction books about a topic of their choice (spiders, space, solar power) and constructed their own lists. While these lists could have been used to begin a short paragraph summary of the book, they used the lists to create poems.

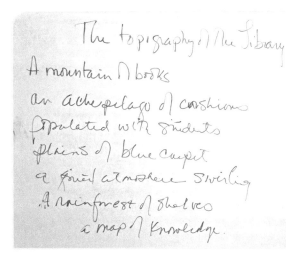 

Picture This: Assessment Checkpoint

SKILL	3	2	1
Identify Key Details	Demonstrates, through classroom discussion and writing, the ability to identify key details in a scene as depicted in an image.	Partially demonstrates, through classroom discussion and writing, the ability to identify key details in a scene as depicted in an image.	Does not yet demonstrate, through classroom discussion and writing, the ability to identify key details in a scene as depicted in an image.
Prioritize Key Details	Demonstrates the ability to choose the most important facts from a list of details that complete the description of an image.	Partially demonstrates the ability to identify key details among a list of many details, occasionally choosing important facts that complete the description of an image.	Does not yet demonstrate the ability to identify key details among a list of many details, and is not yet able to choose important facts that complete the description of an image.
Sentence Construction	Demonstrates the ability to develop full sentences to grow a list of details into a fully formed description of a scene or image.	Partially demonstrates the ability to develop full sentences to grow a list of details into a fully formed description of a scene or image.	Is not yet able to demonstrate the ability to develop full sentences to grow a list of details into a fully formed description of a scene or image.
Speaking Skills	Is willing to share aloud and consistently demonstrates effective presentation skills using good voice projection, inflection, pacing, eye contact, and stance.	Is often willing to share and partially demonstrates effective presentation skills using good voice projection, inflection, pacing, eye contact, and stance.	Is not yet willing to share and/or does not demonstrate effective presentation skills using good voice projection, inflection, pacing, eye contact, and stance.
Listening Skills	Actively participates in discussions about other students' work and is tuned in to student presentations.	Occasionally participates in discussions about other students' work and is tuned in to student presentations.	Does not participate in discussions about other students' work and is not yet tuned in to student presentations.

Pinpointing Vocabulary: Describing Word Meaning

TIME: about 45 minutes   **GRADE LEVEL:** 4 and up

MATERIALS:

- Slides 1–5*
- Pinpointing Vocabulary Go Sheet*
- A list of targeted vocabulary words
- Notebooks, computers, or tablets

*Available online at scholastic.com/ThrivingWriterResources

WHY TEACH THIS?

To take students beyond using a vocabulary word in a sentence to describe how it works in the world in terms of what it can and cannot do.

CONTENT AREA CONNECTIONS: All subjects

Persuasive	Descriptive	Narrative	Procedural	Research	Vocabulary	Figurative Language
	X	X		X	X	X

STEPH REFLECTS ON FRAMEWORK 4

Visualizing is the strategy that brings joy to reading. When we visualize as we read, we create our own movie or slide show in our minds. We keep that projector running unfettered as we read on. To engage readers so completely, writers paint pictures with words by showing, not telling. Taking a word like *happy* and sharing what happy looks like works wonders when teaching kids to show, not merely tell.

We all want to be understood. We want people to get us and get what we are saying. The surest route to understanding is language mastery and a rich vocabulary. In this writing framework, students will discuss word meaning with a partner, write about a word, and share with the class. This framework hits the bull's-eye when it comes to vocabulary acquisition.

Research shows that if a student can tell you what a word does *not* mean, it is a much more accurate indication that they know the meaning of the word (Beck, 2002). It is also noted that visualizing the word and using it in multiple contexts, conversation, and writing also fosters deeper understanding. This is why we are going to describe, instead of merely define, the words.

Sara:	If memorizing word lists worked, I'd be killer at Scrabble. But as much as I try to memorize those lists of obscure small words, they evaporate like rain on hot concrete when the pressure is on. With no context, I can't get them to stick, let alone use them in writing.
Michael:	And adding a one- or two-word definition to unfamiliar words doesn't help much. So rather than define a word, this framework helps students to *describe* a word.
Sara:	Words like *piu* and *wud*?
Michael:	Words like *serf* and *zygote*; words that will help kids communicate their content understanding. I'm not sure anything will help your Scrabble game.
Sara:	Just you wait, 'enry 'iggins, just you wait.

This framework is a great way to work on vocabulary pertinent to content learning, whether they are tier two words—terms that travel across disciplines, such as *revolution* or *point*—or tier three words—content-specific terms, such as *enzyme* or *tundra*. We often personify words in this writing framework, put shoes on them, and walk them around the room to see what the word would and would not do, opening the door for you to reteach the power of that literary device. Allocate plenty of time for sharing as the words begin to come to life, to borrow Beck's terminology, as students think deeply to pinpoint word meaning.

1. Introduce the Framework

Project Slide 1, read it aloud, and introduce the concept of writing about word meaning. Tell students that first they will write about a familiar word to understand the framework, and then they will go on to describe more challenging words from a content area.

2. Discuss Mentor Text

- Project Slide 2, 3, or 4, depending on grade level. We offer three mentor texts: one short poem for primary students that is fun to reread and act out, a short paragraph for intermediate students, and a prose poem for students in grades 6 and up.

- Read aloud the text you chose, and have students reread it. Ask: *What is this text describing?* (It describes what the word *happy* [jubilant] acts like.)

- Ask the students to identify lines in the mentor text that describe what the word does or looks like. Then ask them to identify lines that describe what the word does not do or look like.

- Ask: *Do these descriptions help you to visualize the word in action? Why is that a good thing?* (Because it makes the reader think more deeply about the word than a simple single-sentence definition or synonym.)

Pinpointing Vocabulary:
Describing Word Meaning

What are we going to learn today?

1. We will describe words in terms of what they mean *and* what they don't mean.
2. We will collaborate with a partner to discuss and write about word meaning.
3. We will share our word knowledge.

Slide 1

Happy Moves
by Sara Holbrook

Happy
jumps,
smiles,
fist pumps
and doesn't
wear a frown.
Tickle.
Giggle.
Clap.
And wiggle.
Happy dances
all around.

Slide 2

Happy Glow
by Sara Holbrook

Happy settles, an orange campfire in my chest. It's peaceful, not a scattering wildfire, dangerous and fierce. More like a slow glow, my inner circle, warm, attracting others all around.

Slide 3

Jubilant
by Michael Salinger

Jubilant is
beyond plain old happy
she's dancing in the street.
Doesn't wear a boo-boo lip,
never drags her feet.
Kissing strangers, hands clapping,
on cloud nine,
whooping to the sky,
winning lottery ticket in hand,
out of her mind with delight.
Seeing jubilant you just might,
without being rude,
describe her as being
in a very, very, very
good mood.

Slide 4

---

3. Co-construct Version 1

- Re-create the Pinpointing Vocabulary GO Sheet so it's visible to all.

- Select a word to describe in your co-construct. We usually select a word that students have plenty of prior knowledge about, such as *friendship*, so we can focus on the writing strategy rather than the word's meaning.

- Explain to students that one way to do research is to interview experts, and seeing that they are all experts when it comes to friendship, you are going to interview them to help fill in your GO Sheet.

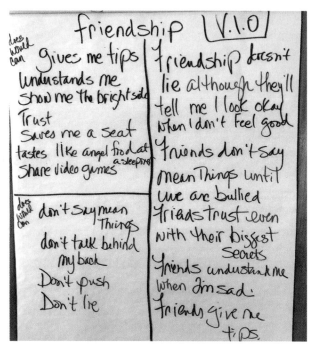

A co-construct from a grade 5 classroom
in New Philadelphia, Ohio.

- Ask students to turn and talk about what a good friend does or does not do. Then take a suggestion of something a friend does—for example, "Save me a seat at lunch"—and write it in the top left-hand box.

- Ask: *What might a friend* not *do?* If you get a general reply, such as "Be mean," prod for a more specific answer (A friend does not trip me in the hall).

- Jump back and forth between the two boxes on the left to encourage students to think about the opposite of what they have just written.

- Collect four or five responses for what a friend does and what a friend doesn't do. Encourage students to think about how this word (*friend*) would act in different environments, such as the lunchroom, a soccer field, or the hallway. Include one sensory observation (smells like, tastes like, etc.).

- Write Version 1. To begin, take suggestions from students about which response to pull over first.

- Write that response in the box on the right and extend it into a full sentence, using a transition word. For example, "A friend shares snacks *when* I'm hungry." Suggest transition words for the first few responses and then ask students to provide them as you continue working.

Transition words (Slide 5) are an essential part of complex sentences, the kinds of sentences mature writers use in essays, reports, and other common forms of writing. Knowing how to use transition words in writing takes practice. We have included a partial list of transition words for students to use as they work on this fundamental skill.

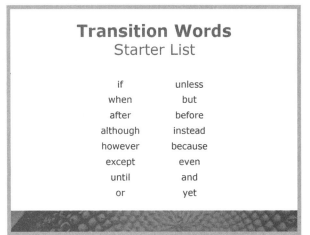

Slide 5

- Continue selecting responses from the *Does* or *Doesn't* boxes, extending them with transition words, until you have four (or so) sentences. Then ask students to come up with a declarative statement to end the text, containing no transition word. The statement should break the established pattern to bring the text to a satisfying conclusion. We never use all the ideas we've gathered in our two boxes; instead we urge students to prioritize and use the most important of those listed.

- When you're finished, read the piece aloud with students. Applaud yourselves. Not bad for Version 1.

4. Hand Out the GO Sheet

5. Have Students Write Their Version 1

- Have students pair up with a writing partner, and provide them with a word to define. Duplicate words are okay; it's good to get varied responses.

- Make sure each student is filling in their own copy of the GO Sheet.

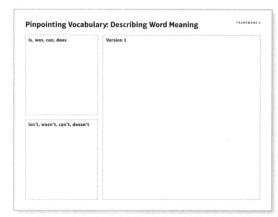

Pinpointing Vocabulary GO Sheet

- Provide research material related to the words they are writing about. For example, if they're writing about receivers, you might provide them with books and handouts on electricity.

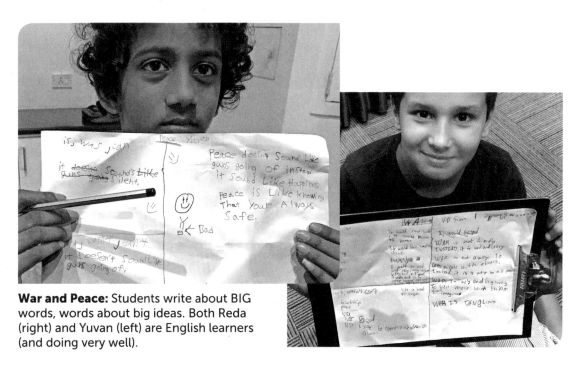

War and Peace: Students write about BIG words, words about big ideas. Both Reda (right) and Yuvan (left) are English learners (and doing very well).

> **"War" by Reda, age 9**
> War is not friendly instead it is sad and crazy.
> War is not a way to communicate with others instead it is a way to kill people.
> War is ugly and frightening even more than things I could imagine.
> War is dangerous.

- Instruct students to fill in the left side of the Vocabulary GO Sheet with five or six responses in each box, based on research they've done. In the upper left-hand box, they list what the word does, is, can, or would do (for instance, *equator* circles Earth, is invisible, and is at the zeroth circle of latitude). In the lower left-hand box, they list what the word doesn't, isn't, can't, or wouldn't do (*equator* is not on the North pole, doesn't run vertically, is not truly fixed). Adjust the number of responses as necessary, based on your students' capabilities. Encourage lots of research and discussion.

- Once the left side of the sheet is completed, give students the option to continue with partners—or split up and write solo. If they continue to work together, have each partner maintain a copy of what he or she is writing. Some students may wish to transition to a notebook, computer, or tablet at this point.

- Set a goal for the number of sentences students create. Three or four is a good starting point for intermediate students and above. One or two is sufficient for primary students.

- Remind students to stretch their ideas with transition words and urge them to include new ideas. We want them to develop their ideas fully, not just stack bullet points.

- When they're finished, have students read their Version 1 aloud, in unison, then have them share them with a classmate other than their writing partner.

- Call on volunteers to read their Version 1 to the class. Discuss the words being described to help solidify understanding.

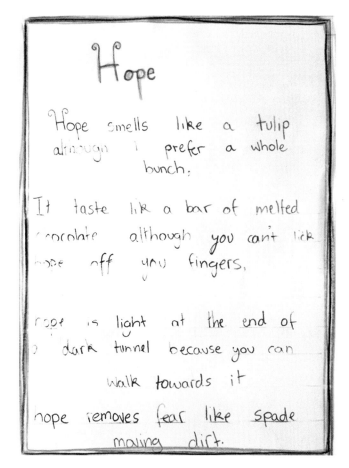

6. Co-construct Version 2

- If you are a content area teacher, you may consider finishing at this point, because co-constructing Version 2 is designed to improve writing skills by adding more detail.

- If you are an ELA teacher, return to your Version 1 co-construct. Review one of your sentences containing a transition word and then ask students to help you come up with a supporting sentence. For example:

  - Version 1 sentence: *A friend shares snacks even when I don't ask.*

  - Supporting sentence: *My friend knows that I love chocolate.*

- Focus on your instructional goals. For example, you may wish to have students add one simile to Version 2, or add a line of dialogue to practice quotation marks.

- Demonstrate by adding the target element to your co-construct, and then set students on their own to revise their Version 1, adding a supporting sentence to add detail.

7. Have Students Write Their Version 2

- Have students work individually on their Version 2 or continue in pairs—it's up to them and you.

- Instruct students to go back to their Version 1 and to insert at least one supporting sentence.

8. Share!

- Note that sharing aloud is especially beneficial here. If students are working on content area vocabulary words, sharing aloud means sharing their learning.

- After each student shares, ask the class: *What does this word mean? What does it not mean?* If more than one student has written about the same word, encourage the class to compare the pieces to boost vocabulary learning.

Lesson Extension Ideas

- Have students use these short texts as a basis for longer works. They can expand on their Version 2 into a more complex prose piece.

- Ask them to distill their texts into poems. See "Found Poem," page 184, for ideas.

- Compile students' texts into a classroom dictionary to support the lesson from which the vocabulary comes. Encourage students to refer to their dictionary during unit study as needed.

- Use this framework to define high-concept words that may be part of your school's ethos (*responsibility, courage, honesty*).

Sample Stages

Working in Theresa Marriott's fourth-grade class in Balikpapan, Indonesia, we first had students write about familiar words to teach them the framework. Then, once they were familiar with how it worked, we moved on to write about content area words from their science unit on electricity, using classroom resources. After co-constructing, students chose from a preselected list of electricity vocabulary words. Afterward we shared, discussing each word's meaning, reinforcing learning and giving Theresa a clear insight into the students' understanding.

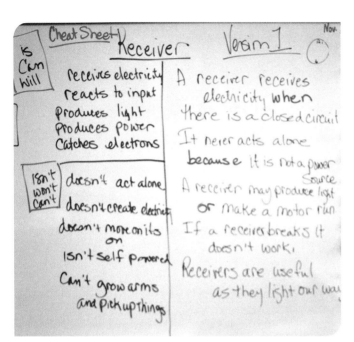

(above) Fourth grader using classroom books to research his text.

(left) Fourth graders co-construct text about a receiver based on their learning about electricity and using transition words to expand their ideas.

PART I: LEARNING ABOUT LANGUAGE

Circuits Version 2

Circuits are circles instead of polka dots
Circuits only work if it is a closed circuit not an open circuit
Electricity flows through a circuit like water through a hula hoop
BUT REMEMBER CIRCUITS ARE TOTALLY CIRCLES!!!!!!!!!!!!!!!!!!!
Lucia, grade four

Force Version 3

Pull the magnet
Push the magnet
Or make it dance around
Because this force is so strong
We use it to power our trains
When we use this strong force
We can power our World!
Tyler, grade four

(left) Lucia is able to evidence her understanding of circuits in the first sentence of her Version 2 text. Using her own words, she is making a conceptual comparison, rather than just repeating a textbook definition.

(right) Tyler gets creative in his Version 3, describing how magnets can both pull and push.

Pinpointing Vocabulary: Assessment Checkpoint

SKILL	3	2	1
Careful Reading	Demonstrates a deeper understanding of words through examining their relationships to other words, research, and common experience.	Partially demonstrates an understanding of word meanings. May not pick up on nuanced meanings and may display some misperceptions when trying to analyze text.	Does not yet demonstrate an understanding of word meanings and is unable to understand texts in which the words appear.
Structure and Organization	Demonstrates the ability to recognize and re-create a writing structure and to craft a strong conclusion. There is a well-developed prewrite, and the finished piece uses transition words followed by the growth of relevant ideas.	Demonstrates a partial ability to recognize and re-create a writing structure and to craft a strong conclusion. The prewrite may be lacking, and transitions may be followed by generalizations that do not add to understanding.	Does not yet demonstrate the ability to recognize and re-create a writing structure. The piece may not be complete, and there may be gross misperceptions regarding word meanings.
Write Informative Explanatory Text	Demonstrates the use of well-researched details and specific examples in support of their word definitions.	Partially demonstrates the use of research, details, and some examples to support their word definitions. May include some clichés or unsupported interpretations.	Demonstrates no apparent research. Shows misperceptions in the meaning of the words. Uses no transitions or follows transitions with non sequiturs.
Speaking Skills	Is willing to share aloud and consistently demonstrates effective presentation skills using good voice projection, inflection, pacing, eye contact, and stance.	Is often willing to share and partially demonstrates effective presentation skills using good voice projection, inflection, pacing, eye contact, and stance.	Is not yet willing to share and/or does not demonstrate effective presentation skills using good voice projection, inflection, pacing, eye contact, and stance.
Listening Skills	Actively participates in discussions about other students' work and is tuned in to student presentations.	Occasionally participates in discussions about other students' work and is tuned in to student presentations.	Does not participate in discussions about other students' work and is not yet tuned in to student presentations.

 From Striving to Thriving Writers copyright © 2018 by Sara Holbrook, Michael Salinger, and Stephanie Harvey. Published by Scholastic Inc.

Personification: A Word Walks In

TIME: about 45 minutes   **GRADE LEVEL:** 4 and up

MATERIALS:

- Slides 1–3*
- Personification GO Sheet*
- Notebooks, computers, or tablets

*Available online at scholastic.com/ThrivingWriterResources

WHY TEACH THIS?

1. To help students see that personification is central to understanding and using figurative language.

2. To show students how to personify a feeling or abstract noun, dressing it up and examining how it looks, moves, and sounds.

CONTENT AREA CONNECTIONS: ELA initially, but you may see other connections as you personify content area terms.

Persuasive	Descriptive	Narrative	Procedural	Research	Vocabulary	Figurative Language
	X	X			X	X

STEPH REFLECTS ON FRAMEWORK 5

As they say, time can fly—it can drag its feet, tap its fingers, or it might even run away. Don't let it run away before you steal a few minutes to teach personification, a very important aspect of writing. In general, helping children learn to use figurative language in their writing also enhances their comprehension of reading as it brings language to life, adding depth, vitality, and meaning to both reading and writing.

If it walks like frustration or sings like joy, then it's personification.

This lesson is designed to encourage students to attach physical characteristics to otherwise intangible emotional states by collecting and citing evidence rather than subjective synonyms. We demonstrate *show, don't tell* by asking students to use objective evidence to tell us *how* (*show* minus the *s*) a particular emotion acts within a well-structured sequence. This way we avoid lines like "I knew he was angry because he had a mad face," or "She was the bravest and stood up fearlessly."

Personification is possibly the most ubiquitous form of figurative language. Words and phrases that animate our descriptions of objects and feelings with human traits help our readers and listeners manufacture a picture of what we are trying to communicate. Time can fly, it can drag its feet, tap its fingers, or it might even run away. That neon sign might be screaming for attention while a bucolic log cabin hides among the pines. Personifying a word requires that the writers cozy up to that word, familiarizing themselves with the nuances of its meaning.

By employing well-grounded personification in their own writing, students will be better able to identify and understand its use in the text they read.

Sara: Personification makes words cartwheel and skip.

Michael: Hopefully in language that doesn't trip over itself.

1. Introduce the Framework

Project Slide 1, read it aloud, and quickly review the concept of personification: giving human characteristics to something that is not human.

Slide 1

2. Discuss Mentor Text

- Project Slide 2, read it aloud, and clarify any unknown words. Ask students to join you in a second read-aloud, and have fun!

- Ask: *Can* Sorry *really sit next to you at dinner? Can it trail after you?* This is personification in action, and it is a tool of writers of fiction, nonfiction, poetry, and other types of text.

- Explain that the author could have personified the word *sorry* by simply writing, *Sorry was really annoying* or *Sorry was bugging me*, but instead she explained how *Sorry* was a pest by describing the annoying actions *Sorry* took. This is what is meant by *Show, don't tell.*

Shy

Jennifer

Shy shuffles her feet,

stares at ground,

nibbling at her bottom lip.

A moth

of washed out grey

among a crowd of brightly colored butterflies.

She was not

standing on stage

applauded

by millions of spectators.

Instead

Shy cowers,

makes herself

as small as possible,

and slips

unnoticed

through the crowd

without a word.

Version 2 of sixth grader Jennifer's personification of the word *shy*. For Version 3, we would help her identify some tense issues and encourage her to experiment by rearranging lines and seeing where she could take this creatively.

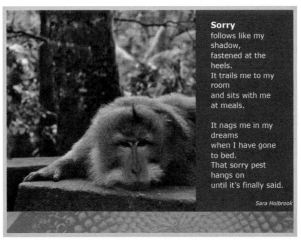

Slide 2

A WORD ABOUT GENDER SENSITIVITY

In the Version 1 co-construct, we refer to the word we are personifying as *he* or *she*. This is just for simplicity's sake, and in the Version 2 co-construct, you and/or students may wish to edit those pronouns out.

We want to work with a singular pronoun for clarity, so *them* doesn't work, and neither does using *it* to describe human qualities. So, in Version 1, we might describe *Flamboyant* as a *she*, as in *She walked in wearing a tutu and a neon pink boa.* By Version 2, we might drop the pronoun altogether: *Flamboyant bounced in wearing a tutu and a neon pink boa*, or change it altogether, giving *Flamboyant* a bright red beard and a top hat. This is the beauty of Version 1; it is infinitely changeable.

All emotions and states of being are, of course, gender neutral. In our co-constructing, we like to challenge gender stereotypes. *Flirty* is not always female and *Powerful* is not always male. We urge you to embrace this thinking as you co-construct your Version 1 with the class, but choose either *he* or *she* to start. At Version 2 and beyond, let writers know that gender is not essential to personification and gender-specific pronouns may be dropped entirely.

3. Build Background Knowledge

How personification works: Before we ask students to describe an abstract noun or a feeling using actions, we want to familiarize them with how actions lead us as readers to infer meaning. The following warm-up exercise helps them differentiate between identifying physical evidence and interpretation or inference. We don't care why *Shocked* is grabbing his hair with his mouth agape, we simply want to describe what we see and leave it to our reader to infer.

- Write three basic emotions or states of being on slips of paper, such as *happy, sad, angry, sleepy, excited, scared.*

- Invite three enthusiastic volunteers to the front of the class, hand each one a slip of paper, and ask him or her, one at a time, to act out the emotion or state of being physically, using no words or cliché movements, such as drawing hearts in the air for "in love."

- As each student performs, ask the class members what they are seeing. Most likely they will initially guess the emotion being acted out: *sad, depressed,* or *unhappy.* If that's the case, push them to articulate the actions that led them to identify that emotion. In other words, have them describe motions, not emotions, evidence rather than interpretation. Volunteers may have to perform their emotion multiple times.

- Allow volunteers to return to their seats after their action has been described and you have recorded class members' responses on the board. Tip: Overacting pays off. Applaud the performers!

- Explain that these are images—not visual images like photos, but word images a reader might encounter in a story.

- Consider your three images and read the first one aloud. Ask: *If you saw this as a character description in a story, what would you infer the character was feeling?* Jot down four or five suggestions from students. If you're working on a projection system, write the images in one color and the emotions in another. (See right.)

- Push beyond everyday vocabulary words, such as *happy*, *angry*, and *sad*. Go for those "five-dollar" words, such as *exuberant*, *reticent*, and *infuriated*.

- To create personification, replace pronouns with emotions and states of being. (*Shy* hid behind her hair. *Rage* stomped. *Elation* leapt.)

① She hid behind her hair, fingers touching her lips, and turned away.

② He stomped, crossed his arms, then punched the air with two fists.

③ He leapt into the air, fist pumping and hollering, hooray!

① She hid behind her hair, fingers touching her lips, and turned away.

② He stomped, crossed his arms, then punched the air with two fists.

③ He leapt into the air, fist pumping and hollering, hooray!

4. Co-construct Version 1

- Pick an emotion or state-of-being word to write about as a group. We like to take three suggestions from the class and then vote on the final word. Assure students whose nomination did not get chosen that they can work with that word when they write on their own.

- Write the word at the top of your co-construct space.

- Remind students to describe *how* the emotion manifests itself. In other words, they should describe the actions of the emotion, and not rename the emotion. *Embarrassed* is not acting *shamed*, for instance.

- Title your text "Version 1" and build the text one line at a time.

- Ask students to come up with a line describing an action the emotion might take. Prompt them by asking a question such as, *How might it enter the room?* Solicit several suggestions and meld them into a line of text.

  Embarrassed: He walked in slowly, head down.

- From there, consider following this line-by-line procedure:

Line 1: Action: Ask students to describe external actions a word such as *embarrassed* might take, or actions we might see (we are not mind readers). For example, *Embarrassed hides his face, sweats profusely.* (*Embarrassed was thinking about what he'd done* is mind reading. *Embarrassed was hiding in his hoodie* is an action.)

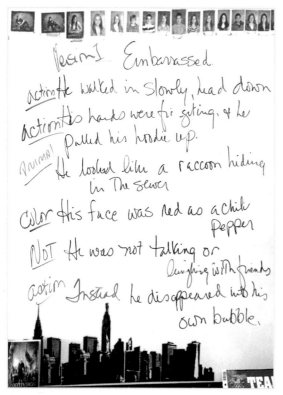

This co-constructed text is from Libbie Royko's seventh-grade class in Eastlake, Ohio.

Line 2: Action: Ask: *What happens next? What's another action that this word may take?* (His hands were fidgeting.)

Line 3: Animal: Ask: *If you were to compare this word to an animal, which would it be?* Have students turn and talk and then take a few suggestions, picking one and adding it to the list of descriptors. (He looked like a raccoon hiding in the sewer.) Ask: *Under what circumstance is the animal behaving this way?* Note: Is that bear you are referencing shuffling out of a cave after hibernating or is it standing on its hind legs clawing the air? Be specific and offer some context to the animal comparison.

Line 4: Color: Bring a little color into the fourth line— color to describe clothing, mood, or an outside force. *His face was as red as a chili pepper.* From gray skies to yellow flowers, color adds tone to any text.

Line 5: Opposite Action: What is your word definitely *not* doing? (He was not talking or laughing with friends.) Using contrast this way helps to clarify your message.

Line 6: Action: Add one more action, starting with a transition word such as *rather* or *instead*. (Instead, he disappeared into his own bubble.)

Read aloud your Version 1 with the class and stand tall. Applause! Great Version 1.

5. **Hand Out the GO Sheet**

6. **Have Students Write Their Version 1**
   - Ask students to pair up with a writing partner or work solo. Have each pair or individual student select one of the remaining emotions or states of being on the board, or come up with their own, as long as it fits the criteria. Have them write that word at the top of their GO Sheets.

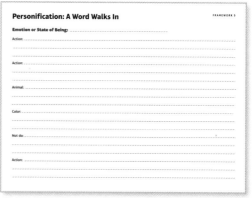

Personification GO Sheet

- Ask students to stand up and act out their word. Encourage them to go over the top and exaggerate movements. Urge them to be conscious of what they are doing with their hands, feet, shoulders, and faces. Doing so will inform their writing.

- Tell students to sit and base their first line on the GO Sheet on one of the actions they just performed. Walk them through the five remaining prompts, one at a time.

    Action: Add at least one more action. Think about eyes, shoulders, feet.

    Animal: Encourage students to think beyond clichés. *Brave* doesn't have to be a lion; it can be a chihuahua. Remind them of birds and insects—mean like a scorpion perhaps, or annoying like a mosquito.

    Color: Dress the word up in a pink tutu or a black cape. Ask if the word might be wearing mismatched red and blue socks, or is the word standing out in the room like an orange traffic cone?

    Not do: *Shy* wouldn't be standing on a chair belting out a song, and *Evil* is not passing out hugs. Ask: *What would your word definitely not do?*

    Action: Begin this line with *Instead* or *Rather,* building a comparison with the previous prompt. Shy was not standing on a chair belting out a song; instead she hid under her desk. Again, students are looking to identify actions, not motivations.

- Remind students to focus on actions, not motivations, thoughts, or feelings— what their words did, not what they were thinking. No mind reading.

- If they get stuck on a particular prompt (animal and color can be tricky at times), encourage peer discussion and/or throw the challenge out to the whole class for ideas, so students see writing as a cooperative effort.

- Once students have completed their six-sentence texts, invite them to read aloud all at once, and then read aloud to a partner.

7. Co-construct Version 2

- Return to your co-constructed Version 1 and look for words that can be eliminated or phrases that can be tightened, beginning with the first line.

- Strengthen verbs.

- For the animal line, consider turning a simile into a metaphor, or a metaphor into a simile. Which works better?

- Don't finish your Version 2 before students begin their own. We usually continue working as students are writing, to model the process.

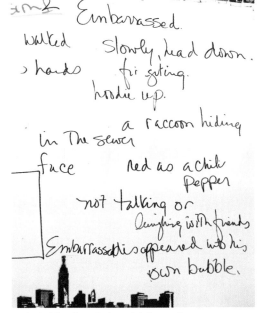

This is Version 2, in which students have eliminated all but, in their opinion, power words.

8. Have Students Write Their Version 2

- Suggest students start their Version 2 by rearranging the lines and picking their strongest line to be used for the lead. Give them a "word elimination" goal, such as removing at least six words from their Version 1.

- Confer with and offer assistance to writers who can use it.

- Encourage subsequent versions. You might ask students to evolve their work into a character description or the opening paragraph to a story. See Slide 3 in which we have turned "Embarrassed" into a short piece of descriptive prose.

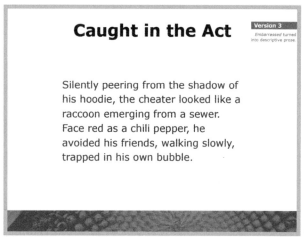

Slide 3

9. Share!

- Ask students to share their work with a student other than their writing partner.

- Ask a few volunteers to share their work with the whole class. Urge them to read with expression! Their body language and the tone of their voices should reflect the personified word. *Evil* should not sound the same as, say, *Jubilant*.

Lesson Extension Ideas

- Consider having students continue to revise their pieces onward, to Versions 3, 4, 5, and so on, clarifying images and honing their visual language. They may add more sensory perceptions or even a line or two of dialogue. In this way they will experience what it means to grow a simple piece of text into a more complex work.

- After substituting the emotion with someone or something concrete, have them use Version 2 text as an opening paragraph or character description, and, from there, continue writing a longer piece.

Content Area Extension Idea

Use this framework to personify important terms in any discipline (e.g., How would *evolution* behave? What would *democracy* do in a lunchroom? What about an *electron*?)

Sample Stages

These personification texts move out and move on, compressing into poetry or morphing into character descriptions or story starters. The framework can even be used to personify content area words, such as *chemical elements,* or social studies words, such as *revolution.* In these samples, students were working with abstract nouns.

> ### Version 2
>
> Brave
> He stands up straight ~~and~~ puffs ~~his~~ chest out
> putting ~~his~~ shoulders up high,
> ~~He~~ looks across the room with a fierce face,
> ~~He was~~ a mama bear fighting for ~~his~~ cubs,
> ~~His~~ clothes were ~~a~~ royal purple making him look fierce,
> ~~He~~ was not wasting time,

In this sample Version 2, a fifth grader is doing a great job eliminating unnecessary words to tighten his text. For Version 3, we would coach him to keep his gender references consistent (*he* can't be a mama bear, for instance), or eliminate the pronouns altogether by crafting a metaphor. Work in progress!

> ### DOUBTFUL   VERSION 1
>
> ACTION SHE TIPTOED IN LOOKING ALL AROUND HOW So
> THE ROOM AND LET OUT A BIG SIGH.
> ACTION SHE STARTED IN ONE DIRECTION THEN HEADED (WALT) Wh
> IN ANOTHER AND SHRUGGED HER HEAD INTO → Far
> HER SHOULDERS. hap
> ANIMAL SHE LOOKED LIKE A JITTERY MOUSE
> IN THE MIDDLE OF AN OPEN FIELD.
> COLOR SHE WAS LIKE A GRAY FOG
> NOT SHE WASN'T STANDING TALL HOLDING
> HER HEAD HIGH POPPING WITH JOY
> ACTION RATHER SHE STAYED ALONE SINKING (WALT) Which
> INTO SILENCE.

Englis]
→ Edit
→ Poetry

This is a sample co-construct written with a fourth-grade class in Frederick, Maryland. *Doubtful* was a word taken from their vocabulary list for that week. The students went on to write definitions of other words on the list.

Personification: Assessment Checkpoint

SKILL	3	2	1
Careful Reading	Demonstrates an understanding of how to use actions to define an emotion in visual language.	Partially demonstrates an understanding of how to use actions to define an emotion in visual language. May confuse more nuanced references.	Does not yet demonstrate an understanding of how to use actions to define an emotion in visual language. Cannot see past literal meaning of text.
Structure and Organization	Demonstrates the ability to recognize and re-create a writing structure and to revise for concision and order.	Partially demonstrates the ability to recognize and re-create a writing structure. May not be able to complete one or two of the sequential steps or instructions.	Does not yet demonstrate the ability to recognize and re-create a writing structure. Is unable to follow most of the sequence and instructions.
Grammar Conventions	Demonstrates an understanding of how to maintain third person throughout the piece. Maintains subject-verb agreement throughout.	Partially demonstrates an understanding of how to maintain third person throughout the piece. Maintains subject-verb agreement most of the time.	Does not yet demonstrate the ability to maintain third person throughout the piece. Confuses subject-verb agreement throughout.
Connotative Word Meaning	Demonstrates an understanding of figurative language, word relationships, and nuances in word meanings when using personification.	Occasionally demonstrates an understanding of figurative language, word relationships, and nuances in word meanings when using personification. May have trouble articulating responses to one or two of the writing prompts.	Does not yet demonstrate an understanding of figurative language, word relationships, and nuances in word meanings when using personification. Cannot articulate responses to any of the writing prompts.
Speaking Skills	Is willing to share aloud and consistently demonstrates effective presentation skills using good voice projection, inflection, pacing, eye contact, and stance.	Is often willing to share and partially demonstrates effective presentation skills using good voice projection, inflection, pacing, eye contact, and stance.	Is not yet willing to share and/or does not demonstrate effective presentation skills using good voice projection, inflection, pacing, eye contact, and stance.
Listening Skills	Actively participates in discussions about other students' work and is tuned in to student presentations.	Occasionally participates in discussions about other students' work and is tuned in to student presentations.	Does not participate in discussions about other students' work and is not yet tuned in to student presentations.

Prepositionally Speaking: Setting the Scene

TIME: about 45 minutes   **GRADE LEVEL:** 5 and up

MATERIALS:

- Slides 1–7*
- Prepositionally Speaking GO Sheet*
- An image showing action. Sports images are a good place to start.
- Notebooks, computers, or tablets

*Available online at scholastic.com/ThrivingWriterResources

WHY TEACH THIS?

1. To provide a framework for students to express content area understanding.
2. To familiarize students with how prepositional phrases work and how they enrich communication by describing in detail context and setting. Using prepositional phrases leads to more sentence and text complexity.

CONTENT AREA CONNECTIONS: Literature, Social Studies, Science, Art

Persuasive	Descriptive	Narrative	Procedural	Research	Vocabulary	Figurative Language
	X	X		X	X	

STEPH REFLECTS ON FRAMEWORK 6

Have any of you ever had any fun while learning prepositional phrases? Not me, that's for sure. Oh, how I wish Sara and Michael had been waving their magic teaching wands when I was slogging through fill-in-the-blank parts of speech worksheets while sleeping through class. The best way to learn the parts of speech is to use them in the service of communicating your own essential message. Indeed, Marcia Hurlow's (2014) research demonstrates that "many errors disappear from student writing when students focus on their ideas and stop trying to 'sound correct.'"

Do your eyes glaze over at the mere mention of a grammar lesson? It's a common affliction among students. About the only thing you have to know about a prepositional phrase is that it is not a complete sentence, more like a sentence plug-in. It contains one preposition (e.g., *along*) and the object it references (e.g., *the yellow line*). Writers use prepositional phrases to describe a person, place, or thing, establishing the time and filling in the background. We have found prepositional phrases to be excellent facilitators of image analysis—fun and effective, even when mixed with (gasp!) a grammar lesson.

Don't despair! This writing framework begins with a refresher lesson on how to construct a prepositional phrase. From there, students are encouraged to look deeper into an image, expressing what they see and what they infer.

This framework is excellent for use in social studies and science as well as in language arts. It encourages students to look closely at an image, inferring information and then dipping back into research in order to complete the framework's GO Sheet. Any subject matter that may be illustrated with an image can be described using prepositional phrases. We start simply and add complexity by presenting multiple versions of a piece of text, then ask students to create their own versions—each version providing material for formative assessment.

According to art expert Brian Kennedy, "Ninety percent of all the information we take in from the world, we take in visually." Visual literacy is defined as the ability to construct meaning out of images, and one way to do that is to discuss and write about images, pausing to read them closely. "Unless we connect cognition and memory, we don't remember what we see," Kennedy points out, recognizing the integration of text and image to be multimodal, multidisciplinary, interdisciplinary, and collaborative. Images are indeed a universal language, open to interpretation and inference, and an inspiration for further research.

1. Introduce the Framework

Project Slide 1 and say something like: *We are going to take a step toward mastering the power of prepositional phrases. We will read an image and sum it up in a simple sentence* (the boy walked, the stream flowed, the refugees fled), *and then compose a list of prepositional phrases to read the image* (along the yellow line, beside the landfill, toward an uncertain future).

Prepositionally Speaking:
Setting the Scene

What are we going to learn today?
1. We will examine an image looking at setting details.
2. We will review what a prepositional phrase is.
3. We will write about an image using prepositional phrases.

Slide 1

2. Build Background Knowledge

* Tell students: *A prepositional phrase describes the time and place something happens.*

* Project Slide 2, the list of common prepositions, and explain that these words can be used to describe just about anything a squirrel can be in a park (e.g., over the lawn, up the tree, beside the pond) and when it does something (e.g., since dawn, until sunset, before winter).

* Project Slide 3 and ask students to mix and match prepositions and objects to create prepositional phrases.

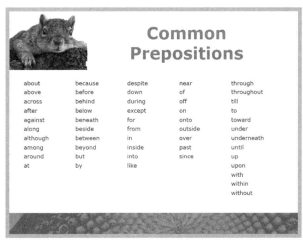

Common Prepositions

about	because	despite	near	through
above	before	down	of	throughout
across	behind	during	off	till
after	below	except	on	to
against	beneath	for	onto	toward
along	beside	from	outside	under
although	between	in	over	underneath
among	beyond	inside	past	until
around	but	into	since	up
at	by	like		upon
				with
				within
				without

Slide 2

Mix 'n' Match
Prepositional Phrases

Prepositions	Objects
without	my friend
over	the lunchroom
beside	the doorway
before	the bell
after	recess
across	the bus
under	the clock

Slide 3

3. Discuss Mentor Image and Mentor Text, Version 1

- Project Slide 4, the image of the squirrel raiding the birdfeeder, and ask a student to read aloud the simple sentence that sums up what's happening. (The squirrel eats).

- Project and read Slide 5, the mentor text. Read the text again with the students.

- Ask: *What role do the prepositional phrases play in the text?* (They describe the setting.) *What about the last line?* (It sums up the piece—it is the theme of the image.)

Slide 4

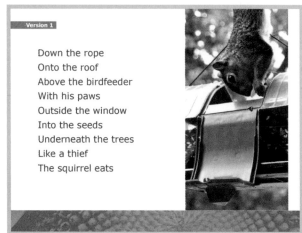

Slide 5

4. Co-construct Version 1

- Share the action image you found or use the one at right and ask students to sum up your image in a simple sentence (*The squirrel climbs*, for instance). In other words, determine the theme.

- Write down the theme at the bottom of your communal writing space.

- Project Slide 2 again, the list of common prepositions. You may also hand out copies of the list for students to refer to and keep in their writing notebooks.

- Prompt students to give you six to eight prepositional phrases describing the image and write them on your shared writing space.

- Read the co-constructed text aloud with your students.

5. Hand Out the GO Sheet

6. Have Students Write Their Version 1

Prepositionally Speaking GO Sheet

- Have students pair up, find an image from a content area unit, and create a Version 1 of their own.

- Ask the pairs to summarize the image in a simple sentence. Ask a few students to read their sentences aloud and offer corrections as needed.

- Prompt students to add seven or so prepositional phrases that describe what they see and what they may infer. Remind students that every line should begin with a different preposition (*along, with, before, after*) followed by the object of the preposition (*the road, his friend, sunset, lunch*). On the GO Sheet, those prepositional phrases would look like this:

Along	the road
With	his friend
Before	sunset
After	lunch

As they write, occasionally call on a few students to read one of their prepositional phrases aloud.

- Have them read their texts aloud, first simultaneously and then individually for the whole class.

> **Tip:** Students may find it irresistible to write in complete sentences rather than in prepositional phrases, such as *The squirrel clung to the branch* instead of simply writing *to the branch*. Or students may begin with a verb, such as *climbing up the tree*, rather than simply *up the tree*. Remind them that in Version 1 they are to begin each line with a preposition. This will get them focused on explicit details. The GO Sheet helps!

7. Discuss Mentor Text, Version 2

- Project Slide 6 and read aloud the mentor text, and then read it again, inviting students to read the red words while you read the black ones.

- Ask: *What has changed?* Details have been added, including action verbs (e.g., *digging*) and adjectives (e.g., *red, green, shady*), and some inferences have been included (e.g., Outside *my* window). Ask: *What do these edits do for the text?*

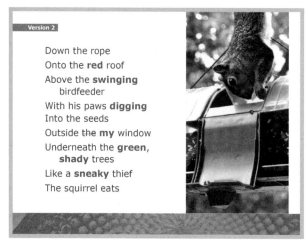

Version 2

Down the rope
Onto the **red** roof
Above the **swinging**
    birdfeeder
With his paws **digging**
Into the seeds
Outside t̶h̶e̶ **my** window
Underneath the **green**,
    shady trees
Like a **sneaky** thief
The squirrel eats

Slide 6

8. Co-construct Version 2

- Return to your co-constructed Version 1 and have students take another hard look at it.

- Take suggestions for just a couple of details to insert into the prepositional phrases.

- Ask students to identify the weakest phrases—ones that could be edited out.

- Don't necessarily "finish" the text with students. Just get started so they can get to their own revising.

- Consider continuing work on the co-constructed Version 1 while students revise their pieces.

9. Have Students Write Their Version 2

- Ask students to continue writing either with their partners or on their own, relabeling their page "Version 2" or using the right side of the GO Sheet. If students have access to technology, this is a good time to transition from paper to a digital platform.

- Ask them to insert details into at least four of their prepositional phrases. Also ask them to cross out the weakest line. Finally, ask them what inferences they can add that show their background knowledge.

- Invite students to share one of their revisions with the class, guiding them as needed.

- When they're finished revising, ask students to read their Versions 2 simultaneously.

10. Discuss Mentor Text, Version 3

- Project Slide 7, read aloud, and discuss mentor text Version 3. Can students identify the prepositional phrases?

- Ask: *Can you give me an example of how the prepositional phrases added to the story?*

- Have students turn the list of prepositional phrases into a story.

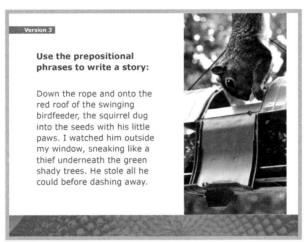

Slide 7

11. Share!

- Ask students to share their Version 2 with a classmate other than their writing partner.

- Have a few volunteers share their work with the whole class.

- Showcase the learning. If students have been writing about multiple images on the same topic, for instance, coral reefs, oral presentation provides an opportunity to share new learning.

Lesson Extension Ideas

- Apply this framework to any discipline where setting and time frame are covered. For example, it could be adapted to get students writing about historical or current events, a scene in literature, or a work of art.

- Have students use their Version 2 as a story starter. Ask them to add in a voice or two from the image. What could the people pictured be saying? What might that dog be thinking? Intersperse the dialogue with the lines of prepositional phrases to start growing a fictional story or perhaps a news article.

Sample Stages

We have used this framework with students in all content areas. Images of the Dust Bowl, income disparity, rocket propulsion, great works of art, and geometric shapes can all be described using prepositional phrases, painlessly teaching a bit of grammar at the same time. Students may seem skeptical at first, but soon will be impressing themselves and others with the detailed descriptions they are able to create about various images.

Here is a co-constructed Version 1. Not one of Sara's proudest moments, but the summary sentence (*The Monkey Grabs the Banana*) is a very fine start. Michael wrote this in a sixth-grade inclusion class at Eastern Middle School in Old Greenwich, Connecticut.

In the upper right-hand corner, his sketch directs students where to place an image into a Google document and begin to write independently.

VERSION 1

ON SARA'S SHOULDER
IN FRONT OF THE TALKING
                    monkey
OUTSIDE OF CIVILIZATION
UNDER THE JUNGLE CANOPY
DURING A TOUR
INSIDE THE JUNGLE
DESPITE THE MONKEY'S GRABBING
BESIDE THE STATUES
WITH A DETERMINED ATTITUDE

THE MONKEY GRABS A
                    BANANA

This sixth-grade swimmer chose a photo of his idol, Michael Phelps. Because the writer had also competed, when we asked him to insert some inferred dialogue, he brought firsthand insight to his prepositional phrases (note text in blue).

Splashling down
USA, USA
Under the water
Kicking harder
Between the lanes
Past the flags
"Hold your breath now"
Toward the wall
 Before the media / crowd
Hoots and hollers
With adrenaline
 For the gold
Is 23 possible?

Through tides of great storms,
Inside the never ending ocean,
The man rows.
Beside icy blue waters,
Against the crashing of waves,
Above the dark monsters that lurk,
The man rows.
Down the whisper of fearsome tides,
Beyond the horizon,
The man rows towards nowhere.

This is a ninth-grade student's writing about Winslow Homer's famous painting *The Fog Warning (Halibut Fishing)*, at mfa.org/collections/object/the-fog-warning-31042. Notice that she used her summary sentence as a refrain. This was probably Version 3 or 4, given the details she has added.

Prepositionally Speaking: Assessment Checkpoint

SKILL	3	2	1
Structure and Organization	Demonstrates the ability to recognize and re-create a writing structure, utilizing prepositional phrases as a means to establish setting and motion. Avoids cliché.	Demonstrates to a degree the ability to recognize and re-create writing structures, utilizing prepositional phrases as a means to establish setting and motion. Occasionally may lapse into cliché.	Does not yet demonstrate the ability to compose a simple sentence with a modifying phrase. May create prepositional phrases that modify nothing.
Grammar Conventions	Demonstrates an understanding of the terms *noun, verb, simple sentence,* and *modifying phrase.*	Demonstrates to a degree an understanding of the terms *noun, verb, simple sentence,* and *modifying phrase.* May occasionally misidentify these terms.	Does not yet demonstrate an understanding of the terms *noun, verb, simple sentence,* and *modifying phrase.* Misidentifies the majority of these terms.
Careful Reading	Demonstrates an understanding of how the use of setting in a text adds to the overall tone. Recognizes prepositional phrases in text and understands their role in modifying nouns and verbs.	Demonstrates to a degree an understanding of how the use of setting in a text adds to the overall tone. Occasionally confuses a phrase with a clause or misidentifies what the phrase is modifying.	Does not yet demonstrate an understanding of how the use of setting in a text adds to the overall tone. Cannot yet distinguish between a phrase and a clause. Cannot yet identify prepositions or explain what they modify.
Speaking Skills	Is willing to share aloud and consistently demonstrates effective presentation skills using good voice projection, inflection, pacing, eye contact, and stance.	Is often willing to share and partially demonstrates effective presentation skills using good voice projection, inflection, pacing, eye contact, and stance.	Is not yet willing to share and/or does not demonstrate effective presentation skills using good voice projection, inflection, pacing, eye contact, and stance.

Virtual Haiku Hike: Words and Images

TIME: about 45 minutes	**GRADE LEVEL:** 4 and up

MATERIALS:

- Slides 1–4*
- Haiku Hike slide show*
- Research materials on the Triangle Slave Trade
- Notebooks, computers, or tablets

*Available online at scholastic.com/ThrivingWriterResources

WHY TEACH THIS?

To stimulate discussion among students, causing them to think and rethink deeply about the subject matter, using precise and concise language, as they read images and restate their thoughts into a structured format.

CONTENT AREA CONNECTIONS: All subjects

Persuasive	Descriptive	Narrative	Procedural	Research	Vocabulary	Figurative Language
	X			X	X	

STEPH REFLECTS ON FRAMEWORK 7

Donald Graves (1986) referred to the "bed to bed" story as one in which children record every event of every day from the moment they pop out of bed to the moment they turn in for the night. Eventually, children learn to focus their writing and zero in on the one event of the day that invites deeper exploration. The Virtual Haiku Hike is a crash course in learning to focus writing. Sara and Michael invite students to focus their minds, examine a topic closely, and understand it so well they can figure out how to capture it in just 17 syllables.

"The whole is greater than the sum of its parts." Aristotle.

Images are windows. In this writing framework, we will stand at a series of windows, talk to a partner about what can be seen, discuss, and then work together to capture each vista in a mere 17 syllables. Haiku is a sparse Japanese form arranged into three lines of five, seven, and five syllables. It's a quick-write with boundaries.

Sara:	Professional poets will tell you that haiku is much more complicated than simply counting syllables.
Michael:	Let's not complicate things. We'll just call this Virtual Haiku Hike an introduction to the traditional Japanese form.
Sara:	We're adapting it for our purposes. Like chop suey.
Michael:	Which the average Chinese citizen wouldn't recognize as Chinese food.
Sara:	You think this explanation will satisfy the haiku purists?
Michael:	Sound of one hand clapping.

Each haiku will convey one vivid idea, which, when added to others on the same topic, will work in concert to create a greater understanding. Part of the magic of this framework is the negotiation the writers go through to pare their ideas to fit the form.

This particular Virtual Haiku Hike explores the human tragedy of slavery. Once you have walked this hike, we hope you will create virtual hikes of your own from, say, pictures of a polluted stream, child labor then and now, circulatory systems, and so on. After that, we further hope you will encourage students to create their own Virtual Haiku Hikes to take their classmates down other learning paths.

As an introduction to this topic, we'd also like to quote South African musician Abdullah Ibrahim, who reminds us, "People say that slaves were taken from Africa. This is not true: People were taken from Africa. . . and were made into slaves."

1. Introduce the Framework

Project Slide 1, read it aloud, and let students know they are entering into a serious discussion about a human tragedy.

Slide 1

2. Build Background Knowledge

- Project Slide 2, read the poem aloud on your own, and read it again with students. Ask: *What is this text about*? (It's like a photograph created with words.)

Slide 2

- Count out the syllables in each line and in the piece overall.

- Note that even though this is sparse text, it conveys a picture. Ask: *What do you see?*

3. Co-construct Version 1

- Project Slide 3 and ask students to turn and talk about what they see in the photo. Then co-construct a haiku poem with them, summarizing what they see.

- Project Slide 4 and read the haiku Sara and Michael wrote about the image.

- Note that although this haiku and the one you co-constructed are different, together they help to make a more complete word picture.

Slide 3

A hands-free approach,
bowl balancing on her head.
Through green leaves, she smiles.

Slide 4

4. Have Students Write Their Version 1

- Pair up students, tell them they're going on a Virtual Haiku Hike, and continue with the rest of the slide show (Slides 5–26).

- Read the text on each slide or engage students in reading.

- Have students work with a partner to synthesize the image and the text into a haiku. Encourage discussion. Some students will work more quickly than others and may wish to write two.

- Ask all students to read their haiku aloud after each slide, thinking about how it is working for them. Ask one or two pairs to share with the class how their words articulate the most important information or correct misperceptions.

- Give students time at the end to play catch up. Most of them will have a few partially written haiku. Encourage discussion as students work on incomplete ones.

5. Co-construct Version 2

Return to the co-constructed haiku about the image of the woman with the copper pot on her head. Ask: *Is there any way you could make this more precise?* Students have a tendency to begin every line with a pronoun, trying to make a sentence. Reaffirm that haiku consists of power words. Pronouns and passive verbs are a waste of syllables!

6. Have Students Write Their Version 2

Ask students to return to their collection of haiku and replace any syllables wasted on repetitive pronouns or articles or verbs that don't move.

7. Share!

- Invite students to read and reflect on their favorite haiku.
- Take this opportunity to discuss the whole picture of slavery in the Americas.
- Acknowledge this is a difficult topic and let students express their feelings.

Cape Coast Castle in Ghana is one of 30 slave castles, large forts on the coast of West Africa.

Slide 6

...ungeons ...omen, and

Slide 15

Those who survived were ultimately led through this door labeled "The Door of No Return." The captives had no idea where they were going.

Slide 21

Lesson Extension Ideas

- Display the haiku with images on a wall or in a hallway. Walls and hallways teach!
- Make a classroom book using an app such as *Book Writer* or have pairs each create books of their own, perhaps with images they find through research.
- Make a haiku Mad Lib book, manipulating the information in all kinds of ways.
- Collect questions from the class about each pair's haiku. Have pairs contemplate the questions and conduct research to help answer them in the form of more haiku.

Sample Stages

These samples are from Libbie Royko's grade 7 social studies classroom, W-E School of Innovation, Eastlake, Ohio. Her students were writing in pairs, some using paper and pencil, and some using shared documents on their Chromebooks.

Libbie reported that after the students took this hike, they had a deeper understanding of the slave trade. Additionally, students were excited to create their own Haiku Hikes on other topics to share with classmates.

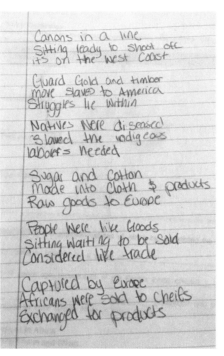

Slaves were property
People thought they were items
Were commodities

Sometimes for Europe
They usually didn't go
They're used to get guns.

Transported in chains
Put in dungeons until gone
Boarded onto ships

Slavers in barracks
Had large windows and seabreeze
Much better than slaves

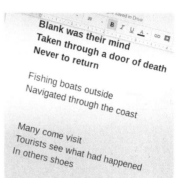

Blank was their mind
Taken through a door of death
Never to return

Fishing boats outside
Navigated through the coast

Many come visit
Tourists see what had happened
In others shoes

This screenshot shows a partially written haiku, which can be finished at the end of the hike.

PART I: LEARNING ABOUT LANGUAGE

Theresa Marriott counts syllables while discussing information with her fourth-grade students at Dostyk American International School in Atyrau, Kazakhstan.

Virtual Haiku Hike: Assessment Checkpoint

SKILL	3	2	1
Word Choice	Demonstrates, through classroom discussion and writing, an understanding of the impact of word choice in detailing a scene as depicted in an image.	Partially demonstrates, through classroom discussion and writing, an understanding of the impact of word choice in detailing a scene as depicted in an image.	Does not yet demonstrate, through classroom discussion and writing, an understanding of the impact of word choice in detailing a scene as depicted in an image.
Content Understanding	Demonstrates a growing understanding of the unit of study as evidenced by classroom discussion and quick-write haiku.	Partially demonstrates a growing understanding of the unit of study as evidenced by classroom discussion and quick-write haiku.	Does not yet demonstrate a growing understanding of the unit of study as evidenced by classroom discussion and quick-write haiku.
Speaking Skills	Is willing to share aloud and consistently demonstrates effective presentation skills using good voice projection, inflection, pacing, eye contact, and stance.	Is often willing to share and partially demonstrates effective presentation skills using good voice projection, inflection, pacing, eye contact, and stance.	Is not yet willing to share and/or does not demonstrate effective presentation skills using good voice projection, inflection, pacing, eye contact, and stance.
Listening Skills	Actively participates in discussions about other students' work and is tuned in to student presentations.	Occasionally participates in discussions about other students' work and is tuned in to student presentations.	Does not participate in discussions about other students' work and is not yet tuned in to student presentations.

Point of View: If I Were...

TIME: about 45 minutes **GRADE LEVEL:** 3 and up

MATERIALS:

- Slides 1–6*
- Point of View GO Sheet*
- A preselected subject matter you wish students to write about
- Research materials for that subject matter
- Notebooks, computers, or tablets

*Available online at scholastic.com/ThrivingWriterResources

WHY TEACH THIS?

To build understanding by writing from an alternate perspective, incorporating facts and details about what the speaker would and would not do or say.

CONTENT AREA CONNECTIONS: Literature, Social Studies, Science, Art

Persuasive	Descriptive	Narrative	Procedural	Research	Vocabulary	Figurative Language
	X	X		X		X

STEPH REFLECTS ON FRAMEWORK 8

We have research that demonstrates a solid link between empathy and hours spent inside the world of Harry Potter locked in a struggle between good and evil (Vezzali & Emilia, 2014). Reading loads of fiction, in general, seems to develop our perception of others' needs and make us nicer, more compassionate people. Is it possible to teach empathy? This framework offers an ideal way for kids to stand in other people's shoes and use writing as a way to develop empathy.

If I Were a Camel...

Visualizing how a person or thing experiences the world gives us insight into another's perspective. This writing framework invites writers to take an alternative point of view with the simple prompt, "If I were."

"Take the information apart, look at its parts, and then try to put it back together again in language that is meaningful to you. The best way to determine that you've really gotten the point is to be able to state it in your own words," advises Susan Gilroy (2004).

Looking at information and issues through different lenses helps us to understand, as well as tempering our views with empathy. A gear, a camel, a tool, or a circle—making a personal connection brings students closer to understanding and teachers closer to measuring their depth of knowledge.

Similar to personification, writing from another's point of view causes us to recognize capabilities and limitations while writers think deeply about the topic. "Kids need an arsenal of tools to think deeply about text" (Harvey & Goudvis, 2013). *Consider this an addition to your arsenal!*

This framework helps our students look at the world through a different pair of eyes, or even to create a pair of eyes, in the case of an inanimate object. Whether that "other" is a character from literature or a peptic enzyme, trying on an outside-of-self point of view will help our students form meaningful connections in their reading and writing.

1. Introduce the Framework

Project Slide 1, read it aloud, and ask students if they have ever wondered what is going on in someone else's head. Let them know they are going to be thinking and writing about this very thing. Although some of the writing they do will be fiction, in which they will put words in their subjects' mouths, it will be grounded in facts.

Point of View:
If I Were...

What are we going to learn today?
1. We will learn about a narrator's point of view.
2. We will discuss how an author's perspective influences text.
3. We will write from another perspective.

Slide 1

2. Discuss Mentor Text, Version 1

- Project Slide 2 and read it aloud. Then ask students to read it with you, and clarify word meaning where necessary.

- Ask: *Who is speaking in this text?* (a gear) *How does the writer embody the gear?* (by explaining what it would or would not do)

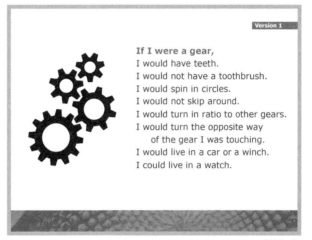

Version 1

If I were a gear,
I would have teeth.
I would not have a toothbrush.
I would spin in circles.
I would not skip around.
I would turn in ratio to other gears.
I would turn the opposite way
    of the gear I was touching.
I would live in a car or a winch.
I could live in a watch.

Slide 2

3. Build Background Knowledge

- Project Slide 3 and explain that this boy's job is to give camel rides to tourists around the pyramids of Giza, outside of Cairo, Egypt. (Feel free to choose your own image. Just make sure it ensures a good discussion of point of view, like this one.)

- Explain that this photo contains people and an animal with different points of view about what's happening, as well as different expectations, needs, and desires.

Point of View?

Slide 3

From Striving to Thriving Writers copyright © 2018 by Sara Holbrook, Michael Salinger, and Stephanie Harvey. Published by Scholastic Inc.

PART I: LEARNING ABOUT LANGUAGE

- Ask: *What do you think the boy wants? What does the camel want? What do the tourists in the background want? What are their hopes and/or concerns about the day? How might each of them feel about that stick?*
- Choose one point of view to be your writer's perspective. We invariably end up writing from the camel's perspective, no matter how much we push the young man with the stick.

4. Co-construct Version 1

- Re-create the GO Sheet on the board. From there, ask leading questions such as: *What does the camel wish for? What does he think of his job? What are his needs? What does he think of the boy on his back and that stick?* Write students' responses in the top-left section.
- Ask leading questions to fill in the bottom-left section: *What does the camel not want to happen? What can the camel not do that he might like to?*
- Don't feel compelled to finish one section before the other—you can bounce back and forth. Sometimes writing down one response inspires a counter response. The more responses the merrier. Writing them all down assures they won't be forgotten.
- Once you have listed several responses, pull some over to the right and co-construct Version 1, starting with the phrase, "If I were..." Compose five or six lines with older writers. For primary writers, three lines is fine, as long as one is about what the camel can't or wouldn't do.
- Finish the text with a statement of fact about the subject.
- Ask the whole class to read Version 1 aloud at the same time.

5. Hand Out the GO Sheet

6. Have Students Write Their Version 1

- Have students pair up with a writing partner. Remind them that although they'll be working together, they should each produce their own copy of the piece.
- Give them the preselected subject they are to write about.

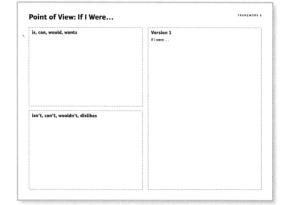

Point of View GO Sheet

- Instruct students to work with their partners to fill in the left side of their GO Sheets. Remind them that they are to put themselves in the subject's shoes. Guide them to do research to help with details. In the upper left-hand box, list what the word is, can, or would do (for instance, *If I were a pyramid I would have four sides, live in the desert, hold a pharaoh*). In the lower left-hand box, list what the word is not, cannot, or would not do (for instance, *If I were a pyramid I could not talk, wouldn't have wheels, would not have windows*).

- Ask periodically for a volunteer to share his or her work. Provide support as needed.

- Once students have completed their prewrites, instruct them to write their Version 1, pulling ideas from the left side of their GO Sheets. They may write in pairs or individually, but each student should write his or her own copy of the piece.

- Have students end their pieces with a statement of fact about the person (or thing) whose point of view they've embraced. Invite all students to read their work aloud at the same time, tuning in to obvious typos. Have they neglected to write down a word they meant to?

- Invite students to read their piece to a classmate, someone other than their writing partner.

- Finally, call on a few volunteers to share aloud with the whole class.

Tip: Sara and Michael have had success using this framework in a variety of content areas. What is particularly helpful is if you are carrying out a unit on a topic with several subtopics. For example, with primary students, we have written about shapes. In intermediate science, we have written about the solar system. In middle school science, we have written about a coral reef (*If I were a coral reef…*). With high schoolers, we have written about characters in Shakespeare plays and elements of ecosystems. One time, with a sixth-grade social studies class, we wrote about ancient worlds, focusing on occupations: *If I were an artisan, a scribe, a pharaoh, a priest, a farmer,* and so on. When students read their pieces at the end of the session, they were able to present a more complete picture of life in ancient Egypt.

7. Discuss Mentor Text, Version 2

- Project Slide 4, read it aloud, and then ask students to read it aloud with you. If time allows, screen this read-aloud by the author: Search "If I were a gear" on YouTube.

- Ask: *How has the piece changed?* (The author turned the bullet points into smooth sentences, removed repetition, and added some rhyme at the end.) How does that help the writing?

- Invite students to have fun with their texts and revise them. You may want to challenge them to add a color or two, maybe a simile, or a sensory image.

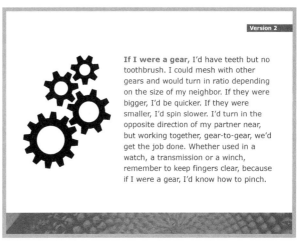

If I were a gear, I'd have teeth but no toothbrush. I could mesh with other gears and would turn in ratio depending on the size of my neighbor. If they were bigger, I'd be quicker. If they were smaller, I'd spin slower. I'd turn in the opposite direction of my partner near, but working together, gear-to-gear, we'd get the job done. Whether used in a watch, a transmission or a winch, remember to keep fingers clear, because if I were a gear, I'd know how to pinch.

Version 2

Slide 4

8. Co-construct Version 2

- Project your co-constructed Version 1 and review it with students.

- Project Slide 5 and let students know that transition words will help them combine lines into compound and complex sentences. Rewrite two or three lines to demonstrate—no need to finish the piece once you have modeled this process.

Transition Words
Starter List

if	unless
when	but
after	before
although	instead
however	because
except	even
until	and
or	yet

Slide 5

9. Have Students Write Their Version 2

Leave your co-constructed Version 2 on display and encourage students to craft fluid sentences from their Version 1, using the list of transition words to help them. They may continue to work in pairs or branch out on their own. Either way, encourage them to talk things out with a partner.

10. Share!

- Ask students to read their pieces aloud periodically, checking on how the writing is progressing.

- Ask them to share their work with a classmate other than their writing partner.

- Ask for volunteers to share with the whole class.

Lesson Extension Ideas

- Consider having students revise their pieces onward from Versions 3, 4, and 5, augmenting them with additional research.

- Ask students to turn their texts into poems by inserting poetic elements and rearranging the lines to make the writing more artistic.

- Encourage them to use their text as a character analysis and develop it into a piece of fiction or nonfiction writing.

 From Striving to Thriving Writers copyright © 2018 by Sara Holbrook, Michael Salinger, and Stephanie Harvey. Published by Scholastic Inc.

Sample Stages

Partly a beginner lesson in personification and very much an artifact of students' understanding, this framework calls on students to take another's point of view. We have used this with success in grades two through six in units as divergent as ancient Egypt, rocket science, and shapes. In the samples below, writers in Annette Holcomb's second-grade class at Dostyk American International School in Atyrau, Kazakhstan, worked in pairs and small groups to read a short nonfiction book on a subject of their choice, discussed the topic between them to complete their GO Sheets, and collaborated to write.

Two students read a short book on wolves, writing that if they were wolves they would want to be free and not threatened by human encroachment. Talking the subject over with them, they said to Sara that they were surprised to find out that the phrase "lone wolf" wasn't accurate at all, as wolves live in packs. After this discussion, the writers decided that fact belonged in their Version 2.

Three students read and reread a short book on puppies to find what is and is not true in order to complete their GO Sheets.

PART I: LEARNING ABOUT LANGUAGE

Point of View: Assessment Checkpoint

SKILL	3	2	1
Careful Reading	Demonstrates an ability to assume another persona and write from that perspective in first person. Maintains a consistent and logical voice.	Partially demonstrates an ability to assume another persona and write from that perspective in first person. Partially maintains a consistent and logical voice.	Is not yet able to demonstrate an ability to assume another persona and write from that perspective in first person. Is not yet able to maintain a consistent and logical voice.
Structure and Organization	Demonstrates the ability to recognize and re-create a writing structure with bullet points and then use them to craft fluid sentences.	Partially demonstrates the ability to recognize and re-create a writing structure with bullet points and then occasionally uses them to craft fluid sentences.	Does not yet demonstrate the ability to recognize and re-create a writing structure with bullet points and then use them to craft fluid sentences.
Textual Evidence to Support Voice of Writing	Demonstrates an understanding of the subject matter through accurate interpretation of facts obtained through research and experience. Is able to articulate findings through a consistent alternative point of view.	Partially demonstrates an understanding of subject matter. May misinterpret a fact or two, or may fail to maintain a consistent alternative point of view.	Is not yet able to articulate an understanding of subject matter or to write from an alternative point of view.
Speaking Skills	Is willing to share aloud and consistently demonstrates effective presentation skills using good voice projection, inflection, pacing, eye contact, and stance.	Is often willing to share and partially demonstrates effective presentation skills using good voice projection, inflection, pacing, eye contact, and stance.	Is not yet willing to share and does not yet demonstrate effective presentation skills using good voice projection, inflection, pacing, eye contact, and stance.
Listening Skills	Actively participates in discussions about other students' work and is tuned in to student presentations.	Occasionally participates in discussions about other students' work and is tuned in to student presentations.	Does not participate in discussions about other students' work and is not yet tuned in to student presentations.

Refrain Again: Finding, Repeating a Theme

TIME: about 30 minutes

GRADE LEVEL: K and up

MATERIALS:

- Slides 1–3*
- Refrain Again GO Sheet*
- Notebooks, computers, or tablets

*Available online at scholastic.com/ThrivingWriterResources

WHY TEACH THIS?

To help students prioritize information into a pattern of writing, using repetition, which prepares them for persuasive writing.

CONTENT AREA CONNECTIONS: All subjects

Persuasive	Descriptive	Narrative	Procedural	Research	Vocabulary	Figurative Language
X	X			X		

Repeat. Replay. Refrain. Remember.

One of the best things about this writing framework is its seeming simplicity. It's a great way to prioritize information and to organize data for presentation. This one starts out modestly but can scaffold into quite the sophisticated piece of text. This framework also lends itself to practically any subject matter. If you can come up with a list of attributes, you can create compelling text using a refrain.

Sara: We used to only use this one with primary students, but then we bounced it up into the upper grades.

Michael: I remember the first time you tried this with high school students reading *Romeo and Juliet*. I was more than a little interested to see how it turned out.

Sara: But the students were great! On their Version 2 they went back into the text to develop their stanzas with the exact words of the Bard.

Michael: And the proof was in the pudding! It gave them an authentic reason to reread the text, prioritizing information.

Since then we have used this framework with success in science, math, and social studies classes as a quick summary of informational text. Have fun—this one is quick and effective.

1. **Introduce the Framework**

   - Project Slide 1, read it aloud, and ask students, *What are parrots famous for?* (Talking.) *But do they make up what they say?* (No, they repeat what's said to them.) *Why do humans teach them what to say?* (They think those words and phrases are important.)

Refrain Again!
Finding, Repeating a Theme

What are we going to learn today?
1. We will examine refrain in writing.
2. We will write using a refrain.
3. We will see the power of repetition.

Slide 1

- Ask students what the word *repeat* means. Then ask them what *replay* means. Connect what they say to the word *refrain*.

- Explain that a refrain is a repeated phrase in writing, often used in commercials, songs, and poems.

2. **Discuss Mentor Text, Version 1**

- Project Slide 2 and read it aloud. Then read it again, with students reading the refrain—I am not afraid—in red. Ask students to re-read the piece, perhaps dividing the class to read the different parts.

- Ask: *What is this poem about?* (Scary things.) *Do you see a pattern? What is it? Why might the author have decided to use repetition?* (To make the piece musical and memorable.) *How do you think the author decided on the last line?* (It makes for a strong conclusion.)

> **Brave**   Version 1
> *by Sara Holbrook*
>
> Look both ways.
> I am not afraid.
> Sleepovers.
> I am not afraid.
> Movie monsters.
> I am not afraid.
> **SPIDERS!**

Slide 2

- Explain that repetition suggests importance. The author repeats a concept that he or she thinks is worth repeating. Explain that the conclusion breaks the refrain, signaling that the end, or a change, has arrived.

3. **Co-construct Version 1**

- Pick a topic for your co-construct. The playground, the classroom, or even the mud table (see photos below) are great places to start.

- Divide your writing space into two sections with a vertical line (like the GO Sheet).

- Brainstorm a list of six to 10 attributes for the topic, and list them on the left side of your writing space.

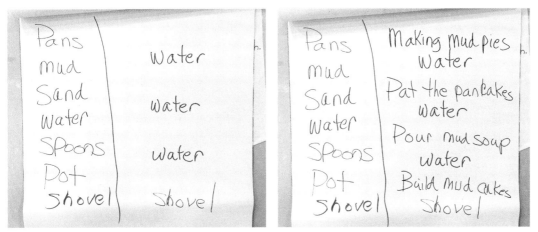

Kindergarten students at the American School in Chennai, India, co-constructed a text about their mud table, using refrain.

- When you're finished, read the list with students and ask them to decide the two most important attributes. In Version 1, one of those attributes will become the repeated refrain and one will become the conclusion. As a class, decide which will be which.

- Begin co-constructing by writing the refrain three times on the right side of your writing space, leaving room between lines, and finish with the conclusion.

- Read this aloud with students.

- Return to create stanzas by plugging in lines before the first refrain, between the second and third refrains, and before the conclusion. Refer to your list of remaining attributes for ideas.

- When you're finished, read the piece aloud with the students. We read it several times with primary students, alternating parts among them, encouraging them to use hand motions, and having a lot of fun in the process!

4. Hand Out the GO Sheet

5. Have Students Write Their Version 1

Refrain Again GO Sheet

- Have students pair up with a writing partner and ask them to select a topic or assign topics to them.

- Have them write their topic at the top of the page, brainstorm six to eight details or attributes for that topic, and list them in the left column on their GO Sheets. Each student should write his or her own piece.

- Ask a few students to share their topics and attribute lists with the class.

- Direct students to select the two most important attributes and assign one to be the refrain and the other to be the conclusion.

- In the right column of their sheet, have them write the refrain three times, leaving space in between for stanzas, and then the conclusion.

- Instruct students to insert a stanza before the first refrain, after the second and third refrains, and before the conclusion.

- When they're finished, ask students to read their Version 1 to a neighbor.

6. Discuss Mentor Text, Version 2

- Project Slide 3, read it aloud on your own, and then read it again with students.

- Ask: *What do the added details do for the text?* (They provide more information within the established format.)

- Tell students that they are going to practice adding details to an existing text of their own.

7. Co-construct Version 2

- Project Version 1 of your co-construct and review it.

- Add a detail or two, taking suggestions from the students and focusing on the attributes that did not make it in the first time.

- Note that the co-construct is still a work in progress, but adding details brings it closer to final.

- You needn't finish this piece—just get students started, priming the pump for their Version 2.

8. Have Students Write Their Version 2

- Instruct students to relabel their GO Sheets "Version 2" and add one or two details.

- When they're finished, ask them to read their Versions 2 at the same time. Then ask them what they think. Does their piece need more work? Do they see the value in using refrain?

9. Share!

- Ask students to read their pieces aloud, periodically checking on how the writing is progressing.

- Ask them to share their work with a classmate other than their writing partner.

- Ask for volunteers to share with the whole class.

> ### Brave
> *by Sara Holbrook*
>
> Version 2
>
> Red means stop.
> Look both ways.
> I am not afraid.
> Sleepovers
> And school bus rides.
> I am not afraid.
> Escalators.
> Wiggle teeth.
> Thunderstorms.
> Rollercoasters.
> Movie monsters.
> Scraped-up knees.
> I am not afraid.
> **SPIDERS!**

Slide 3

Lesson Extension Ideas

- Have students illustrate their pieces with crayons or a photo.

- Engage them in choral reading, alternating between stanza and refrain. Hand motions add a dose of fun.

- Post pieces on walls and in hallways. Walls and halls teach!

- Take the framework into a content area lesson.

Sample Stages

The key to a successful text using a refrain is a good, solid list of key words. This is true whether students are in first grade studying seeds and growing things or in high school delving into the words and themes of Shakespeare. We have used this framework at all grade levels and in every content area. After a recent professional development session in Bucharest, Romania, two physical education teachers rushed up to us to announce they were doing this with their students on Monday as part of their unit on nutrition. Unfortunately, we weren't able to see the outcome of that writing session, but we were certain that their enthusiasm would carry the day.

From Striving to Thriving Writers copyright © 2018 by Sara Holbrook, Michael Salinger, and Stephanie Harvey. Published by Scholastic Inc.

Violence coursing through Verona's veins,
A fire burning in Verona's heart.
For centuries two families causing pain,
No one knows when was the start.
Vendetta.
Two children born,
One Capulet, one Montague,
For them fate shall fall askew,
Star-crossed victims of the fire.
Vendetta.
Quiet hearts found, both lovers hounded,
At last,
Letter too late, poison to the lips too soon
A dagger plunged in sorrow
Families shocked, unsteady hearts shared
Wailings from both houses.
Peace forged.
Tragedy?

Vendetta between ancient rivals.
Love.
A bloody feud arises.
Love.
Two youths lust for each other.
Love.
An unlikely coincidence brings death.
Tragedy.

Here are two samples from an eighth-grade class at the French International School of Hong Kong. The class read *Romeo and Juliet* and summarized the theme of Shakespeare's play into a piece of text using refrain. Note the differences in sophistication as one student revisited the text to enrich her piece with words taken directly from the play. The second text is less sophisticated, but still evidences the student's understanding of the play.

A seventh-grade class wrote about the middle school classic, *The Outsiders,* by S. E. Hinton. Following the co-construct, students worked in pairs to discuss and write about characters and scenes in the book, coming together at the end to share, giving everyone a fuller appreciation of the entire novel. Students pulled exact language from the text to write their stanzas.

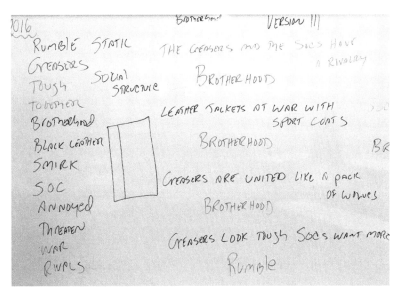

Refrain Again: Assessment Checkpoint

SKILL	3	2	1
Careful Reading	Demonstrates an understanding of the impact of specific word choice and the relationship between the refrain and the intervening lines.	Partially demonstrates an understanding of the impact of specific word choice, but may have a weak conclusion, or perhaps may not have chosen the most appropriate words for the refrain.	Does not demonstrate an understanding of the impact of a specific word choice when choosing a refrain. May not follow an established pattern, and intervening lines may not be relevant.
Structure and Organization	Demonstrates the ability to recognize and replicate a writing structure. Includes an apt refrain and a strong conclusion.	Partially demonstrates the ability to recognize and replicate a writing structure, but may misstep by forgetting or inadvertently repeating an intervening line.	Does not demonstrate the ability to recognize and replicate a writing structure. The piece has no refrain or intervening lines.
Connotative Word Meaning	Demonstrates an understanding of connotative word meanings when selecting words for the refrain and the conclusion. Crafts relevant intervening lines.	Occasionally demonstrates an understanding of connotative word meanings. May have a conclusion or an intervening line that is weak.	Does not demonstrate an understanding of connotative word meanings. The choice of refrain and/or intervening lines shows no evidence of thoughtful word choice.
Speaking Skills	Is willing to share aloud and consistently demonstrates effective presentation skills using good voice projection, inflection, pacing, eye contact, and stance.	Is often willing to share and partially demonstrates effective presentation skills using good voice projection, inflection, pacing, eye contact, and stance.	Is not yet willing to share and/or does not demonstrate effective presentation skills using good voice projection, inflection, pacing, eye contact, and stance.
Listening Skills	Actively participates in discussions about other students' work and is tuned in to student presentations.	Occasionally participates in discussions about other students' work and is tuned in to student presentations.	Does not participate in discussions about other students' work and is not yet tuned in to student presentations.

Harnessing Rhyme: Making Words Memorable

TIME: about 45 minutes

GRADE LEVEL: 2 and up

MATERIALS:

- Slides 1–4*
- Harnessing Rhyme GO Sheet*
- Preselected topics from a current content area study
- Notebooks, computers, or tablets

*Available online at scholastic.com/ThrivingWriterResources

WHY TEACH THIS?

To convey meaning while using rhyme.

CONTENT AREA CONNECTIONS: All subjects

Persuasive	Descriptive	Narrative	Procedural	Research	Vocabulary	Figurative Language
X	X	X		X	X	

STEPH REFLECTS ON FRAMEWORK 10

Rhymes resonate! My three-year-old granddaughter, Riley, loves chanting the ABCs, which she can't identify but knows by the rhyme. Rhymes also help young children with prediction. One of Riley's favorite books, *Yawn* (2011) by Sally Symes, features an animal on each page yawning and then another one yawning on the next page, "*The mole gave a yawn then rested from her dig. Guess who she gave it to—a snorty, snouty pig.*" Riley shrieks with delight and turns the page, which confirms she is right! Teaching kids to rhyme and make sense is a wise thing to do; plus, as Tim Rasinski (2018) reminds us, "Rhymes and poems for children are excellent and joyful choices for developing fluency"—both in reading and in writing.

Rhyming makes words memorable. From "See the USA in your Chevrolet" and "*i* before *e* except after *c*" to "The Star-Spangled Banner" and Mary and her fleecy lamb, rhymes stick in our heads. Rhymes are fun, and kids are naturally attracted to them, falling down in giggles like little funny bunnies.

Sara: Rhymes are easy. I know this because my daughter Katie invented calling her younger sister Kelly Jelly Belly when she was only three years old.

Michael: Rhyming isn't the problem for kids. The problem arises when they attempt to take a string of rhyming words and make meaning out of them. It's better if they start with meaningful text and work in the rhyme.

Sara: Which is why we are going to use nonfiction details as a foundation for our text and then add one or two rhymes.

Michael: Do we call that poetry?

Sara: Not necessarily. Rhyming structure can be a component of poetry, but just constructing rhyming text does not a poem make.

In this writing framework, our goal is to harness rhyme to convey meaning, which means our details are of utmost importance and the rhyme supports them and is (hopefully) fun. Rhymes at their best are not predictable, but rather a little surprising. Because of this, the very act of rhyming can stretch vocabularies as we use tools such as rhyming dictionaries and thesauruses to find just the right word to suit our dual purpose of rhyme and meaning. We do not want to give rhyme free rein to go galloping off into nonsense.

We were reading the hallways in a school once and came across rhyming text in which students were writing about their unit on oceans. Cool! One writer had written a brilliant line: *The ocean is our storage tank*. Wonderful. Unfortunately, that was followed by, *where I go to fish with Hank*. Ugh. A fake rhyme is like a fake smile—obvious and unbelievable. We are going for rhyming text that is both meaningful and memorable.

The way to do that is to start with a list of careful details.

1. Introduce the Framework

Project Slide 1 and read it aloud. Ask students if they like to rhyme. Some may express trepidation, having attempted it and gotten stuck. Others may embrace it happily, rhyming anything, even making up words that don't exist.

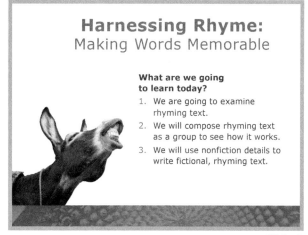

Slide 1

2. Discuss Mentor Text

- Project Slide 2 and read the poem aloud. Then ask students to read it with you.

- Ask: *How many rhymes are in this piece of text?* (only two) When beginning writers attempt rhyme, they often try to rhyme too many words. Students will be familiar with this simple rhyme pattern (a quatrain, ABCB pattern) as it sounds like a nursery rhyme or song lyrics. What they may never have realized is that there is only one rhyme per stanza.

- Project Slide 3 for a breakdown of how the rhyming pattern works.

Slide 2

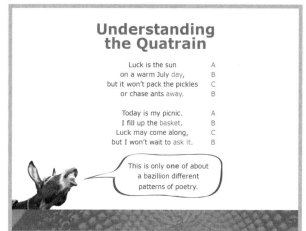

Slide 3

From Striving to Thriving Writers copyright © 2018 by Sara Holbrook, Michael Salinger, and Stephanie Harvey. Published by Scholastic Inc.

Tip: Believe it or not, rhyming text is a bit controversial in the land of writing instruction. Well-meaning educators may encourage kids to read rhyming poetry and then discourage (or forbid) them from trying to write it. Unfair!

There are important lessons we can learn from writing rhyming text, lessons that expand our vocabulary and evidence our content knowledge. Let's not forget, kids love rhyming words!

But rhyming well requires discipline, which is why this framework is important. It walks students through the process step by step, showing them how to harness the power of rhyme.

3. Co-construct Version 1

- Choose a writing topic that is familiar to students. We've had success with topics such as a bathtub, the playground, the view from the window, and the library.

- Divide your writing space into two columns. (See the GO Sheet, page 114.)

- Think about your topic and take no more than a couple of minutes to list in the left column factual details about it.

- Choose a few of the details and list rhyming words alongside them. (See sample, right.) This step has a dual purpose: It can expand vocabulary as students reach for just the right words, and it can stimulate ideas for where to go next with the text.

- Begin by putting one of the details into a simple sentence and writing it in the right column. No rhymes allowed.

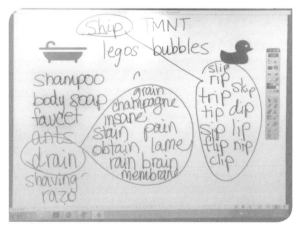

- Continue by adding two more sentences to create a stack of three sentences with NO RHYMES!

From Striving to Thriving Writers copyright © 2018 by Sara Holbrook, Michael Salinger, and Stephanie Harvey. Published by Scholastic Inc.

- Add a fourth sentence that *does* rhyme—specifically with the last word in sentence 2. (See sample below.)

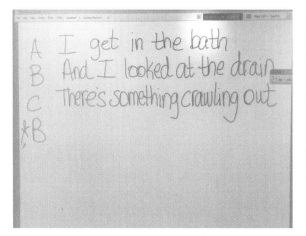

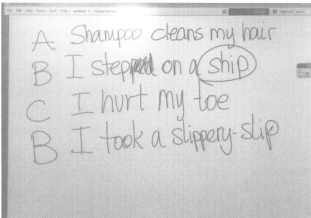

Tip: If you can't logically rhyme the last word in sentence 2, rearrange the sentences and choose a different word. Think of the sentences and words as building blocks—play with them until they fit together right.

What if I can't rhyme the word I want to rhyme to make my pattern?

Don't be stubborn as a mule! Rearrange your lines and pick a different word.

- Add another four lines, following the same steps.
- When you're finished, read aloud your Version 1 with students and celebrate. You have written two quatrains!

From Striving to Thriving Writers copyright © 2018 by Sara Holbrook, Michael Salinger, and Stephanie Harvey. Published by Scholastic Inc.

4. Hand Out the GO Sheet

5. Have Students Write Their Version 1

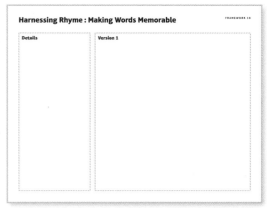

Harnessing Rhyme: Making Words Memorable FRAMEWORK 10

Details	Version 1

Harnessing Rhyme GO Sheet

- Have students pair up with a writing partner and lead them to choose a topic related to a subject you are studying. Sometimes we write topics on slips of paper and have students draw them from a basket.

- Instruct them to begin by listing factual details about their topic, not opinions, in the left column on their GO Sheets. Have research materials handy.

- Ask students to read items off of their lists occasionally, checking to make sure they are including facts only. There should be no words such as *cute, wonderful, terrible,* or *ugly.*

- Ask them to choose a detail and create a cluster of words that rhyme with it, using a rhyming dictionary if necessary. Then have them do it for a couple more details.

- Ask students to begin writing in the right column on their GO Sheets. Ask them to write down a first line (no rhymes). Then ask for a second line (no rhymes), and finally a third (no rhymes). Stick to the facts. Excitement builds as writers hold back the urge to rhyme. As they write, periodically ask students to read a line or two aloud.

- Ask students to add a fourth and final line that rhymes with the last word of line 2, encouraging them to rearrange lines and/or words if necessary. If students get stuck, urge them to confer with each other for ideas and to consult a rhyming dictionary to stretch vocabulary.

- Encourage students to experiment. Be sure they understand that the rhyme should somehow support the text's meaning, therefore no nonsense rhymes are allowed.

6. Co-construct Version 2

- Project your co-constructed Version 1 and review it to see if you can work in more details—colors, similes, sensory details, and such. Add at least two details, and if necessary, revise lines for rhythm and flow.

- Strengthen verbs. Try to make one change that makes your text jump!

7. Have Students Write Their Version 2

- Challenge students to clarify their message by adding at least two details and revising the text as necessary.

- Challenge them to strengthen their verbs.

- Encourage repeated read-alouds to determine if the piece is working for them.

8. Share!

- Ask students to share their work with a classmate other than their writing partner.

- Ask volunteers to share with the whole class.

- Encourage students to speak for word meaning rather than emphasizing the rhyme. There is an unfortunate tendency when reading rhyming text to heavily accent the rhyming words. Resist! Remind students they are trying to convey an idea. The rhyme may support that idea, but it is not the most important part.

Lesson Extension Ideas

- Have students turn the text into song lyrics, or perhaps a jingle to promote, for instance, preservation of rain forests.

- Have them illustrate the text with drawings or captured images to enhance its impact.

- Have them pare the text down, removing the rhyme to create a free-verse poem.

Sample Stages

Rhyming can be a rollicking good time, as long as the resulting text makes sense. Here again, the key to writing is first gathering a strong list of facts. Although rhyme is often relegated to the humor section, in works ranging from *The Charge of the Light Brigade* by Alfred, Lord Tennyson, to *In Flanders Fields* by John McCrae to *Rhymes of a Red Cross Man* by Robert W. Service, rhymes have also been used over the centuries to commemorate serious events. In Katie Lufkin's class at Hillside Elementary in Virginia, students used rhyme to synthesize their learning about segregation and the catastrophic inequity of Jim Crow laws.

```
A  We studied segragation
B  I learned it was unfair
C  Jim Crow laws were terrible
B  But most whites didn't care

A  Segragation is so bad
B  The worst was Jim Crow
C  They could of acted better
B  But they just didn't know

A  Life back then was so unfair
B  Most people were so cruel
C  You ride a fancy horse
B  While I ride a dirty mule
```

(top) Students in Katie's class come from a wide variety of backgrounds, including first- and second-generation immigrants. For all of her students, this topic was new to them, not at all part of the schema of equality and diversity in this present-day classroom. The writing process gave students the opportunity to discuss in detail the concepts and reading that they had been doing in class.

(left) This fourth grader captures the essence of the cruelty of Jim Crow laws. Katie reported that the word most used among the students in their writing was *unfair*.

Harnessing Rhyme: Assessment Checkpoint

SKILL	3	2	1
Careful Reading	Can recognize a rhyme pattern and identify key words that make the pattern work.	Can occasionally recognize a rhyme pattern and identify key words that make the pattern work.	Cannot yet recognize a rhyme pattern or identify key words that make the pattern work.
Visual Language	Demonstrates the ability to create a list of factual details about a subject using research materials, and distinguishes between fact and opinion.	Partially demonstrates the ability to create a list of factual details about a subject, occasionally using research materials, and often distinguishes between fact and opinion.	Does not yet demonstrate the ability to create a list of factual details about a subject using research materials, and/or does not yet distinguish between fact and opinion.
Structure and Organization	Is able to create patterned writing that includes rhyme and conveys an idea.	Is partially able to create patterned writing that includes rhyme and conveys an idea.	Is not yet able to create patterned writing that includes rhyme and conveys an idea.
Speaking Skills	Is willing to share aloud and consistently demonstrates effective presentation skills using good voice projection, inflection, pacing, eye contact, and stance.	Is often willing to share and partially demonstrates effective presentation skills using good voice projection, inflection, pacing, eye contact, and stance.	Is not willing to share and/or does not yet demonstrate effective presentation skills using good voice projection, inflection, pacing, eye contact, and stance.
Listening Skills	Actively participates in discussions about other students' work and is tuned in to student presentations.	Occasionally participates in discussions about other students' work and is tuned in to student presentations.	Does not participate in discussions about other students' work and is not yet tuned in to student presentations.

PART I: LEARNING ABOUT LANGUAGE

Infomercial: Learn It! Know It! Sell It!

TIME: about 45 minutes, plus 15 minutes for video performances	GRADE LEVEL: 5 and up

MATERIALS:

- Slides 1–4*
- Infomercial GO Sheet*
- An infomercial video (see the following page for ideas)
- Preselected topics from a current content area study

*Available online at scholastic.com/ThrivingWriterResources

WHY TEACH THIS?

To demonstrate students' understanding of a topic by having them "sell it" with an infomercial they create, a form of persuasive writing.

CONTENT AREA CONNECTIONS: Literature, Social Studies, Science, Art

Persuasive	Descriptive	Narrative	Procedural	Research	Vocabulary	Figurative Language
X	X	X		X		

STEPH REFLECTS ON FRAMEWORK 11

This is one of my all-time favorite lessons! I first saw Sara and Michael teach this framework a few years ago. What an ingenious way to engage kids in persuasive writing. And, if you have not seen a Billy Mays infomercial, you are in for a real treat! So have a go at this one. You won't regret it, except that your kids may want to do this every day. And come to think of it, what's wrong with that?

Don't be left out! All the cool teachers are using infomercials for persuasive writing! Act now!

Everyone has heard an infomercial, but have you ever dissected one? In this writing framework, we take a slightly different entry into the lesson as our mentor text is going to come from YouTube. There are (roughly) a gazillion infomercials out there from which to choose. One of our favorites is an advertisement for a product called *What Odor?* performed by that iconic fast-talking salesman, Billy Mays. (Search "What Odor? by Billy Mays.")

The GO Sheet is key to this lesson. As students complete the organizer, they will readily see the pattern for their subsequent writing. Money-back guarantee, this will not be boring!

We have heard students selling everything from the Cultural Revolution in China to computer components and pyramids. *Are you tired of that mummified pharaoh smelling up your kitchen? You need a pyramid!*

Sound fun? Add some research and enthusiastic performance and you have yourself a meaningful and memorable good time.

1. **Introduce the Framework**

   - Project Slide 1, read it aloud, and ask students what they know about infomercials.

   - Ask: *How do infomercials differ from regular commercials?* (They are a bit longer, but not too long or else people tune out. Less than two minutes is a good rule, around 300 to 350 words.)

   - Tell students it is a challenge to compress ideas into few words, but sometimes it's a real-world writing requirement, particularly when it comes to persuasive writing. We are bombarded with sales messages, a form of persuasive writing, continually, and we are wired to tune out quickly if they are boring.

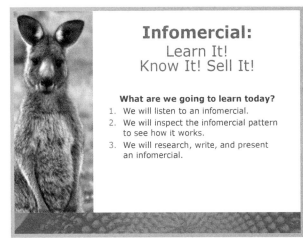

Slide 1

2. Build Background Knowledge

- Find an infomercial on YouTube and screen it for the class. *What Odor?* by Billy Mays is a real crowd-pleaser, only 1:48 minutes long!

- Ask: *What is the product and what problem does it solve? How do you remember the name of the product?* (Repetition!)

- Keep in mind, infomercials are a form of patterned writing, and they contain elements designed to persuade the audience to buy a product (see the GO Sheet). Writers use peer pressure and sympathize with their audience. ("We know you're busy, but this product will help!") Amazingly, every product also contains a secret ingredient, some quality that makes it unique.

- Tell students that infomercials always end with "the ask": buy this product, vote for me, tune in on Thursday. Ask: *What is "the ask" in this video?*

3. Co-construct GO Sheet Entries

- Project the GO Sheet and fill it in with your students, as if you are selling a kangaroo (or choose another animal or product that is *not* a subject you are studying), modeling the framework.

- Work through the process with students, using words and phrases. There is no need for complete sentences. Be creative! What problem could a kangaroo solve? What would be a memorable, concise name for your product? *Kanga 3000*, or *KangaEX*, for instance.

4. Hand Out the GO Sheet

- Pair students with writing partners. Or, with older students, create small groups of no more than four members. We want to encourage discussion.

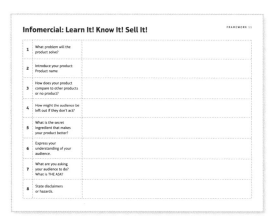

Infomercial GO sheet

- Ask students to choose a topic from a content area study. For instance, during a study on ancient Egypt, students might choose from these topics: pyramids, mummification, pharaohs, scribes, artisans, and so on. Have topics and research materials available.

- Direct each student to complete a GO Sheet for their topic, filling in the eight boxes related to their product, whether they're working with a partner or in a group.

- Encourage creativity by asking students to name their products. At the same time, their writing should ring true. For instance, a scribe from Ancient Egypt would not be using a computer.

5. Co-construct Version 1

- Model how to turn entries from your co-constructed GO Sheet into sentences. However, do not do it for every entry.

- Project Slides 2 and 3, which contain an infomercial developed from GO Sheet entries. Read the infomercial quickly and leave it on display for students to reference as they begin their own writing.

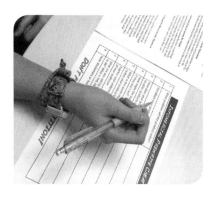

Infomercial `Version 1`

Are you broke from paying for expensive babysitters? Do you have trouble reaching that top closet shelf? Are you tired of carrying a purse, tote bag, or briefcase? You need a **Kanga3000**.

The Kanga3000 can jump six feet high—nothing will ever be out of your reach again. The Kanga3000 comes with a handy pocket where you can safely store your baby and other important items.

The Kanga3000 is the most useful pet on the market. Forget lazy cats that sleep all day or robot toys that require batteries. The Kanga3000 is almost maintenance-free, and unlike plastic toys, the Kanga3000 is 100% natural and totally safe for the environment. Don't be seen as old-fashioned or out of touch. When you upgrade your golden retriever to the Kanga3000, your neighbors will be impressed.

page 1 of 2

Slide 2

Infomercial `Version 1`

The Kanga3000 is unlike any other product. What makes it unique is a secret ingredient: springiness. Morning, noon, and night, the tireless Kanga3000 never loses its jump.

Babysitters can charge $5, $10, or even $20 an hour. You may think that you can't afford a new pet, but with the money the Kanga3000 will save you on babysitters, you will be dollars ahead in no time.

Buy a Kanga3000 now and improve your life. Visit www.kanga3000.com and place your order now or call 888-BUY-KANGA; operators are standing by. Buy within the next three hours and you will receive a package of Kanga3000 diapers absolutely free.

Warning: Seller is not responsible for damage to breakable household items or costs from Kanga3000's speeding tickets in school zones.

page 2 of 2

Slide 3

---

6. Have Students Write Their Version 1

- Ask students to turn entries from their GO Sheets into sentences. Some entries may fall away and others may be added—and that's okay. Reinforce that this is part of the process, choosing the best ideas and using them to come up with even more ideas!

- Ask students to read their Version 1 aloud periodically. There is a rhythm to good writing; reading their work aloud gives students the opportunity to listen for that rhythm.

7. Co-construct Version 2

- Project Slide 4, an excerpt from the kangaroo infomercial. Read it aloud on your own and again with a student, with each of you taking a different part. (Note that in anticipation of the performance, we have blown up the font size.)

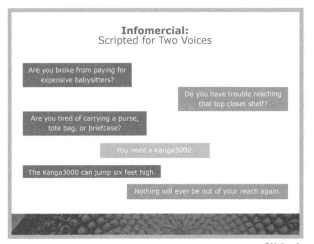

Infomercial:
Scripted for Two Voices

Are you broke from paying for expensive babysitters?

Do you have trouble reaching that top closet shelf?

Are you tired of carrying a purse, tote bag, or briefcase?

You need a Kanga3000.

The Kanga3000 can jump six feet high.

Nothing will ever be out of your reach again.

Slide 4

- Encourage expression and enthusiasm. Leave the slide on display so students can refer to it as they write their Version 2.

- Ask students to look at their Version 1 and think about how it could be scripted for two or more voices.

8. Have Students Write Their Version 2

- Ask students to script their infomercial for two or more voices.

- When they're finished, encourage repeated reading. Warning, this should be a noisy process. If it isn't, it's not working.

- Emphasize that the final scripts don't need to be fancy, but they do need to be readable. So students should use large print: 20-point type at least.

9. Share!

- Jump on this opportunity for students to hone their oral communication skills! It is practically impossible to read an infomercial in a monotone. Encourage students to turn up the inflection and sell it!

- Elicit responses to every presentation by asking at the end: *What are the benefits of this product? Why do we need it? Where can we get it?*

> **Tip:** Use your classroom projection system as a teleprompter by turning everyone's seats around and having the presenters stand in the back of the room. This will give the presenter full view of the projection board, enabling a hands-free presentation.

Lesson Extension Ideas

- Videotape a performance, or have students perform live. Include images, props, and music. Invite in another class to up the excitement and applause.

- Go on to have students write infomercials about real events in the community and have them ask for change. Broadcast the announcements.

- Call your local cable station and see if you can get some studio time or even local air time for students to showcase their persuasive talents.

Sample Stages

The infomercial is not only a great introduction to persuasive writing, it is also a practice in patterned writing. Students funnel background knowledge onto a GO Sheet in order to sell a concept to an audience in a predetermined style. These are fun and a great way to practice inflection as students perform their infomercials with gusto. We tell students to have fun, but they must remain true to the facts. Since every great performance is based on good writing, we begin there.

Here, middle school students at Shanghai American School work in small groups, referencing background information handouts, in order to complete their GO Sheets before crafting infomercials, each group writing to sell one of the 16 points of the Chinese Cultural Revolution.

Here, an eighth grader at Dostyk American International School in Atyrau, Kazakhstan, keeps his GO Sheet handy as he begins to craft an infomercial selling the U.S. Constitution.

Are you tired of suffering at the hand of your supreme leader? Do you want stability and representation? Well, the U.S. Constitution is the document for you! There is no other document like the constitution it in the world. And it has already successfully built a government. With the constitution you won't have to watch other countries rejoice in freedom you can do it too. We know you hate your current dictator! Unlike any other constitution this was made by the founding fathers and their wisdom. So buy the Constitution now for the low price of the U.S. national debt plus 58 dollars shipping. Pick one up now at your closest American embassy.

remember the United states government is not liable if your document does not arrive on time or at all, does not help your country, is damaged during shipping, enrages your dictator, somehow makes things worse for you or causes death.

(above) Here is a close-up of an eighth grader's Version 1 of her infomercial for the U.S. Constitution.

(left) Three sixth grade students rehearse their infomercial selling enzymes, reading and rereading in a science class in Indianapolis, Indiana.

Infomercial: Assessment Checkpoint

PART I: LEARNING ABOUT LANGUAGE

SKILL	3	2	1
Content Area Knowledge	Demonstrates an understanding of content area knowledge and applies it clearly and logically.	Partially demonstrates an understanding of content area knowledge and occasionally applies it clearly and logically.	Infomercial contains content area inaccuracies and student cannot yet apply his or her understanding.
Structure and Organization	Demonstrates the ability to re-create the pattern of an infomercial, particularly setting up a logical reason the product is needed and an informed product description.	Partially demonstrates the ability to re-create the pattern of an infomercial, particularly setting up a logical reason the product is needed and an informed product description.	Is not yet able to re-create the writing pattern of an infomercial, is not yet effective at setting up a logical reason the product is needed and/or does not yet give an informed product description.
Creativity	Shows creativity in composing an infomercial about content area learning, varies vocabulary choices, and demonstrates deep understanding of topic.	Sometimes shows creativity in composing an infomercial about content area learning, occasionally varies vocabulary choices, and demonstrates some understanding of topic.	Is not yet able to show creativity in composing an infomercial about content area learning, does not yet vary vocabulary choices nor demonstrates deep understanding of topic.
Speaking Skills	Is willing to share aloud and consistently demonstrates effective presentation skills using good voice projection, inflection, pacing, eye contact, and stance.	Is often willing to share and partially demonstrates effective presentation skills using good voice projection, inflection, pacing, eye contact, and stance.	Is not willing to share and/or does not yet demonstrate effective presentation skills using good voice projection, inflection, pacing, eye contact, and stance.
Listening Skills	Actively participates in discussions about other students' work and is tuned in to student presentations.	Occasionally participates in discussions about other students' work and is tuned in to student presentations.	Does not participate in discussions about other students' work and is not yet tuned in to student presentations.

Part II: Learning Through Language

Reading, writing, and speaking are our most potent tools for learning and sharing about the world. We want children to understand how to use all three to ask their own questions and follow a line of inquiry that will lead to new revelations—and to new questions.

▶ scholastic.com/ThriveResources

Then and Now: Charting Change

TIME: about 45 minutes (and, if you choose, 45 minutes for content-area extensions)	**GRADE LEVEL:** 1–8

MATERIALS:

- Slides 1–6*
- Then and Now GO Sheet*
- Notebooks, computers, or tablets

*Available online at scholastic.com/ThrivingWriterResources

WHY TEACH THIS?

To help students put into words the transition "from then to now," whether they are talking about themselves, a fictional character, or coral reefs, because nothing in life stays the same.

CONTENT AREA CONNECTIONS: Literature, Social Studies, Science

Persuasive	Descriptive	Narrative	Procedural	Research	Vocabulary	Figurative Language
	X	X		X		

STEPH REFLECTS ON FRAMEWORK 12

What's more important than preparing kids for change? So many of us struggle with change. I believe that the more time spent focused on the inevitability of change, the easier it will be for most of us to handle it. Writing about how we change over time is a powerful way to start out. It is generally easier to transfer to a less familiar topic once we have written from our own experience.

The Earth literally has the ability to move mountains. Our planet, its residents, and its components are in a constant state of flux. In a world where nothing stays the same, being able to observe change and then translate our findings into words is the job of the careful writer. This skill is crucial in every type of writing, from literary analysis to delineating scientific and historical findings, and even in tracking our fitness goals.

In this writing framework, we will first write about how we have changed as individuals and then research and write about an area of content learning. Beginning writers will need to be coached into providing a strong basis for comparison with unambiguous facts detailing both what was and what is. A potential pitfall is when students begin with a statement such as: *I used to wear diapers* and then follow that up with *Now I don't*. You will want to coach them to strengthen the "Now" column to include a detail such as *Now I wear jeans*.

Throughout, there will be a focus on explicit details followed by a strong conclusion. The framework may grow into an essay or a memoir, or may distill into a poem. What is important is that the initial framework is strong.

1. **Introduce the Framework**

   - Project Slide 1, read it aloud, and discuss how nothing in this world remains the same. Things are constantly changing.

   - Encourage students to offer examples of what is changing or has changed in the world.

   - Let them know they will be writing a simple framework and then building on that framework by adding details.

Then and Now:
Charting Change

What are we going to learn today?
1. We will look at how we have changed.
2. We will write about our changes, growing our writing by adding details.
3. We will research and write about how something else has changed.

Slide 1

2. Discuss Mentor Text

- Project Slide 2, read it aloud, and ask: *Do you recognize a pattern? What words does the writer repeat, and how many times does he repeat them?*

- Ask: *What happens at the end?* (The pattern is broken.) Writers do this all the time. They create patterns and break them. In a way, it is a power play because it really gets the reader's attention.

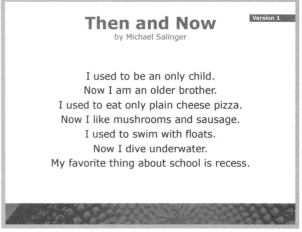

Slide 2

- Let's look at what is not happening in this piece of text. The author did not write, *I used to be an only child, now I am not,* or *I used to eat only plain cheese pizza, but not anymore.* He used details on both sides of the comparison to make it stronger.

3. Co-construct Version 1

- Introduce the Then and Now GO Sheet.

- Ask students to turn and talk to a partner for a couple of minutes about how they have changed since they were little. What did they do for entertainment? What foods did they eat? What books did they like?

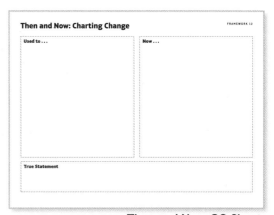

Then and Now GO Sheet

- Ask: *Who has an example?* (I used to watch *Dora*, live in Peru, wear diapers). Add examples to upper left box. Draw out a few examples—so many choices! Ask another student to supply entries for the "Now" box. (Now I watch *Star Wars*, live in Houston, wear blue jeans). Solicit three sets of three examples.

- Time to break the pattern! Add one declarative sentence—or "True Statement"— to the bottom box, such as: *I am a third grader, I love to laugh,* or *I'm on my way.* Finish with a read-aloud.

- Point out what you did not write: *I used to watch Dora, now I don't.* Instead you added strong details to both sides of the comparison.

- Read the piece aloud again.

4. Hand Out the GO Sheet

5. Have Students Write Their Version 1

- Ask students to write down four or more examples of things they used to do versus things they do now in the top two boxes on their GO Sheets. They should produce more writing than they need so they can practice editing. Here are some ideas for topics if they are stuck: foods, TV shows, cartoons, video games. *Have you moved? Do you have more cousins or siblings? Did you gain or lose someone or a pet in your family?*

- Encourage conversation, but don't allow them to explode into complex storytelling. We are still building our story ideas!

- Ask students to break the pattern and complete the section of the GO Sheet labeled "True Statement," a sentence that tells the reader an important detail about themselves. Perhaps: *I am an athlete. My creativity knows no limits. I know how to bounce back.*

6. Co-construct Version 2

- Project Slide 3 and read it aloud with the class. You read the black type and have students read the added details in orange type.

- Ask students to discuss what the author has done to strengthen his Version 1. (added details)

- Note that the author also made a change to the last line, indicating that this is a work in progress and he is striving to improve his word choice, as well as add details.

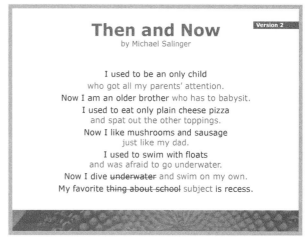

Slide 3

7. Have Students Write Their Version 2

- Instruct students to go back to their Version 1 and add details.

- Encourage use of colors, senses, numbers—any detail that would make their comparison more precise. Some ideas may fall away. Some may be replaced. Remind students that moves like that are part of the process, choosing the best ideas and using them to come up with more ideas.

- Ask students to look closely at the concluding sentence and strengthen it, if possible.

- Ask them to read their Version 2 aloud, first everyone at the same time and then to a neighbor.

8. Share!

- If they wish, have students publish their piece as it is, but add illustrations or photos from home.

- Encourage students to share in multiple ways—everyone stand and read aloud at the same time, find a partner across the room and take turns reading to one another, and take turns reading to the class. Each sharing has students rereading their own words.

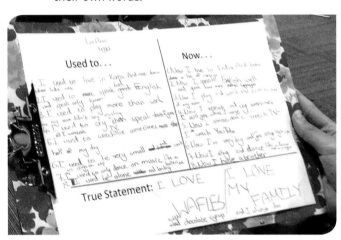

Reading over this fourth grader's shoulder, we can see that she used to live in Korea and didn't know where India was. Now she lives in India. She used to not speak English well. Now she does, in addition to a couple more languages. Notice how she has added details to expand her text: She loves waffles (with chocolate syrup) and she loves her family (and always will).

Lesson Extension Ideas

- Ask students to revise Version 3 and versions beyond. Add (perhaps) one simile, one sensory term, or some hyperbole for humor.

- Have them consider choosing a couple of lines and developing them into a poem or song.

- Use this framework as the basis for writing a paragraph or expanding into a memoir.

- Bring this framework into a content area unit in literature, science, or social studies (see below).

- In upper grades, we have had success converting our Then and Now frameworks into metaphors, combining this framework with either Mentoring Metaphor or Extended Metaphor. Use Elizabeth Thomas's poem (Slide 4) as a mentor text. For student samples, see page 135.

Content Area Extension Ideas

Of course, we are not the only things changing in our world. Here is an extension idea based on the story of the American bison.

- Discuss Content Area Mentor Text, Versions 1 and 2 (Slides 5 and 6).

- Project Slide 5 and read it aloud. Then project Slide 6 and read the black type aloud and ask students to read the added details in blue. Ask: *What has happened to the American bison?*

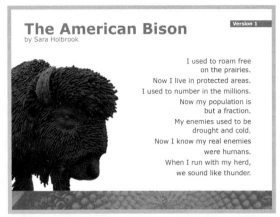

Slide 5

Slide 6

- Ask students to identify some of the added details in Version 2. Then read the author notes: *The author researched one source for Version 1, but she researched three sources for Version 2, which included Americanbison.com, Smithsonian.com, and National Geographic.*

- Ask students if those sources sound reliable. Then ask them if they can name other creatures that have a similar story to the American bison's. Draw a parallel to content learning, such as an evolving character in a novel, a famous person from history, rain forests, coral reefs, energy sources, and so forth.

- Use these slides as a model for students to research and write about your current area of study. We have used this framework to write about cultural change, coral reefs, and even characters in fiction.

- When they're finished, have students share their pieces aloud, everyone at the same time. Then have them share them with a classmate.

- Encourage students to refine their pieces for publication, or turn them into digital presentations, monologues, or persuasive essays. Students can share their understanding of change in any number of ways. Use presentation time to reinforce key points in your area of study.

- Post. Walls and halls teach!

This is an example of a co-construct Sara and Michael wrote with Theresa Marriott's fourth-grade class in Balikpapan, Indonesia. The students were reading *Number the Stars* by Lois Lowry and used the Then and Now framework to summarize how life changed for the main character, Ellen. Note there are some subject-verb agreement issues in the co-construct. But guess what? It's only Version 1! We can fix them later.

> Ellen
> I used to be free to run
>   The streets
> but now I was caught by soldiers
> I used to have the right to speak
> now I am silent
> I used to be safe with my family
>   but now we are separate.
> I wear a Jewish star.

PART II: LEARNING THROUGH LANGUAGE

Sample Stages

We have used this framework with success in grades 1 and up. Students reflect on their personal growth, which makes it both a great getting-to-know-you and end-of-the-year activity. Combined with a content area lesson, it can evidence change in a person, place, or thing. In upper grades, we have combined this one with Framework 24, Mentoring Metaphor, to add depth and sophistication to the students' writing.

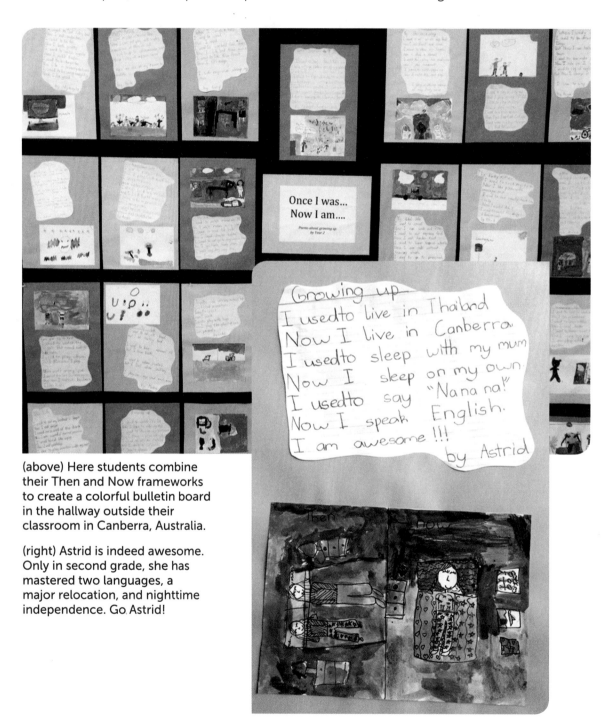

Growing up

I used to live in Thailand
Now I live in Canberra.
I used to sleep with my mum
Now I sleep on my own.
I used to say "Na na na!"
Now I speak English.
I am awesome !!!

by Astrid

(above) Here students combine their Then and Now frameworks to create a colorful bulletin board in the hallway outside their classroom in Canberra, Australia.

(right) Astrid is indeed awesome. Only in second grade, she has mastered two languages, a major relocation, and nighttime independence. Go Astrid!

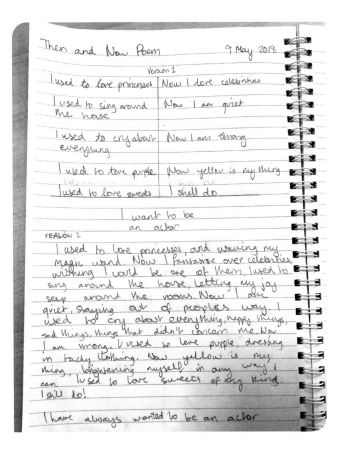

(left) This eighth grader, Rosie, from Jakarta Intercultural School, used her Then and Now prewrite to illustrate her growth through middle school, later sharing her polished Version 2 at a commemorative assembly celebrating her upcoming transition into high school. She first developed her ideas in her writer's notebook, noting how she had changed, and adding details.

(bottom) Next, Rosie converted her Then and Now framework into metaphors. What you see here is a work in progress. Her teacher, Jennifer Hopp, noted that she has a great diversity of language skills in her class and what she liked most about this framework is that "it gave all my students an opportunity at success. Some, like Rosie [whose work is pictured], are able to work easily with metaphor; other students might only have one metaphor in their piece, and that's okay. It's a process." Agreed!

Then and Now Version 1

I used to be a storybook. Bright and open, willing to be read. Playing with different characters and different scenarios all in my head.
Now, I fantasise over celebrities, wishing, if only I could be one of them.

I used to be a trumpet, blaring songs and noises of any kind around, wherever I was. Letting my joy seep into those around me.
Now I am a muted bee, struggling to be heard and occasionally letting out a feeble cry. For voice.

I used to be a tap, gushing with water. Letting myself go, with my emotions. Happy ones, sad ones, ones that even I was confused about.
Now I am a statue, standing tall and strong, not noticed by those around me.

Then and Now: Assessment Checkpoint

SKILL	3	2	1
Content Area Knowledge	Demonstrates an understanding of content area knowledge and applies it clearly and logically.	Partially demonstrates an understanding of content area knowledge and occasionally applies it clearly and logically.	Writing contains content area inaccuracies and student cannot yet apply his or her understanding.
Structure and Organization	Consistently demonstrates the ability to re-create the pattern of a comparison charting a change in a person, place, or thing.	Occasionally demonstrates the ability to re-create the pattern of a comparison charting a change in a person, place, or thing.	Is not yet able to re-create the pattern of a comparison charting a change in a person, place, or thing.
Research Skills	Chooses valid research sources and is able to cite them accurately.	Mostly chooses valid research sources and is occasionally able to cite them accurately.	Is not yet able to choose valid research sources and is occasionally able to cite them accurately.
Speaking Skills	Is willing to share and consistently demonstrates effective presentation skills using good voice projection, inflection, pacing, eye contact, and stance.	Is often willing to share and partially demonstrates effective presentation skills using good voice projection, inflection, pacing, eye contact, and stance.	Is not willing to share and/or does not yet demonstrate effective presentation skills using good voice projection, inflection, pacing, eye contact, and stance.
Listening Skills	Actively participates in discussions about other students' work and is tuned in to student presentations.	Occasionally participates in discussions about other students' work and is tuned in to student presentations.	Does not participate in discussions about other students' work and is not yet tuned in to student presentations.

Wonder of Wonders: Collecting Questions

TIME: about 45 minutes   **GRADE LEVEL:** 4 and up

MATERIALS:

- Slides 1–3*
- Research materials such as handouts, textbooks, short nonfiction text, and websites
- Small slips of recycled paper, sticky notes, or index cards, about 6 to 8 per student
- A topic for a co-constructed questioning text. (See page 140 for some ideas.)
- Notebooks, computers, or tablets

*Available online at scholastic.com/ThrivingWriterResources

WHY TEACH THIS?

1. To help students reveal their background knowledge and wonderings through questioning.
2. To inform your instruction based on what you learn.
3. To introduce a new unit of content area learning.

CONTENT AREA CONNECTIONS: Literature, Social Studies, Science, Art

Persuasive	Descriptive	Narrative	Procedural	Research	Vocabulary	Figurative Language
		X		X		

PART II: LEARNING THROUGH LANGUAGE

STEPH REFLECTS ON FRAMEWORK 13

Passion and wonder are contagious! Curiosity comes in all forms. Nothing is too trivial to spark wonder and questions—and, in fact, kids have questions about all sorts of things. A good thing since question-asking is linked to cognitive development. Children who are able to ask questions about the world around them develop the cognitive tools they need "in order to learn about the world and solve problems in it" (Chouinard, 2007).

The wonder of wonder comes to life in this writing framework.

Have research materials handy and let students paw, flip, and skim through an upcoming unit of study, or perhaps even view a video. Then put them in small groups and have them generate questions, not just for themselves, but to share in a mini classroom performance. Sound effects and interpretive dance are encouraged. And here's the best part—no one has to know the answers to the questions. Yet.

This framework is a small-group effort, which will benefit students in a variety of ways according to two of our favorite educators, Harvey and Elaine Daniels. It is their experience (and ours) that co-composing provides multiple benefits, including replacing sleepy lessons with thoughtful, meaningful interaction; creating vigorous discussion; and encouraging buy-in while it gives a voice to reticent participants and helps develop healthy relationships (Daniels & Daniels, 2013).

Not only will this framework get students engaged and thinking about their upcoming lesson, it will also provide a periscope into their prior knowledge and pique their curiosity. After the sharing performance, post the questioning texts around the room. You can refer to them as you proceed with your instruction, showing that their questions are directing the lesson. This works with standard lessons and project-based learning and generates teamwork—and maybe even some classroom fun.

1. **Introduce the Framework**

    Project Slide 1, read it aloud, and explain to students that you are interested in their questions. By sharing questions, we can determine what we know and what we want to know.

Wonder of Wonders:
Collecting Questions

What are we going to learn today?

1. We will think about and document what we wonder.
2. We will collect and prioritize our questions in small groups.
3. We will arrange our questions creatively to share with others.

Slide 1

2. Discuss Mentor Text

- Project Slide 2, read it aloud, and clarify any unknown words. Have students reread the text, perhaps taking turns reading individual lines.

- "Perform" the text: Have a few students make wind or rain sounds; reach for the sky; assume the roles of clouds, rain, sun; and so forth.

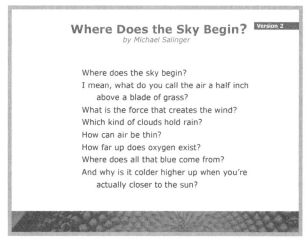

Slide 2

- Note that this text is all questions, no answers. Also note that it is labeled "Version 2," and indicate that you are now going to follow in the steps the author took to construct it.

3. Co-construct Version 1

- Project Slide 3 and tell students that the first step in writing a piece like the mentor text is assembling questions. Explain that these are some questions the author of the mentor text may have asked himself before writing the piece.

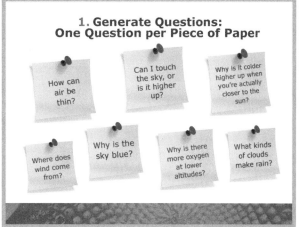

Slide 3

- Brainstorm a list of questioning words. The five Ws—who, what, where, when, and why—are helpful, of course. But don't forget other words such as how, does, can, would, could, has, and will. Tell students that their questions should begin with one of these words.

- Pick a subject for your co-construct of Version 1. The theme should be different from the unit theme you are going to ask the students to write about.

In a third-grade class, Sara co-constructed a list of questions on the topic of zombies. First, they generated a list of questioning words on the whiteboard. Based on that list, students came up with questions to co-construct a Version 1.

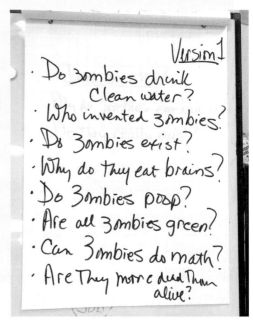

- Solicit questions from students, using the list of brainstormed questioning words. Scribe questions on the board as you collect them. As you do, you may want to ask: *How many of you have the same question?* This encourages participation and shows kids they are not alone in their wonderings.

- After you have listed 10 to 12 questions, read them aloud with students.

4. Have Students Write Their Version 1: A Two-Step Process

Step 1: Generate Questions on Targeted Content

- Distribute slips of paper and divide students into small groups. With primary students, we recommend pairs or groups of three. With intermediate students, we recommend groups of up to six.

- Assign the whole class the same broad topic (reptiles, for instance) or each group a subcategory of a broad topic (snakes, alligators, crocodiles, lizards, turtles).

- Ask each student to generate six to eight questions on the topic. Students may need to do some research in order to think of questions. Have resources available.

- Periodically ask students to read questions aloud and give encouragement.

Step 2: Collaborate to Construct Version 1

- Project Slide 4 and instruct students to collaborate to combine and reword questions, edit out duplicates, and reassemble them into a bulleted list. Each student should wind up with a copy of the list. Students may create a shared online document, or each one may write his or her own copy.

- When students are finished, invite each group to read its list aloud.

5. Co-construct Version 2

- Project Slide 2 again, the mentor text *Where Does the Sky Begin?* Note that the author provides complete sentences, not bullet points.

- Turn to your co-constructed Version 1 and ask which of the bullet points would make a strong first line, and then ask students to transform that point into a complete sentence.

- Do this for a couple of lines—no need to create the entire text. After you have modeled the process, it's time for students to work on their own.

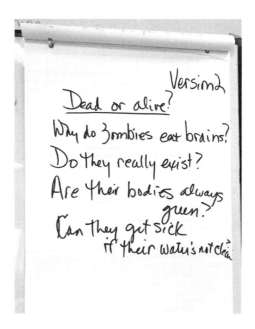

6. Have Students Write Their Version 2

- Ask groups to revise their bullet points into sentences. To inspire the best work possible, ask: *Can the questions be rearranged for drama? Could you insert a statement, rather than a question, here or there to give your piece a more narrative quality? Or could you add a refrain?* (See "Refrain Again," page 101.)

- When they're finished, have students script the text for recitation by multiple voices, including sound effects and hand motions. Give them about two minutes to rehearse.

7. Share!

- Have fun with this.

- Be sure everyone in the group has a role in the performance, even if it is just tapping out a beat.

- Record performances and share them with parents, or invite another class in for the performances.

Lesson Extension Ideas

- Ask students to illustrate their questioning texts with drawings and/or photographs, and display them in the room.

- As you proceed through your study, remind students to refer back to their questions to see if they've found the answers.

Sample Stages

Working in small groups to prioritize and sort their questions to create their Wonder of Wonders framework, students gear up and develop ownership in upcoming lessons. We have successfully implemented this strategy across grade levels and subject matters. Who doesn't like having their questions given such significance in the classroom? (This is a rhetorical question, of course.)

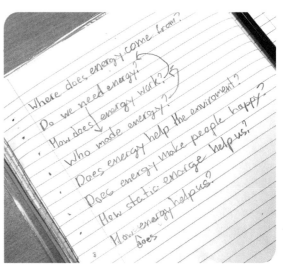

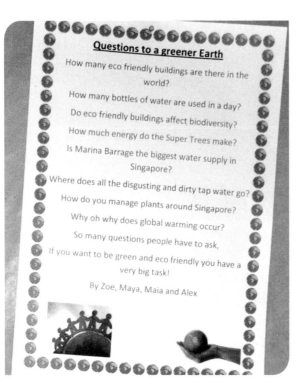

(above) Here, a third-grade group of students at the Anglo American School of Moscow compile their questions about an upcoming unit on energy.

(left) Michael had a quick lunchtime chat with a sixth-grade science teacher at the United World College of Southeast Asia in Singapore and explained how his students might compile questions into a piece of short text. This group of students decided to rhyme the last two lines for a dramatic ending.

Seventh-grade students in Anchorage, Kentucky, co-constructed a questioning text about Hinduism as part of their unit on India. Interestingly, we did the same framework with some students in Singapore. Both groups of students ended with the same question: "What happens when you die?" proving that some questions are indeed universal.

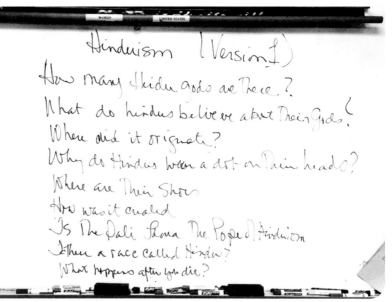

Wonder of Wonders: Assessment Checkpoint

SKILL	3	2	I
Careful Reading	Demonstrates through classroom discussion and writing an understanding of the impact of word choice in crafting questions.	Partially demonstrates through classroom discussion and writing an understanding of the impact of word choice in crafting questions.	Does not yet demonstrate through classroom discussion and writing an understanding of the impact of word choice in crafting questions.
Content and Organization	Demonstrates the ability to recognize and re-create a writing structure composed of questions that genuinely reflect the theme, using available resources for cursory research.	Partially demonstrates the ability to recognize and re-create a writing structure composed of questions that genuinely reflect the theme, using available resources for cursory research. May include duplicate questions or questions that are not pertinent.	Does not yet demonstrate the ability to recognize and re-create a writing structure composed of questions that genuinely reflect the theme, may have neglected to use available resources for cursory research and/or includes duplicate questions or questions that are not pertinent.
Writing Collaboratively	Demonstrates the ability to engage in collaborative civil discourse and discussion that results in a piece of writing with shared authorship.	Shows some evidence of collaboration, but discussion and output are obviously not a group effort.	Group is unable to collaborate. Work produced is obviously created by one author or is unfinished.
Speaking Skills	Is willing to share and consistently demonstrates effective presentation skills using good voice projection, inflection, pacing, eye contact, and stance.	Is often willing to share and partially demonstrates effective presentation skills using good voice projection, inflection, pacing, eye contact, and stance.	Is not yet willing to share and does not yet demonstrate effective presentation skills using good voice projection, inflection, pacing, eye contact, and stance.
Listening Skills	Actively participates in discussions about other students' work and is tuned in to student presentations.	Occasionally participates in discussions about other students' work and is tuned in to student presentations.	Does not participate in discussions about other students' work and is not yet tuned in to student presentations.

PART II: LEARNING THROUGH LANGUAGE

The Academic Essay: A Four-Square Prewrite

TIME: about 1.5 hours (Consider carrying out this framework over two days or more.)	**GRADE LEVEL:** 5–8

MATERIALS:

- Slides 1–13*
- Research materials such as handouts, textbooks, websites, and other references
- The Academic Essay GO Sheet for students, or they can make their own*
- Notebooks, computers, or tablets

*Available online at scholastic.com/ThrivingWriterResources

WHY TEACH THIS?

To provide a beginner lesson on how to craft a five-paragraph essay. It is a toe-dip into academic writing.

CONTENT AREA CONNECTIONS: Literature, Social Studies, Science, Math

Persuasive	Descriptive	Narrative	Procedural	Research	Vocabulary	Figurative Language
X	X	X		X		

STEPH REFLECTS ON FRAMEWORK 14

The author and essayist Neil Gaiman once wrote of writing, "This is how you do it: You sit down at the keyboard and you put one word after another until it's done. It's that easy, and that hard." It's especially hard when you don't know your topic well enough to know what should even come first. Sara and Michael have it right: First become thoroughly acquainted with the content of your essay—and then you can figure out how best to frame and introduce it.

The assignment. The blank page. The blinking cursor. The struggle to draft the perfect thesis statement. The head on the desk. The blood on the forehead. STOP RIGHT THERE.

Essay writing doesn't have to be that wrenching. Instead, we are going to gather our ideas together around a statement of purpose, do some research, develop bullet points for each paragraph, loosely draft a conclusion, identify a few citations, and then, finally, we will draft the introduction with a hook to engage the reader and the all-important thesis statement.

This is a flipped classroom approach to drafting an essay. While all of our frameworks are designed to be done in the classroom and not as dreaded homework assignments, this lesson also flips the standard approach to writing an essay. We do *not* begin with an introduction, nor do we draft disembodied thesis statements. First, we gather the results of our research and organize it, and then we craft our introductory language.

> A statement of purpose is the thought that inspires the research and the subsequent essay. It could be a question: *Is apple juice healthy?* An argument: *Apple juice IS healthy.* A marketing goal: *Get more people to drink apple juice.* A scientific result: *Apple juice does not cause sugar spikes.* Or it can even be an engineering outcome: *Using our newly designed "quick press" causes less waste in the production of apple juice.*

Michael: *Subsequent* is the key word here.

Sara: Right. Attempting to draft a thesis statement before delving into research and organizing our thoughts using a detailed prewrite is a lesson in frustration for many students.

Michael: Beginning an essay by starting with the introduction is dangerous for two reasons: 1. The writer may be tempted to direct research to support a poorly crafted or even inaccurate thesis statement succumbing to confirmation bias; and 2. It's just plain hard to do.

Sara: There may be blood.

We recommend a less painful process. We base our writing frameworks on our own experience. We write educational essays for publication, Sara worked as a speechwriter, Michael did technical writing for engineers, and even in the writing of this professional book, we did not begin writing with the introduction. An introduction is an invitation that entices readers into the text. How can we entice if we aren't clear what's on the menu?

This lesson is not designed to guide your students through the entire essay process. Instead it is a framework to help them to organize their thoughts, those 47 sticky notes, and a few citations into a manageable blueprint for writing.

1. **Introduce the Framework**

   Project Slide 1, read it aloud, and emphasize the importance of prewriting when starting in on a large writing project. Although it may seem like more work, prewriting streamlines the writing process.

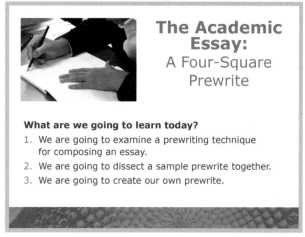

Slide 1

2. **Build Background Knowledge**

   - Review the meaning of the word *verifiable* (able to be checked or demonstrated to be true with a citation). Ask the students to say the word aloud a couple of times. Then invite them to offer a couple examples of verifiable facts: *The temperature is 56 degrees today. Dogs are mammals.*

   - Review the meaning of the word *citation* (an attribution of quoted material from a reference source). You may wish to consult your librarian to further students' background knowledge of how to identify and craft an academic citation.

3. **Hand Out the GO Sheet**

   - Note, there is no mentor text for this framework because the emphasis is on prewriting. Instead, we have assembled a series of slides showing the progression of the prewrite, with one or more talking points for each slide.

   - Project Slide 2 and distribute the GO Sheet.

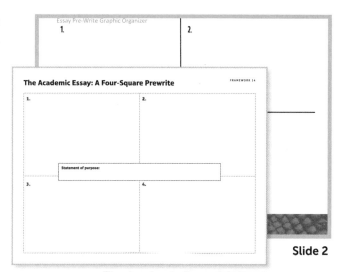

Slide 2

The Academic Essay GO Sheet

- Proceed with the lesson, reading aloud the following slides and pausing to work with students to compose their prewrites as you proceed. Reminder, students need a topic before this process begins.

4. State Your Purpose

- Project Slide 3, read the step at the bottom of the slide, and then read the sample statement of purpose: *Schools are good places to learn.* Note that a statement of purpose is the thought that inspired the research. It may or may not prove to be true and become part of the thesis—we don't know yet.

- Note that it could be formatted as a question, an argument, a goal, a scientific hypothesis, or an engineering outcome. We are using the term *statement* here as a synonym for *premise* or *impetus*.

- Read aloud the sample statement of purpose.

- Inform students that all further details added will have to relate to this statement of purpose.

- Ask students to write a statement of purpose on their chosen topic in the box in the center of their GO Sheets.

5. Add Three True Statements

- Project Slide 4 and call on a student to read the step at the bottom of the slide: *After some initial research, add three true statements (one to each of boxes 1, 2, and 3).*

- Have students read aloud the three sample true statements. Note how each one relates to the statement of purpose.

- Ask students to add three true statements to their GO Sheets.

6. Add Verifiable Supporting Facts

- Project Slide 5 and call on a student to read the next step: Add two verifiable facts below each true statement.

- Remind students that a verifiable fact is not an opinion. For instance, if your statement of purpose is "Saltwater crocodiles don't make

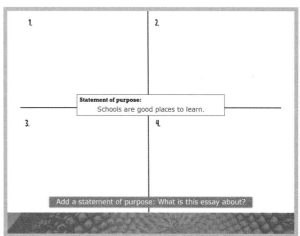

Slide 3

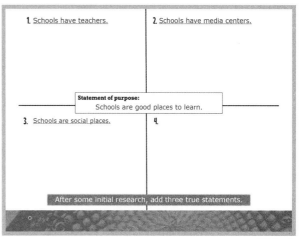

Slide 4

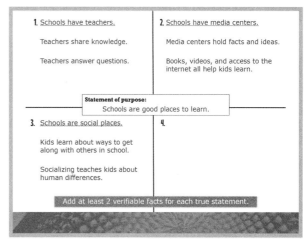

Slide 5

good pets," "Saltwater crocodiles are scary" is not a verifiable fact that supports it. It is an opinion—a perfectly valid opinion, but an opinion nonetheless. "Saltwater crocodiles have powerful jaws" is a verifiable fact, meaning we could find a citation and source to support it, for example, "Saltwater crocodiles have 3,700 lbs. per square inch of bite force" (source: "Crocodiles Have Strongest Bite Ever Measured, Hands-on Tests Show." *National Geographic*, National Geographic Society, 6 Apr. 2016, news.nationalgeographic.com/news/2012/03/120315-crocodiles-bite-force-erickson-science-plos-one-strongest/).

- Read (or select a student to read) the sample verifiable facts on Slide 5. Discuss what sources students might investigate to research supporting citations on a couple of those facts. Show them how recording a citation might look on the GO Sheet, as done, for example, in Slide 6.

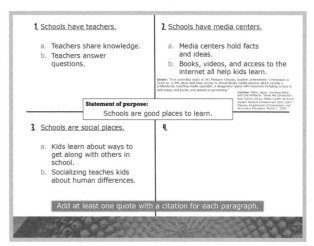

Slide 6

- Ask students to add two verifiable facts to each of the three sections of their prewrites. Then have them read aloud at the same time all the information on the sheet.

7. Add Citations

- Read aloud the quote and citation on Slide 6 and discuss why it supports the verifiable fact.

- Add citations. If the GO Sheet is getting crowded at this point, index cards may be employed.

8. Add a Conclusion, Version 1

- Project Slide 7 and call on a student to read the next step. Then read the sample conclusion that summarizes all of the true statements and verifiable facts.

- Note that the conclusion references each of the three true statements. Ask students to identify them in the conclusion. Also note that the true statements are not presented verbatim, but have been blended and tightened to create a coherent sentence.

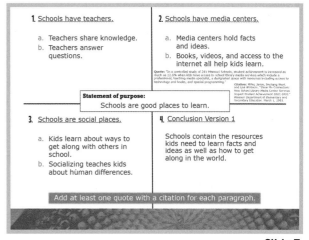

Slide 7

From Striving to Thriving Writers copyright © 2018 by Sara Holbrook, Michael Salinger, and Stephanie Harvey. Published by Scholastic Inc.

- Ask students to draft a Version 1 conclusion using only information from their prewrites. Tell them there should be no new statements or facts in their conclusion. They should write this conclusion in Box 4 on their GO Sheets.

- Circulate the room and lend support as students weave their three true statements into one or two concluding sentences. Watch for students who just copy their statements without distilling them into a coherent sentence.

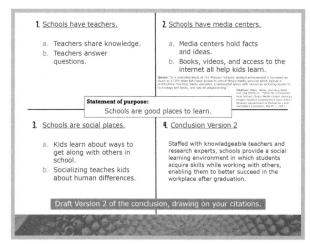

Slide 8

9. Revise Conclusion

- Project Slide 8, read the revised conclusion, and discuss what makes this stronger. (It's more fluent, contains more sentence variety, and contains more details drawn from the research.)

- Ask students to revise their conclusions, adding details from their citations.

- Remind students not to add any new statements or facts to the conclusion.

- If you wish, have students transition to a spreadsheet at this point in the lesson. We like to give students an option. See Slide 9 for a model on how to set that up. The main advantage of a spreadsheet is that it will help students keep all their data in one place. Some students may wish to continue sketching things out by hand.

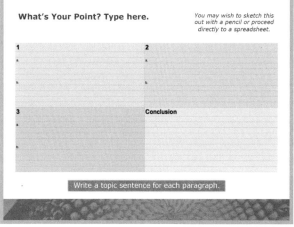

Slide 9

10. Add Introduction

- Project Slide 10, which contains two attempts at introductions. Read them aloud or have students read them. Ask students to turn and talk about which one is stronger and why. (The second one is stronger because it has a strong hook to engage the reader.)

- Have students open a new document and begin to draft Version 1 of their essay. Specifically, ask them to draft an introductory sentence or two that contains a hook to engage the reader. It could be a question: Can you imagine a world without schools? An important fact: Schools help students succeed. *Or* a call to action: Communities need to support their schools.

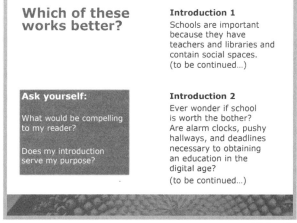

Slide 10

11. Add Thesis Statement

- Project Slide 11 and read it aloud. Then invite students to read the sample thesis statement. Answer any questions they may have about the purpose or placement of a thesis statement. More models of thesis statements can be found online, but don't overwhelm students by showing them too many.

- Note that the thesis statement should reference each of the three true statements, which provide the backbone of the essay—one paragraph is devoted to each statement.

- Guide students as they craft their own thesis statements. This is a big nut to crack. We suggest pairing them and letting them talk their way through their Version 1.

Thesis statement:
1. Comes at the end of the introductory paragraph.
2. Summarizes the contents of the three body paragraphs.
3. Takes a stand that is (most often) arguable.

Schools offer students the benefit of teacher support, crucial media resources, and a social environment, all of which combine to facilitate learning.

Slide 11

Four-Square Essay

1. State your purpose.
2. Add three supporting ideas in boxes 1, 2, and 3.
3. Add (at least) two supporting reasons for each of your three ideas.
4. Draft a conclusion based on your supported reasons.
5. Add one or more citations for each reason.
6. Finally, draft your introduction with a strong hook to engage your reader as well as a thesis statement.

Slide 12

12. Use the Summary Checklist

Project Slide 12 and review the checklist of how to create a prewrite for an essay. You may wish to duplicate the checklist for students to keep in their writer's notebooks.

Lesson Extension Ideas

- Have students complete the essay. Next steps include adding to the GO Sheet topic sentences for each body paragraph and drafting the body paragraphs. Tell students to keep their prewrites handy as guides.

- Have students turn their completed essays into speeches and presentations to share the learning.

The Academic Essay: Assessment Checkpoint

SKILL	3	2	1
Content and Structure	Is able to complete the four-square prewrite, including a clear statement of purpose and three main ideas of support.	Is partially able to complete the four-square prewrite, including a clear statement of purpose and three main ideas of support.	Is not yet able to complete the four-square prewrite in a meaningful way.
Research	Demonstrates the ability to research a topic and include valid citations that support the statement of purpose.	Partially demonstrates the ability to research a topic and include valid citations that support the statement of purpose.	Is not yet able to research a topic and include valid citations that support the statement of purpose.
Lead Writing	Demonstrates the ability to write a strong introduction that engages the reader, including a thesis statement.	Partially demonstrates the ability to write a strong introduction that engages the reader, including a thesis statement.	Is not yet able to demonstrate the ability to write a strong introduction that engages the reader, including a thesis statement.
Speaking Skills	Is willing to share aloud and consistently demonstrates effective presentation skills using good voice projection, inflection, pacing, eye contact, and stance.	Is often willing to share and partially demonstrates effective presentation skills using good voice projection, inflection, pacing, eye contact, and stance.	Is not yet willing to share and/or does not yet demonstrate effective presentation skills using good voice projection, inflection, pacing, eye contact, and stance.
Listening Skills	Actively participates in discussions about other students' work and is tuned in to student presentations.	Occasionally participates in discussions about other students' work and is tuned in to student presentations.	Does not participate in discussions about other students' work and is not yet tuned in to student presentations.

From Striving to Thriving Writers copyright © 2018 by Sara Holbrook, Michael Salinger, and Stephanie Harvey. Published by Scholastic Inc.

What's the Story? The Five-Sentence Narrative

TIME: about 35 minutes	**GRADE LEVEL:** 4 and up

MATERIALS:

- Slides 1–7*
- What's the Story? GO Sheet*
- Preselected subject matter for the co-construct
- Research materials such as handouts, articles, and websites pertaining to content areas
- Notebooks, computers, or tablets

*Available online at scholastic.com/ThrivingWriterResources

WHY TEACH THIS?

To show students how to craft a narrative. From friendly conversations to critical, academic, and business communications, knowing how to craft a narrative helps writers to be understood. A good story also gives people a reason to listen.

CONTENT AREA CONNECTIONS: Literature, Social Studies, Science, Art

Persuasive	Descriptive	Narrative	Procedural	Research	Vocabulary	Figurative Language
		X		X		

STEPH REFLECTS ON FRAMEWORK 15

"After nourishment, shelter, and companionship, stories are the thing we need most in the world" (Pullman, 2013). Kids are naturally drawn to stories. We all learn from stories. Stories are the beating heart of the human condition. We all have our own stories to tell. Teaching students to recognize the power of story will help them make their way through the world.

And then what happened?

"Great leaders are great storytellers," says business communications guru Dr. Nick Morgan. He insists that in our YouTube, Instagram, news-alert age, business leaders "won't be heard unless they're telling stories."

"Facts and figures and all the rational things that we think are important in the business world actually don't stick in our minds at all," Morgan says. But, he continues, stories create "sticky" memories by attaching emotions to things that happen. According to the *Harvard Business Review*, that means those "who can create and share good stories have a powerful advantage over others" (O'Hara, 2014).

A good story, easy enough to appreciate, can be hard to replicate, making the craft of storytelling worth study. "Stories and novels consist of three parts: narration, which moves the story from point A to point B and finally to point Z; description, which creates a sensory reality for the reader; and dialogue, which brings characters to life through their speech," says master storyteller Stephen King. He believes good stories are situational, stating, "A strong enough situation renders the whole question of plot moot," which he says is fine with him (2010).

In this writing framework, we are going to follow Stephen King's lead and encourage our writers to look at a situation with an eye toward describing it and articulating a conflict and a resolution, with just enough detail to connect with our reader. This structure, like the underpinning melody to a jazz solo, can be the jumping-off point to longer or shorter texts.

We are well into this new century, and sometimes it seems as if we are still trying to figure out what 21st-century learning is all about. The way we consume and archive information has changed dramatically in our lifetimes. Education tech guru Jeff Utecht has said that jobs in the future won't expect employees to have all the pertinent problem-solving facts in their heads at any one time, but they *will* expect employees to be able to come up with the right answer in five minutes.

Michael: And we heard him first say that 10 years ago.

Sara: The future is now.

Steph: It is not effective teaching to just feed students information; we need to give them the skills to find information on their own.

Additionally, students must learn to verify that information.

1. Introduce the Framework

- Project Slide 1, read it aloud, and ask students to turn and talk about all the places they hear stories (library, movies, TV shows, video games, relatives, morning announcements, and so on). The confused fellow in the picture is an orangutan. More on him later.

- Explain that *narrative* is just a two-dollar word for *story*.

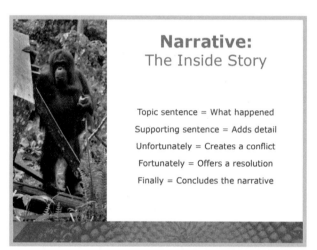

Slide 1

2. Build Background Knowledge

- Project Slide 2 and explain that this is the structure we are going to use to build our story.

- Ask if any students have ever read books in a series, such as Captain Underpants, Harry Potter, and Ramona, and note that while these books often contain the same characters, each one has a different "Unfortunately"—or a different conflict, a different problem that needs to be addressed, which may even require different settings. But at the crux of every narrative is the "Unfortunately."

- Explain that they are going to start out writing nonfiction, but later they will have the opportunity to fictionalize their pieces. If they ask, "What's with the orangutan?" respond, "Just wait."

Slide 2

3. Discuss Mentor Text, Version 1

- Project Slide 3 and read aloud the story of Hurricane Harvey in Houston. Select volunteers to reread the story.

- Ask: *What is this story about?* (Hurricane Harvey in Houston) Note that Version 1 is a bit vague and doesn't tell everything about the hurricane. However, it does provide a quick summary of the situation.

- Ask what the words *Unfortunately, Fortunately,* and *Finally* do for this short narrative. (They help present a conflict, a resolution, and a conclusion—the three essential components of compelling narratives.)

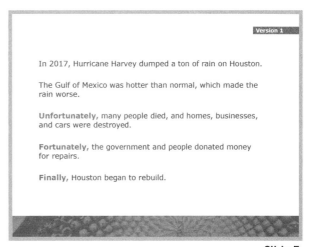

Slide 3

- Note that Version 1 does not provide the number of homes destroyed or people injured, but that can be fixed in Version 2, after a little research.

- Note that Version 1 also contains no opinions. Nowhere does it say that Hurricane Harvey was **horrible** or that **good** people donated money. This short narrative sticks to the facts.

4. Co-construct Version 1

- Project Slide 4 and announce that it is finally time to write about these orangutans who've been hanging around.

- Note that at first it may seem that orangutans are a whole lot funnier than a hurricane. Say something like: *Let's look into this and see what the story is with orangutans.*

- Pair up students and give them five minutes to go online to find some facts about these (as their name translates from Malay) "old men of the forest." Set a timer for drama.

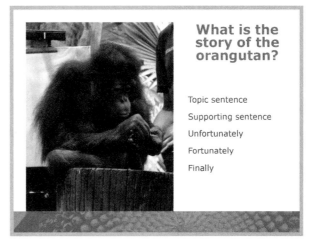

Slide 4

- Ask partners to jot down at least three facts about orangutans. In fact, the story of orangutans is pretty tragic. Their habitats are disappearing because of deforestation, causing their numbers to dwindle, and they're being preyed upon by black-market animal traders. Let students find out facts like that on their own.

- Invite students to offer facts for your first line. Combine a couple to create your topic sentence and write it down.

PART II: LEARNING THROUGH LANGUAGE

- Continue this process to create your second, supporting sentence. Remind students that the third sentence must begin with the word *Unfortunately*, the fourth with *Fortunately*, and the final one, *Finally*. As with the story about Hurricane Harvey, students may have to think hard to come up with a *Fortunately* sentence for your co-constructed story about the orangutans.

Orangutans' live in Indonesia in rainforests
their arm span is 8 ft.
Unfortunately hundreds of Orangutans are taken from the wild for the pet trade
Fortunately there are conservationists trying to help
Finally their numbers continue to drop.

Test: ?/
Meet orientation 3/28
Roll a word 3/2

A co-construct from a fifth-grade class in Kirtland, Ohio.

- When you're finished, read your Version 1 aloud with students.

Working with a grade 4 class in Zimbabwe, we co-constructed a narrative about rhinos. Version 1 was pretty straightforward. As the class and Sara revised Version 2, the text became a call to action.

Rhinos are large gray mammals
Their name means horned nose in Greek
Unfortunately people hunt them for their horns
fortunately they are still alive because they can charge their enemies
Finally Some people protect them

Version 1

Rhinos are large gray animals. Their name means "horned nose" in Greek. **Unfortunately,** people hunt them for their horns.
Fortunately, they are still alive because they can charge their enemies.
Finally, some people protect them.

Version 2

Rhinos
Large, gray.
Hunted for their horns.
Still alive,
Charging their enemies.
Protect them.

5. Hand Out the GO Sheet

6. Have Students Write Their Version 1

- Have students collaborate with a writing partner to research and write their Version 1. Each student should have their own copy of the work as it is being written.

- Guide students to pick a topic related to a content area of study. When we were working with Katie Lufkin's fourth graders, who were studying Chesapeake Bay, the students researched and wrote about fishing, clams, recreation, water quality, the bridge, and other related topics. Compiling and listening to the students' topic-specific stories about the bay created a more complete narrative about it.

- Prompt students through each sentence of the structure on their GO Sheets, one at a time. Pause now and then to have students read individual sentences aloud. Walk them through these prompts one at a time (Topic sentence, Supporting sentence, Unfortunately, Fortunately, Finally).

- Upon completion, have the whole class read their narratives aloud at the same time. Then invite students to read them to someone other than their writing partner. Then ask a few students to read aloud to the whole class.

What's the Story? GO Sheet

7. Discuss Mentor Text, Version 2

- Project Slide 5 and read through Version 2 with students. Ask: *What has changed?* (Details have been added, including numbers and temperatures.)

- Note that the helper words *Unfortunately*, *Fortunately*, and *Finally* have been deleted. We don't need them anymore because the piece works well without them. The idea of Unfortunately, Fortunately, and Finally is still apparent even if the words have been edited out.

- Note that Version 2 references a source. Let students know how you want them to format their references.

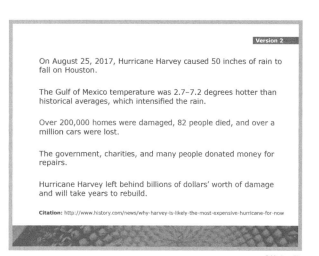

Version 2

On August 25, 2017, Hurricane Harvey caused 50 inches of rain to fall on Houston.

The Gulf of Mexico temperature was 2.7–7.2 degrees hotter than historical averages, which intensified the rain.

Over 200,000 homes were damaged, 82 people died, and over a million cars were lost.

The government, charities, and many people donated money for repairs.

Hurricane Harvey left behind billions of dollars' worth of damage and will take years to rebuild.

Citation: http://www.history.com/news/why-harvey-is-likely-the-most-expensive-hurricane-for-now

Slide 5

8. Co-construct Version 2

- Return to your co-constructed Version 1 and invite students to suggest verifiable facts to add to it.

- Ask students where they obtained facts. No need to write down references, just keep them part of the conversation at this point.

- Add a fact or two to model the revision process. Don't spend time finishing up the piece. Once the students understand where this is headed, set them loose on their own pieces.

9. Have Students Write Their Version 2

- Ask students to revisit and discuss their research findings with their partners.
- Ask them to add a fact to each of the five sentences to create their Version 2. If students are working on summarizing a piece of text, you may want to ask them to go back into that text and include page numbers for their references.
- Students may wish to split from their partners to write on their own and/or transition to a computer or tablet.
- Ask periodically for read-alouds.

10. Share!

- Ask students to share their work with another student.
- Ask volunteers to share with the whole class.
- As students share, point out how their stories relate to your content area studies.

Lesson Extension Ideas

- Invite students to use this framework for different content area topics, including events from history, scenes in literature, and changes caused to the earth. This framework is also good for classes such as physical education and health. *Ice cream tastes good, but unfortunately it's fattening and bad for your teeth.*
- Grow the piece into a story by introducing a character. See how the Hurricane Harvey story changes when we introduce Isabella. Add some sensory details like sounds and colors and you have added tone to the narrative. Rearrange the five lines. Have fun—this is where we can let our creativity fly.
- Project Slide 6 and read aloud or have students read. Ask: *Do you want to know what happens next for Isabella?* Ask students to identify facts from Version 2 and see how they were woven into the story.
- Project Slide 7 to see how writers might begin to shrink the text into a poem by applying the Found Poem format from Framework 19.

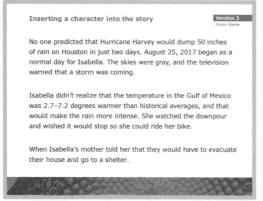

Slide 6

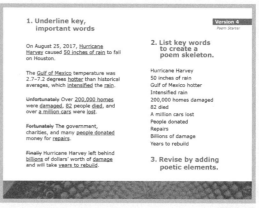

Slide 7

Sample Stages

Synthesizing and summarizing using this framework, students can quickly demonstrate their understanding in five lines. As they progress, refining their versions, they may grow the text by adding more information or render it into a poem or a caption. Or the five-sentence narrative story can just serve as a quick formative assessment as it stands. You set the goals to fit the needs of your classroom and your individual students.

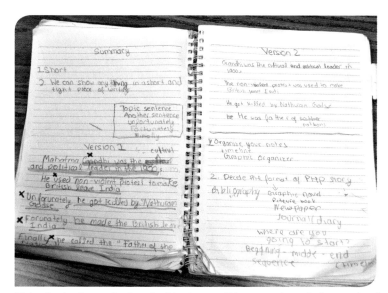

This student was instructed to keep all her versions in her writer's notebook as she progressed. We can track her progress as she crafted her narrative first with the Unfortunately, Fortunately, and Finally prompts, through selecting the most important words and crafting a text, which relates a conflict and resolution without the helper words. A fifth grader, she was doing independent research on Gandhi at the Harare International School in Zimbabwe.

Here, a second-grade student from Kirtland, Ohio, tells his first-person story of learning cursive, throwing a rhyme in at the end. Fun!

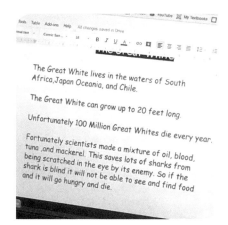

A fifth grader from Kirtland, Ohio, summarizes his reading about sharks.

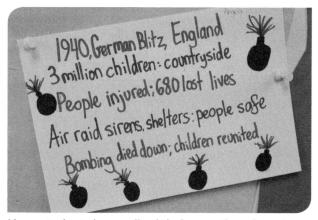

Here, students have edited their narratives down to postcard size using color and graphics to augment the evidence of their learning. These samples came from a sixth-grade writing workshop led by our great friend Stevi Quate at the Jakarta International School.

PART II: LEARNING THROUGH LANGUAGE

What's the Story? Assessment Checkpoint

SKILL	3	2	1
Content Knowledge	Demonstrates an understanding of content area information and is able to identify the main idea.	Demonstrates some understanding of content area information and is able to identify the main idea. May include one or two details that are not pertinent to the main theme of the piece.	Includes inaccuracies when writing about content area information and is not yet able to identify the main idea.
Narrative Structure	Consistently and accurately develops a narrative story using the prescribed pattern.	Partially develops a narrative story using the prescribed pattern. Perhaps a line does not reflect its prompt or is irrelevant to the narrative.	Does not yet develop a narrative story using the prescribed pattern.
Revision	Effectively develops the nonfiction summary framework by adding details and a citation.	Partially develops the nonfiction summary framework by adding details and a citation.	Does not yet develop the nonfiction summary framework by adding details and a citation.
Speaking Skills	Is willing to share aloud and consistently demonstrates effective presentation skills using good voice projection, inflection, pacing, eye contact, and stance.	Is often willing to share and partially demonstrates effective presentation skills using good voice projection, inflection, pacing, eye contact, and stance.	Is not yet willing to share and/or does not yet demonstrate effective presentation skills using good voice projection, inflection, pacing, eye contact, and stance.
Listening Skills	Actively participates in discussions about other students' work and is tuned in to student presentations.	Occasionally participates in discussions about other students' work and is tuned in to student presentations.	Does not participate in discussions about other students' work and is not yet tuned in to student presentations.

Inside Outside: Here's Lookin' at You, Kid

TIME: about 30–40 minutes

GRADE LEVEL: 1–4

MATERIALS:

- Slides 1–3*
- Inside Outside GO Sheet*
- Notebooks, computers, or tablets

*Available online at scholastic.com/ThrivingWriterResources

WHY TEACH THIS?

To help students look at themselves in terms of what others see, what they know about themselves, and what their goals and dreams are.

CONTENT AREA CONNECTIONS: ELA

Persuasive	Descriptive	Narrative	Procedural	Research	Vocabulary	Figurative Language
	X			X		

From Striving to Thriving Writers copyright © 2018 by Sara Holbrook, Michael Salinger, and Stephanie Harvey. Published by Scholastic Inc.

STEPH REFLECTS ON FRAMEWORK 16

Identity matters! Our first job is to get to know our striving readers and writers and to find a way into their hearts and minds. In *From Striving to Thriving: How to Grow Confident, Capable Readers*, Annie Ward and I suggest a number of ways to get to know kids ASAP (Harvey & Ward, 2017). This framework suggests a powerful way to get to know kids better through their writing and to help them understand themselves as well. Ultimately, we want all students to develop strong identities as capable, confident readers and writers.

Who am I? The age-old existential question. This writing framework takes account of what others see, what they may not see, and goals and dreams for the future. Together, these elements create a quick snapshot of the student.

The second benefit is that it is a way to teach or reteach the concept of using bullets and a four-square as a prewrite strategy. This is a precursor for organizing a five-paragraph essay as shown in Framework 9. In fact, our Version 1 simply consists of bullets. Depending on the grade level, it can also be a quick, formative assessment of the students' mastery of simple and compound sentences, including capitalization and punctuation.

This is a great Get to Know You exercise as mentioned in *From Striving to Thriving: How to Grow Confident and Capable Readers*. When we introduced the framework to Katie Lufkin to use with her fourth graders, she decided to use it as an icebreaker (pun intended) in January to talk about New Year's resolutions and goals for the remainder of the year. The students then took their prewrites, illustrated the squares, and used them to decorate square tissue boxes.

Michael:	I'd call that a multipurpose classroom strategy given January is in the middle of tissue-using cold season.
Sara:	We love when teachers take one of our strategies and customize them for their own classrooms.
Michael:	Nothing to sneeze at.
Sara:	You did not say that.

1. Introduce the Framework

Project Slide 1 and read it aloud.

2. Discuss Mentor Text, Version 1

- Project Slide 2 and have fun reading and rereading the little poem.

- Divide the class into four groups and have different groups read aloud different parts (red group, blue group, etc.). Turn it into a round. Add hand motions. Ham it up.

- Discuss the meaning of each stanza: *I am you see*—what others can see about you just by looking, *I am what's me*—what you know about yourself that others cannot tell by looking, *I am not done*—personal goals that you may wish to accomplish, and *I am to be*—what you wish to become.

- Read through mentor text Version 1 and note what is evident to others and what the writer knows personally.

3. Co-construct Version 1

- Project or re-create the Inside Outside GO Sheet (see next page) and brainstorm details about your class for each of the four sections, for example: What others can see (Room 408, third grade, lots of windows), what others may not see (we are friends; we are jazzed about books; we love our mascot, Elmo), and so forth.

- Entertain lots of ideas. It will be hard to confine yourself to three details.

- Remind students that you are looking for facts, not opinions—no words such as *cool*, *sweet*, or *horrible*.

Inside Outside:
Here's Lookin' at You, Kid!

What are we going to learn today?
1. We will read a poem.
2. We will learn what a four-square framework is.
3. We will look inside and outside to write about ourselves.

Slide 1

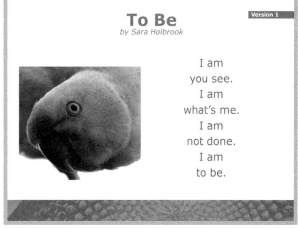

To Be
by Sara Holbrook

Version 1

I am
you see.
I am
what's me.
I am
not done.
I am
to be.

Slide 2

4. Hand Out the GO Sheet

5. Have Students Write Their Version 1

Inside Outside GO sheet

- Have them turn and talk to someone near about what they intend to write.

- After the students have discussed their ideas for a bit, it is time to get started writing.

- Ask students to complete the GO Sheet by writing three details in each square. Note: Details are not complete sentences, just quick notes.

- Remind them to avoid opinion words such as *awesome, cool,* or *boss.*

- Periodically invite students to read a bullet point they have completed, and accept or guide as warranted.

6. Discuss Types of Sentences

Project Slide 3 and review the definitions of simple sentences and compound sentences. Students may create simple sentences on a single detail or create compound sentences by combining details, using conjunctions.

Slide 3

7. Co-construct Version 2

- Project your co-constructed Version 1 and entertain ideas about how to make complete sentences out of a couple of your details.

- Demonstrate how to write at least one simple sentence and one compound sentence.

- Have the class read the sentences aloud as you write them. Point out punctuation and conjunctions.

8. Have Students Write Their Version 2

- Ask students to relabel their text "Version 2." They may continue writing on their GO Sheets or transition to a notebook, computer, or tablet.

- Ask students to craft complete sentences from their details.

- Invite them to read one of their sentences aloud.

9. Share!

- Ask students to share their work with a classmate.

- Ask volunteers to share with the whole class.

- Illustrate and post the Version 2 with photos of the students.

Lesson Extension Ideas

- Grow the bullets into mini-stories. (See "What's the Story," page 152–160.)

- Have older students use this framework to write an analysis of a literary character or famous person from history.

- Cut the four sections of the Version 1 and use them to decorate a box, such as a square tissue box.

Sample Stages

This getting-to-know-you framework can work at any time of year. It's a way of looking at ourselves, noting what others can see and the dreams and plans we hold inside. Even though these are personal, they are not too personal to share, which makes the results fun to post in the room or hallway, complete with illustrations.

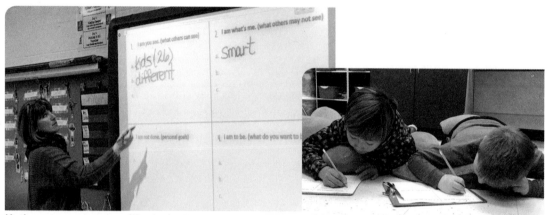

Katie co-constructs with students on a smartboard, taking input from the students.

Students engage in side-by-side writing.

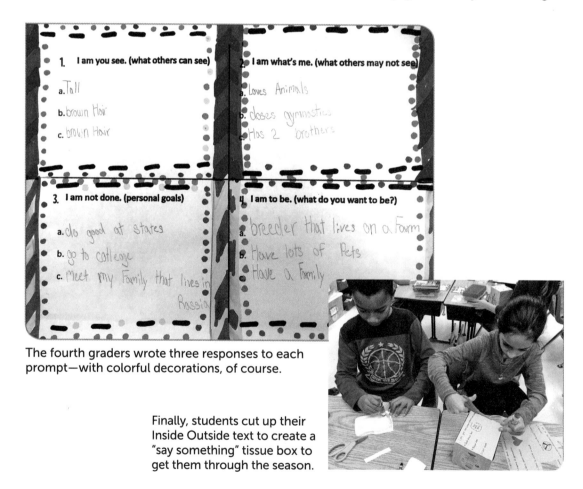

1. **I am you see. (what others can see)**
   a. Tall
   b. brown Hair
   c. brown Hair

2. **I am what's me. (what others may not see)**
   a. Loves Animals
   b. closes gymnastics
   c. Has 2 brothers

3. **I am not done. (personal goals)**
   a. do good at states
   b. go to college
   c. Meet my Family that lives in Russia

4. **I am to be. (what do you want to be?)**
   a. breeder that lives on a Farm
   b. Have lots of Pets
   c. Have a Family

The fourth graders wrote three responses to each prompt—with colorful decorations, of course.

Finally, students cut up their Inside Outside text to create a "say something" tissue box to get them through the season.

Inside Outside: Assessment Checkpoint

SKILL	3	2	1
Format	Demonstrates an understanding of how bullets work and the difference between facts and opinions.	Mostly demonstrates an understanding of how bullets work and the difference between facts and opinions.	Doesn't yet demonstrate an understanding of how bullets work or the difference between facts and opinions.
Sentence Structure	Can compose simple and compound sentences including capitalization and punctuation.	Inconsistently composes simple and compound sentences including capitalization and punctuation.	Does not yet compose simple and compound sentences.
Sharing	Uses creativity in showcasing work, including illustrations, hand motions, or photos that add to the theme.	Uses some creativity in showcasing work, including illustrations, hand motions, or photos that add to the theme.	Doesn't yet demonstrate creativity in showcasing work, including illustrations, hand motions, or photos that add to the theme.
Speaking Skills	Is willing to share aloud and consistently demonstrates effective presentation skills using good voice projection, inflection, pacing, eye contact, and stance.	Is often willing to share and partially demonstrates effective presentation skills using good voice projection, inflection, pacing, eye contact, and stance.	Is not yet willing to share and/or does not yet demonstrate effective presentation skills using good voice projection, inflection, pacing, eye contact, and stance.
Listening Skills	Actively participates in discussions about other students' work and is tuned in to student presentations.	Occasionally participates in discussions about other students' work and is tuned in to student presentations.	Does not participate in discussions about other students' work and is not yet tuned in to student presentations.

From Striving to Thriving Writers copyright © 2018 by Sara Holbrook, Michael Salinger, and Stephanie Harvey. Published by Scholastic Inc.

PART II: LEARNING THROUGH LANGUAGE

Compare/Contrast: Same or Different?

TIME: about 45 minutes	GRADE LEVEL: 4–8

MATERIALS:

- Slides 1–5*
- 2 Compare/Contrast GO Sheets you will want to duplicate in advance*
- Preselected topics from your content area of study
- Notebooks, computers, or tablets

*Available online at scholastic.com/ThrivingWriterResources

WHY TEACH THIS?

To help students craft sentences that explain what is the same and what is different about things.

CONTENT AREA CONNECTIONS: Literature, Social Studies, Science, Math

Persuasive	Descriptive	Narrative	Procedural	Research	Vocabulary	Figurative Language
X	X			X		

STEPH REFLECTS ON FRAMEWORK 17

Understanding comparison is a critical skill. It is fundamental to economics, science, history, politics, art—and just about anything else that we come across. Kids need to understand how to do it and why it's important. But I confess to a bias here regarding the notion of compare and contrast, since the definition of *compare* is "to measure or note the similarity or dissimilarity between something." In other words, *compare* by its very nature includes contrasting. Standardized tests promote the view that comparing and contrasting are opposites. I'll go with it, but just wanted to weigh in. :)

Kind of the same, but a little different? Very different with one thing in common? Comparisons help writers clarify meaning. Who is taller, what animal is faster, and what was true in 1776 that isn't true today? In history, science, literature, and even gym classes, well-drawn comparisons help writers communicate more effectively.

Comparisons are a type of patterned writing using common transition words: flashing signals that easily set the reader up for what is being compared or contrasted. Learning how to craft these associations is crucial for a successful communicator. This lesson begins with a slide that defines the words *compare* and *contrast*.

We have combined this writing framework with a quick review of the value of a strong topic sentence.

Sara: A strong topic sentence is like a label on the storage bin in your closet—it says what's inside.

Michael: Too many striving writers try to begin writing a paragraph by drafting the topic sentence first.

Sara: A habit known to cause lip biting, nail biting, and pencil biting. How do you put a label on an empty bin?

Michael: Avoid a classroom of biters! The topic sentence comes together easily after the content of the paragraph has been established.

We have used a Venn diagram—a visual depiction of which characteristics are different and which are shared—as a prewrite for this framework. Use this as an initial introduction to or review of the Venn diagram, depending on your students' prior knowledge.

1. Introduce the Framework

Project Slide 1, read it aloud, and introduce the topic of compare/contrast. As an invitation to the lesson, ask students if they think lizards and chickens have anything in common.

2. Build Background Knowledge

Compare/Contrast:
The Language of Comparisons

What are we going to learn today?
1. We will compare and contrast a lizard and a chicken.
2. We will look at the language of comparison.
3. We will write a comparison.

Slide 1

- Project Slide 2 and discuss further the terms *compare* and *contrast*. We like to have the students say the words aloud and define them to make them more memorable.

- Discuss Mentor Text, Version 1.

- Project Slide 3 and read it aloud, clarifying any unknown words. Then have students read it aloud to familiarize themselves with the pattern of writing. Read it aloud one more time, with one group of students reading the orange words and another the black words.

To **compare** is to explain what is the **same** between things.

To **contrast** is to explain what is **different** between things.

Slide 2

Version 1

Both chickens and lizards have feet, **but** the chicken has two and the lizard has four.
Chickens are warm-blooded **while** lizards are cold-blooded, **but** they **both** have hearts and circulatory systems.
The chicken has feathers, **unlike** the lizard, which has scales.
Chickens **as well as** lizards lay eggs.

Slide 3

- Ask: *What is the same about chickens and lizards?* Ask a student to identify and read out a sentence comparing the two.

- Ask: *What is different about chickens and lizards?* Ask a student to identify and read out a sentence contrasting the two.

n the mentor text for this framework, we compare a lizard and a chicken. As Sara was researching lizards and chickens, she found several references to how they relate to dinosaurs. This made us want to do more research to find out which animal came first and who was descended from whom.

While working with Katie Lufkin's fourth graders, we compared life in the 1970s to life today to build background knowledge for a read-aloud of *The Pinballs* by Betsy Byars. Imagine life before hip hop and video games. (Pac-Man wasn't released until 1980!) One startling contrast we found was that TV remote controls were not commonly used in the 1970s. Folks actually had to get up out of their chairs and walk across the room to change channels. Horrors! This led us to wonder when remote controls were invented, what early ones looked like, and when they came into common use. (It was not until around 1990!)

As a lesson extension, you may ask students to indicate what they further wonder about the topic(s) they are comparing. This makes this a perfect addition to any unit of inquiry.

3. **Review a Sample Prewrite**

- Project Slide 4, tell students it's a sample prewrite, and explain the concept of a Venn diagram.

- Read through the prewrite and note what the author could observe (e.g., number of feet) and what the author needed to research (e.g., cold-/warm-blooded).

- Note that the details contain observation words, not opinion words such as *cute*, *ugly*, *funny*, or *nice*. We want to stick to the facts.

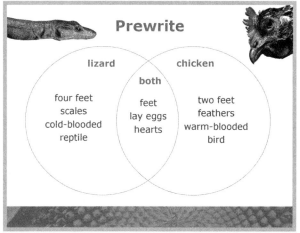

Slide 4

4. **Co-construct a Prewrite**

- Draw a Venn diagram on your writing space or pull up the GO Sheet on the projection system. (See GO Sheet next page.)

- Compare a topic unrelated to whatever they are studying in a content area. We have had success comparing a basketball to a baseball or a soccer ball.

- Remind students that they may have to do some research. (*A basketball is filled with air. What is a baseball filled with?*)

- Fill in your Venn diagram with three or four bullet points in each of the three labeled spaces.

PART II: LEARNING THROUGH LANGUAGE

5. **Hand Out the Venn Diagram GO Sheet**

6. **Have Students Prewrite**
   - Ask students to pair up and use the Venn Diagram GO Sheet to prepare a prewrite on a content area topic. Although they're working together and thus have the same bullet points, each student should prepare his or her own prewrite.

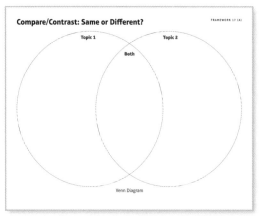

Venn Diagram GO Sheet

   - Have them list at least three facts in each section of the Venn diagram: the facts that apply to "Topic 1," "Topic 2," and "Both" topics. Encourage research.
   - Remind students to avoid opinions (*cute, ugly, awesome, scary*), but to use objective details.
   - Ask students to read their lists aloud once they're compiled.
   - This is their prewrite.

7. **Co-construct Version 1**
   - Project the Compare/Contrast Version 1 GO Sheet. Introduce the lists of compare and contrast words.
   - Referencing your co-constructed Venn Diagram prewrite, use these compare and contrast words to pull ideas from the class.
   - Compose at least three sentences that either compare, contrast, or, with the addition of a conjunction, do both, such as *Chickens and lizards both have feet, but only chickens have a hard beak.*

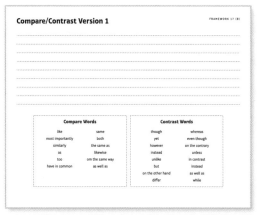

Compare/Contrast Version 1 GO Sheet

   - When you're finished, read the sentences aloud with the class so students hear the pattern.

8. **Have Students Write Their Version 1**
   - Distribute copies of the Compare/Contrast Version 1 GO Sheet. Make sure students have their completed Venn Diagram prewrite on hand to help them compose their sentences.

- Instruct students to compose at least three sentences comparing and contrasting the information from their Venn diagrams. Urge them to use the lists at the bottom of the sheet to make their sentences as strong as possible. Students may choose to continue writing in pairs or go solo. Either way, encourage conversation by asking them to read aloud to one another.

- Have students read aloud periodically as they write.

9. **Discuss Mentor Text, Version 2**

- Project Slide 5 and read aloud the topic sentence the author has added.

- Ask: *What is the job of the topic sentence?* (It informs the reader what the paragraph is about.)

- Return to your co-constructed Version 1 and, with input from the students, compose a topic sentence.

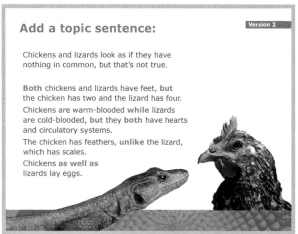

Add a topic sentence: Version 2

Chickens and lizards look as if they have nothing in common, but that's not true.

Both chickens and lizards have feet, **but** the chicken has two and the lizard has four.
Chickens are warm-blooded **while** lizards are cold-blooded, **but** they **both** have hearts and circulatory systems.
The chicken has feathers, **unlike** the lizard, which has scales.
Chickens **as well as** lizards lay eggs.

Slide 5

10. **Have Students Write Their Version 2**

- Ask students to return to their Version 1 and relabel it "Version 2." Have them add a topic sentence. They may wish to transition to a notebook, computer, or tablet, keeping their completed GO Sheets handy for reference.

- Ask them to polish up their writing, checking for spelling, capitalization, and other conventions.

- Celebrate the fact that students have written an entire compare/contrast paragraph. Voila!

11. **Share!**

- Ask students to share their work with another student.

- Ask volunteers to share with the whole class.

Lesson Extension Ideas

- Ask students if writing the compare/contrast sentences unearthed any questions that would require further research (see box).

- Make comparisons the basis of a longer nonfiction text or even a jumping-off point for some fiction.

Sample Stages

Learning to compare and contrast is necessarily a lesson in sentence structure. Understanding the structure of these sentences comes with practice. We practice composing these sentences so writers will be more able to compose more complex comparisons in longer pieces of text. We begin by writing about chickens and lizards, naturally transitioning into comparisons in a content area of study.

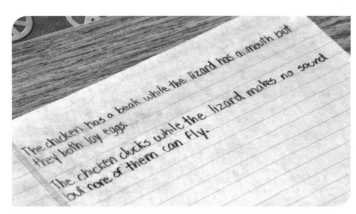

Students worked in pairs in a fourth-grade class in Lusaka, Zambia, to compare chickens and lizards. In this particular class, several students were learning English as an additional language, and we took a hard look at how comparative sentences were structured.

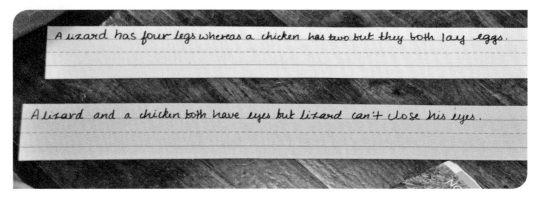

Next, we transitioned into writing comparative sentences about India, which was what they were studying in social studies.

Compare/Contrast: Assessment Checkpoint

SKILL	3	2	1
Format	Demonstrates an understanding of how the Venn diagram works and is able to complete it with pertinent facts.	Mostly demonstrates an understanding of how the Venn diagram works and is able to complete it with pertinent facts.	Doesn't yet demonstrate an understanding of how the Venn diagram works and is not yet able to complete it with pertinent facts.
Sentence Structure	Can compose simple and compound sentences, including capitalization and punctuation, that compare and contrast two topics.	Can sometimes compose simple and compound sentences, including capitalization and punctuation, that compare and contrast two topics.	Does not yet compose simple and compound sentences, including capitalization and punctuation, that compare and contrast two topics.
Topic Sentences	Crafts a topic sentence that clearly articulates pertinent information contained in the compare/contrast sentences.	Crafts a topic sentence that partially articulates pertinent information contained in the compare/contrast sentences.	Doesn't yet craft a topic sentence that clearly articulates the information contained in the compare/contrast sentences.
Speaking Skills	Is willing to share and consistently demonstrates effective presentation skills using good voice projection, inflection, pacing, eye contact, and stance.	Is often willing to share and partially demonstrates effective presentation skills using good voice projection, inflection, pacing, eye contact, and stance.	Is not yet willing to share and/or does not yet demonstrate effective presentation skills using good voice projection, inflection, pacing, eye contact, and stance.
Listening Skills	Actively participates in discussions about other students' work and is tuned in to student presentations.	Occasionally participates in discussions about other students' work and is tuned in to student presentations.	Does not participate in discussions about other students' work and is not yet tuned in to student presentations.

PART II: LEARNING THROUGH LANGUAGE

From Striving to Thriving Writers copyright © 2018 by Sara Holbrook, Michael Salinger, and Stephanie Harvey. Published by Scholastic Inc.

Recipes for Success: Measuring Learning

TIME: about 45 minutes	**GRADE LEVEL:** 4 and up

MATERIALS:

- Slides 1–5*
- Recipes for Success GO Sheet*
- Preselected topics from content area study
- Notebooks, computers, or tablets

*Available online at scholastic.com/ThrivingWriterResources

WHY TEACH THIS?

To inform students that recipes are a form of procedural text. Steps must follow a logical order and contain the correct ingredients in the proper amounts. This will feed the creative spirits of your writers.

CONTENT AREA CONNECTIONS: All subjects

Persuasive	Descriptive	Narrative	Procedural	Research	Vocabulary	Figurative Language
	X		X	X		X

STEPH REFLECTS ON FRAMEWORK 18

Recipes for anything! I love this. What a great idea. As always, Sara and Michael's poems offer terrific mentor texts for kids to see the recipe format as something beyond cooking. Most kids have never thought of this before and love the idea. The GO Sheet is particularly helpful as kids come up with standard measurements and then insert their own topics. And this is especially effective for content learning, as the example at the end so powerfully illustrates.

Gather your spoons and measuring cups, this is a recipe for—well, anything! The results are tasty and packed with nutrition for our writers!

Writers organize details and use the recipe format to write about a theme such as sportsmanship, the French Revolution, patriotism, an ecosystem, or your topic of choice. The framework can be used to analyze themes as diverse as the treachery of *Macbeth* to peer pressure in *Don't Let the Pigeon Drive the Bus*. A seed is often seen as the original metaphor for anything that is growing; a recipe can be a metaphor for any type of analysis.

Since the range of capabilities in this writing framework is so broad, we have provided two mentor texts: one for middle and high school students, and one for elementary. Take a minute and review both, then choose which you think is most appropriate for your classroom.

Adding measurement terms to any analysis affords the writer an opportunity to weigh the evidence. A close relative to the 100% Me writing framework, the recipe framework necessitates looking at a topic in terms of relative importance and adding action verbs to whip up a concise understanding.

This framework produces an extended metaphor in the form of procedural writing. Sequence, quantity, and action, along with relevant word choice, combine to make a delicious artifact of learning.

PART II: LEARNING THROUGH LANGUAGE

1. Introduce the Framework

Project Slide 1, read it aloud, and ask: *What is needed in a good recipe?* Gather responses, then announce to students that they are going to whip up a recipe of their learning into a tasty dish worthy of the most picky guest.

2. Discuss Mentor Text, Version 1

- Project Slide 2 or Slide 3. Choose either *Recipe for a Tall Tale* for younger students or *Mountain Bike Soufflé* for older students.

- Read the text aloud and then ask volunteers to reread it aloud.

- Ask: *What is this piece about? In what format is this written?* (a recipe). *What action verbs and phrases indicate that it is a recipe? Why are measurements used in recipes? What do the measurement terms add to your understanding?*

Creating Recipes for Success:
Measurement terms meet content learning

What are we going to learn today?
1. We will examine how recipes work.
2. We will discuss how to use measurements to weigh evidence.
3. We will write recipes.

Slide 1

Recipe for a Tall Tale | Version 1
by Sara Holbrook

Mix a cup of plot
with a handful of characters
in a bowl with a single hero.
Season with a pinch of description.
Add one half teaspoon of evil
and a tablespoon of lies then
blend with a barrel of bravery.
Pour in a pinch of predictions.
Stir in a gallon of exaggeration.
Sprinkle with laughter
and bake in a circle of friends.
Serves everyone in the room!

Slide 2

Mountain Bike Soufflé
by Michael Salinger

Take a good-sized bowl,
dust edges with tree trunks.
Grease bottom with melted mud
and pepper with roots and rocks.
Drop and mix in a full suspension
mountain bike.
Pound pedals in a circular motion,
spinning tires 'til legs are nearly
whipped.
Mix in bunny hops to separate
wheels from ground as you shred
the single track.

Set fear aside to cool.
Fold in ramps and banked turns.
Toss yourself once or twice over
handlebars.
Sift out embarrassment.
Dissolve doubt then point entire
mixture toward the finish line.
Increase heat till calves scald
and forearms sear.
Once mixture is thoroughly baked,
after an hour or two, set out to cool.
Garnish with plum colored bruises
and battered shins.
Serve with beverage of choice.

Slide 3

3. Co-construct Version 1

- Choose a familiar topic about which the students already have some background knowledge to facilitate teaching this frameworks procedure. We have had success using the topic *sportsmanship*.

- Prepare your co-construct space by replicating this lesson's GO Sheet. Be sure you have enough space and it's large enough for all to see.

- Starting with the Measurements column, ask students to give suggestions, which will most likely be the standard *cup, tablespoon, liter, pinch,* etc.

- After you have listed eight to 10 standard recipe measurements, ask students to add a few more that apply to the topic. For example, if you chose sportsmanship, measurements might be *a quarter, an inning, a yard, a point, a run, a touchdown, a field,* etc.

- Brainstorm a list of actions, starting with traditional recipe verbs: *sauté, sift, bake, sear, grate,* etc., and write them in the second column. Then add some actions apropos to your topic: *run, kick, score, tackle,* etc.

- In the third column, list ingredients pertaining to your topic. If it's sportsmanship, you might include *fair play, competition, sweat, high-fives, intensity, bruises, cheers,* and so forth.

- Once your organizer is filled out, begin co-constructing your recipe with students. Keep the organizer on display, and draft in a space where you can easily refer to it.

- Use measurements, actions, and ingredients from your organizer. As you write, encourage students to consider the quantity of each ingredient, as well as the order in which they are introduced.

- Be sure to include a sprinkling of the measurements and actions that are pertinent to the topic to stretch and extend the topic-specific allusions.

- Finish your Version 1 and read it aloud with the class. Applause! Good job.

4. Hand Out the GO Sheet

5. Have Students Write Their Version 1

Recipes for Success GO Sheet

- Instruct students to use the GO Sheet to organize their prewrites. They may wish to have a real recipe or two handy to help with procedures and action verbs. Content area research materials will help in listing the ingredients.

- Have students select their topics, or provide several choices from a subject they're studying. Ask them to write their topic on the top of the GO Sheet.

- Students may fill in their organizer with a partner or do it solo—it's up to you. Partnering leads to important discussion about the topic.

- Ask students to fill in the Measurements column. Remind them to also include measurements that are particular to their topic.

- Instruct them to fill in the Action Verbs column, again reminding them to also include verbs particular to their topic as well as traditional recipe terms.

- Guide them to fill in the Ingredients column—the topic should really provide inspiration.

- As students are writing, periodically have one of them read aloud a line from their in-progress recipe, and comment accordingly.

- Once Version 1 is complete, invite everyone to read theirs aloud at the same time— and then to a classmate. Lastly, have a few volunteers read theirs aloud to the class.

6. Discuss Mentor Text, Version 2

For this lesson, we have given you two slides for younger students: a Version 2 on its own, and Versions 1 and 2 together for the purpose of comparison.

- Project Slide 4 and read it aloud. Then ask students to read it aloud with you.

- Project Slide 5 and ask students to turn and talk about the differences between Versions 1 and 2. Note the measurements are proportional: 1/2 cup of truth and 3 cups of exaggeration. A tall tale takes a small amount of truth, then stretches it with hyperbole to become something that is greater than its parts. So it's logical to use more exaggeration than truth when creating one.

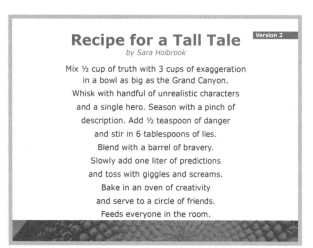

Slide 4

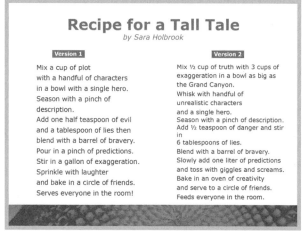

Slide 5

- Encourage students to examine sequence and quantity to understand how the author used them to strengthen the recipe metaphor.

- Ask which version is best and why. Ask if they have ideas on how to sharpen your co-constructed text.

7. Co-construct Version 2

- Project your Version 1 co-construct and read the first line aloud with students. How might it be improved? Could a detail be added?

- Now read through the whole piece in unison with students. Are there any spots leaping out at you that need a tweak? Do the measurements and sequence seem logical?

- With questions like those in mind, instruct students to go back to their Version 1 and garnish as needed.

8. Have Students Write Their Version 2

- Continue writing while students revise their recipes, or circulate the room, doing some drive-by assessment. A little of both seems to work best.

- As you circulate, ask volunteers to share some of their edits aloud with the class. Comment accordingly.

9. Share!

Have students first stand and read aloud to a partner, and then invite several to read aloud to the class. See below for more ideas.

Lesson Extension Ideas

- Gather all of your students' recipes and publish a cookbook. It will make a great mentor text for future classes. It is preferable that the mentor text not be on the theme your current groups of students are working on. This cuts down on copy/paste syndrome.

- Have students create videos of themselves preparing their recipes, in the style of a cooking show, including images and sound.

Content Area Extension Idea

Use the recipe format with any subject matter in which sequence and "ingredients" play a major role. This means pretty much all subject matter!

Sample Stages

A recipe is a procedural text that almost all students readily understand. We enjoy measuring, simmering, and serving up all kinds of concoctions with students, incorporating ingredients from all content areas—from environmental science to Shakespeare. Below are a few samples from primary, middle, and high school students.

The environment recipe

Whip in a gallon of fossil fuels and burn it on the stove
Stir in a cup of lying politicians
Add a tablespoon of tainted drinking water
Blend in a spoonful of people who are in denial
Unfortunately, they are not in short supply
Add a drop of people trying to make a change
Mix in a dash of renewable energy
Cover the top up in Saran and pop it into the oven

After 15 minutes the stench of the pot should smell like chemicals
Making it hard to breath
This is the current state of the earth
It makes it hard to live

We need to make some changes to this recipe
And it starts with you and me

(left) This recipe is from a sixth grader at Eastern Middle School in Greenwich, Connecticut. She used her research on the environment from science class and created this recipe in her language arts class. Fair to say, this dish had a bite to it. After writing, teacher Bridget Suvansri pulled the entire sixth grade together, making an impromptu performance space out of a borrowed music room—a tasty performance after which everyone applauded the cooks.

Recipe for Power
From Lady MacBeth, version 1

In a chalice, add
2 tbs of blood and wealth,
beat till it turns into a murderous paste.
Slice a crownful of greed
and a mound of murder.
Then add a government of defiance
and a pinch of revenge.
Moving back to the paste,
Stuff with pride and layer
the paste with ambition
Mix in a gram of darkness...

(above) In this class, students first identified themes from *Macbeth* at Graded: The American School of São Paulo, Brazil. They then discussed their recipe ingredients in pairs before writing independently. This student can be seen taking risks, crossing out and experimenting with her text as she composes her Version 1.

(right) A recipe for fun in the sun on the playground, co-constructed with kindergartners in Chennai, India. As the lesson progressed, we read and reread aloud, frequently helping students with word recognition. Finally, we put some hand motions with our recipe and read the piece a couple more times.

measurement	verb	ingredient
cup	Pour	blocks
sprinkle	tip	house
spoon	mix	legos
bowl	beat	Slide
handful	fry	games
bucket	bake	swing
pinch		basketball

In a playground
Pour in a barrel of basketball add in a handful of sliding. Mix with a bucket of legos. Sprinkle with games and grille in the sun for 20 minutes and serve with fun.

Recipes for Success: Assessment Checkpoint

SKILL	3	2	1
Careful Reading	Demonstrates an understanding of how a sequence of events and the relative importance of each lead to a logical outcome or conclusion. Recognizes all of the elements of a pattern sequence.	Partially demonstrates an understanding of how a sequence of events and the relative importance of each lead to a logical outcome or conclusion. May have trouble recognizing some of the elements of a pattern sequence.	Does not yet demonstrate an understanding of how a sequence of events and the relative importance of each lead to a logical outcome or conclusion. Cannot make meaning by connecting an abstract idea to a sequenced pattern of writing.
Structure and Organization	Demonstrates the ability to recognize and re-create a writing structure comprising measurements and logical sequence, based on examples.	Partially demonstrates the ability to recognize and re-create a writing structure comprising measurements and logical sequence, based on examples. May have trouble weighting an element or two or may have a misstep in the sequence.	Does not yet demonstrate the ability to recognize and re-create a writing structure comprising measurements and logical sequence, based on examples. Is not yet able to re-create a recipe of an abstract idea or estimate relative importance of ingredients.
Informative Explanatory Texts	Creates a piece of writing that demonstrates understanding of the subject matter, including pertinent facts, appropriate weighting of details, and logical sequence.	Creates a piece of writing that demonstrates partial understanding of the subject matter. Some facts may be misrepresented, or the weight of their importance may be skewed.	Creates a piece of writing that shows no basis in fact. Measurement of components is not yet valid for weighting of importance. Sequence is not yet logical.
Speaking Skills	Is willing to share aloud and consistently demonstrates effective presentation skills using good voice projection, inflection, pacing, eye contact, and stance.	Is often willing to share and partially demonstrates effective presentation skills using good voice projection, inflection, pacing, eye contact, and stance.	Is not yet willing to share and/or does not yet demonstrate effective presentation skills using good voice projection, inflection, pacing, eye contact, and stance.
Listening Skills	Actively participates in discussions about other students' work and is tuned in to student presentations.	Occasionally participates in discussions about other students' work and is tuned in to student presentations.	Does not participate in discussions about other students' work and is not yet tuned in to student presentations.

From Striving to Thriving Writers copyright © 2018 by Sara Holbrook, Michael Salinger, and Stephanie Harvey. Published by Scholastic Inc.

PART II: LEARNING THROUGH LANGUAGE

Found Poem: A Product of Close Reading

TIME: about 45 minutes	GRADE LEVEL: 4 and up

MATERIALS:

- Slides 1–8*
- Found Poem GO Sheet*
- Preselected text(s) from content area study (you may want several selections from the same book, or selections from a variety of books on the same theme, fiction or nonfiction)
- Notebooks, computers, or tablets

*Available online at scholastic.com/ThrivingWriterResources

WHY TEACH THIS?

To encourage close reading by giving students an authentic reason to read and reread a text and having them select the most important words and phrases.

CONTENT AREA CONNECTIONS: Literature, Social Studies, Science, Art

Persuasive	Descriptive	Narrative	Procedural	Research	Vocabulary	Figurative Language
	X	X		X	X	X

STEPH REFLECTS ON FRAMEWORK 19

Nancie Atwell (2016) uses poetry to help students delve into close reading. It's an opportunity, she explains, to explore the "words, lines, patterns, and devices without killing a child's love of poetry." Sara and Michael do much the same with writing. They engage students in a close read of rich content to inspire poetry writing—with the same outcome that Nancie promotes: a chance to study closely the "descriptive language, inferences, and essential details that develop the author's theme."

Like our hippo friend in the first slide, there's whole lot below the surface in a rich piece of writing—descriptive language, inferences, and essential details that develop the author's theme. When we read, we gain knowledge and understanding and we also learn about the craft of writing.

This writing framework is the impetus for some really close reading. In order to ensure success, it is necessary to preselect the text from which the students will be writing, preferably a page or two of image-rich copy. Once the students have done this framework a couple of times, they will gain an eye and ear for self-selecting passages in the future.

Michael: Remember that time in Indiana when we were working with writers in a grade 6 social studies class?

Sara: The social studies teacher was working from a textbook and they were beginning a unit on Ancient Worlds. Hard to say what was dustier, the textbook or the subject matter.

Michael: We divided the introduction to the chapter into chunks of several paragraphs, giving each selection to a small group of students to write a found poem.

Sara: Not only were the poems terrific in summarizing the content, the students were excited to share their new knowledge with one another, providing the class with a succinct overview.

Michael: The teacher remarked that in years of teaching, he believed it was the first time all of his students actually read the chapter introduction.

As readers sift through text, they work like archaeologists, separating what is most valuable from mounds of words. Recording their findings is a lot like note-taking, identifying pivotal and key phrases, artifacts of their study. Once again, we are guiding students to prioritize information as they dig in to extract the most important words and ideas.

1. Introduce the Framework

- Project Slide 1, read it aloud, and ask: *What is similar between this hippo and an iceberg?* (Both have a lot below the water's surface.)

- Tell the class that it's going to look at some text deeply, going beneath the surface.

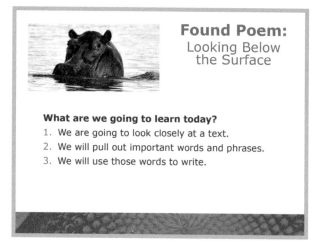

Found Poem:
Looking Below
the Surface

What are we going to learn today?
1. We are going to look closely at a text.
2. We will pull out important words and phrases.
3. We will use those words to write.

Slide 1

2. Build Background Knowledge

- Explain to students they are about to read a poem by Michael distilled from an excerpt from Sara's novel, *The Enemy: Detroit 1954*. In the excerpt, Marjorie, who is in sixth grade, is hiding from the new girl, Inga, who is German. Marjorie is afraid that if she is friends with Inga, she will lose all of her other friends, who have rejected Inga because she is different. Her mother, Lila, is questioning Marjorie's behavior.

- Explain that after reading the poem, they will explore Michael's writing process.

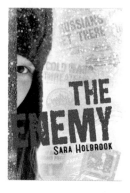

3. Discuss Mentor Text

- Project Slide 2 and read the poem aloud, clarifying any unknown words and briefly discussing content. Let students know that this is Michael's (the poem's author) Version 2.

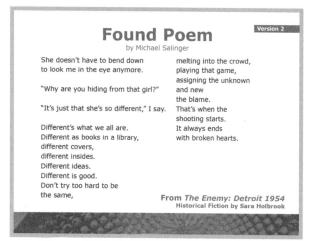

Found Poem

Version 2

by Michael Salinger

She doesn't have to bend down
to look me in the eye anymore.

"Why are you hiding from that girl?"

"It's just that she's so different," I say.

Different's what we all are.
Different as books in a library,
different covers,
different insides.
Different ideas.
Different is good.
Don't try too hard to be
the same,

melting into the crowd,
playing that game,
assigning the unknown
and new
the blame.
That's when the
shooting starts.
It always ends
with broken hearts.

From *The Enemy: Detroit 1954*
Historical Fiction by Sara Holbrook

Slide 2

"Are you hiding from that girl, Inga? You're acting ridiculous." She whips the curtains back. "That's enough of that."

I drop to a crouch and stare down at my stocking feet. "Mom!" I screech. "What are you doing?"

"What are you doing?" she asks, looking down at me. "I thought you were friends with her."

"No! I mean, not really. It's just, you know . . . she's so different." I peek over the windowsill just in time to see Inga turn the corner. I duck back down.

"Up off your knees, young lady." Mom grabs me by the sleeve. "Up!" I stumble to my feet; glad to see that Inga and her mother are out of sight. "You listen to me. Different's what we all are. Or what we should be." Mom looks at the ceiling. We can hear Dad moving in their bedroom over our heads. She puts her hands on both of my shoulders, the blue booties scratching my ear. I must be growing taller, because she doesn't even have to bend over to look me straight in the face.

She talks fast, "You asked me why I went to college and the answer is because Grandpa Henry told me to go. But you didn't ask me what I learned there. I learned this: Books, like the books upstairs, they stretch your brain, so there's enough room in your skull for lots of ideas: good ideas, bad ideas, ideas different than the ideas you grow up with. From those ideas you can make your own ideas, different ideas. Different is a good way to be. Don't let anyone tell you otherwise. When people try too hard to be the same, that's when the shooting starts."

First, read the passage through once.

Slide 3

- Project Slide 3, the excerpt from the novel, and explain that this is what the author based his poem on. Have students take turns reading aloud sentences from the excerpt. After that, read the excerpt aloud on your own, fluently. Explain that you are now going to explore Michael's writing process.

- Project Slide 4 and ask: *Why do you think these words and phrases are highlighted?* (Because they are the power phrases—the most meaningful parts of the text.)

- Project Slide 5, the author's Version 1, and note that it is simply a list of the highlighted words and phrases. Michael rearranged items on the list to create the version of the poem on Slide 2. We often call this a "poem skeleton," the bare bones of a poem. It needs to be fleshed out and given a heartbeat.

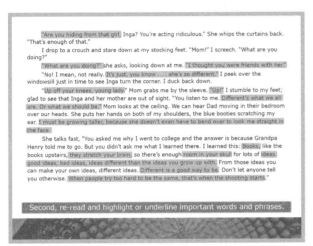

Slide 4

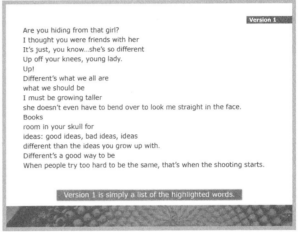

Slide 5

4. Co-construct Version 1

- Share a piece of text with your students, either by projecting it or handing out copies. Slide 6 contains an excerpt from the nonfiction book *Twelve Days in May, Freedom Ride 1961* by Larry Dane Brimner. Feel free to choose a different fiction or nonfiction excerpt of approximately the same length.

- Have students take turns reading through the excerpt, and then read it aloud on your own, clarifying any unknown words.

- Ask the students to help you select the excerpt's power phrases. Guide them to select the most meaningful parts of the text. And guide them to be stingy; a good rule of thumb is no more than 20 percent of the original text. Slide 7 provides a sample. Your selections may vary from ours,

May 8: On Monday the Freedom Riders make it to Charlotte, North Carolina. Charles Person notices his shoes need a shine, and at Union Station he takes a seat in the shoeshine chair. He isn't thinking of this as a test of the law or a challenge to local customs. He only wants his shoes shined, but he is refused service. The chair is for WHITES only. Person does not move. He stays where he is. Within minutes, a police officer arrives and threatens to handcuff him and take him to jail. Person moves to avoid arrest, but he hurries to tell the other riders what has happened. The riders decide Joe Perkins should test the law at the shoeshine chair. It is the South's first-known Shoe-In.

From *Twelve Days in May, Freedom Ride 1961* by Larry Dane Brimner, Sibert Award 2018, Calkins Creek Press

Slide 6

PART II: LEARNING THROUGH LANGUAGE

and that's okay. List the phrases so that each one is on its own line. When you're finished, label the list "Version 1."

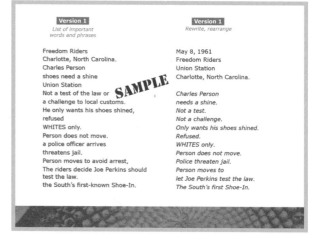

Slide 7

- Read the list aloud and ask: *Have we captured the gist of the text?*

- Tell students that some might consider this list a poem, but we aren't done. We will be coming back to this list to refine it.

5. **Hand Out the GO Sheet**

6. **Have Students Write Their Version 1**

Found Poem GO Sheet

- Have students pair up with a writing partner and pass out copies of the text(s) you want them to work with. When working from a common text, we recommend selecting several passages so that when the final pieces are read aloud, students share the learning, there's more variety, and listeners learn something new through different interpretations of several portions of the larger text.

- Instruct partners to read their text. When they're finished, have them identify the most meaningful phrases by circling, highlighting, or underlining them. Remind them to be stingy.

- Once students have finished selecting power phrases, instruct them to list them on their GO Sheets in the Version 1 column.

- Ask students to read their Version 1s aloud at the same time and then to a classmate.

7. **Co-construct Version 2**

Content area teachers: If students have crafted pieces that adequately reflect their understanding of the text, consider ending the lesson here and move directly to Share!

Language arts teachers (or poetically minded content area teachers):

- Ask the students to elect one of the stronger items on their list to become the seed for the first line of their poem.

- Inform students they are going to use some literary, artistic, or poetic elements. Project Slide 8 and review those elements.

- Take the first item or two of your Version 1 co-construct and expand it, using one of the elements on Slide 8.

- Solicit ideas from the class for the next line to expand.

- Continue to craft your Version 2 co-construct as the students write their own, as well as circulate looking for opportunities to confer and guide writers.

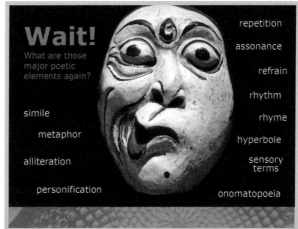

Slide 8

8. **Have Students Write Their Version 2**

- Students may wish to work in the Version 2 portion of their GO Sheets or transition to a notebook, computer, or tablet, and continue working with their writing partner or break out on their own. If they continue working with their partner, have each student create his or her own piece.

- Start by asking students to begin rearranging their text, choosing a different first line (see fiction and nonfiction samples).

- Ask the students to pick a power phrase from their Version 1 and expand it, using a literary element. Instruct them to continue working on their piece, looking for opportunities to use literary elements.

- Ask occasionally for students to share a line aloud and to identify the element they used.

- Set a time limit for students to finish up their Version 2. Five to 10 minutes usually suffices, but you know your students.

9. **Share!**

- Ask students to share their work aloud with a classmate other than their writing partner.

- Ask groups and individuals to share with the whole class, pointing out literary elements used.

Lesson Extension Ideas

- Have students discuss the similarities and differences among each group of poems inspired by the same passage.

- Challenge students with random poetic "throw-downs"—for example: *Craft your piece into three stanzas of four lines apiece.* Or: *The first word of each line must be the same.* Or: *Create a piece with two six-line stanzas—the last two lines rhyme.* Honestly, whatever you can think of. Amuse yourself while getting your students to take risks and experiment with language. We are often amazed by how well the writers take to these challenges. Have fun. We have found that kids are more willing to take risks with text they have created on the spot, rather than text they have worked on for long periods of time.

Sample Stages

Found poems give students the motivation to reread, looking closely at the nuances of language from word choice to content. Sometimes we work from classics, and other times students are able to choose from the text of their choice. Although these samples are all taken from works of fiction, please keep in mind this strategy works equally well with nonfiction text.

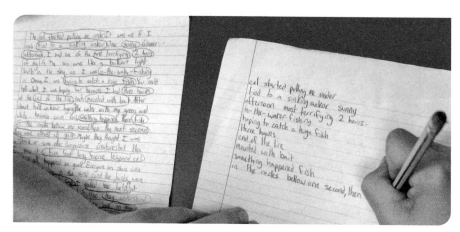

In this sample, a student is turning his own piece of writing into a found poem.

A student transitions to a computer to write her found poem, Version 2.

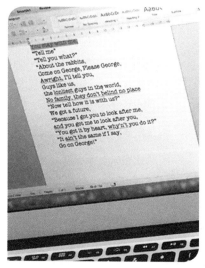

(above) This student is creating a found poem from *Of Mice and Men* by John Steinbeck.

(left) Writing partners collaborate to select power phrases from *The Power of One* by Bryce Courtenay.

Found Poem: Assessment Checkpoint

SKILL	3	2	1
Careful Reading	Demonstrates the ability to determine the theme or central idea of a text and understand how it is conveyed through particular details.	Partially demonstrates the ability to determine the theme or central idea of a text and understand how it is conveyed through particular details.	Does not yet demonstrate the ability to determine the theme or central idea of a text and understand how it is conveyed through particular details.
Word Meaning	Demonstrates knowledge of the technical, connotative, and figurative meanings of words and phrases as they are used in the text. Analyzes how specific word choices shape meaning or tone.	Partially demonstrates knowledge of the technical, connotative, and figurative meanings of words and phrases as they are used in the text. Partially analyzes how specific word choices shape meaning or tone. May miss an important detail when selecting the most important words.	Does not demonstrate knowledge of the technical, connotative, and figurative meanings of words and phrases as they are used in the text. Is unable to analyze how specific word choices shape meaning or tone.
Relevant Content	Effectively selects terms from a particular text or research source that are informative and that convey relevant ideas, concepts, and information.	Partially selects terms from a particular text or research source that are informative and that convey relevant ideas, concepts, and information. May include an extraneous idea or fail to connect the selected ideas with smooth transitions.	Does not select terms from a particular text or research source that are informative and that convey relevant ideas, concepts, and information.
Speaking Skills	Is willing to share and consistently demonstrates effective presentation skills using good voice projection, inflection, pacing, eye contact, and stance.	Is often willing to share and partially demonstrates effective presentation skills using good voice projection, inflection, pacing, eye contact, and stance.	Is not yet willing to share and/or does not yet demonstrate effective presentation skills using good voice projection, inflection, pacing, eye contact, and stance.
Listening Skills	Actively participates in discussions about other students' work and is tuned in to student presentations.	Occasionally participates in discussions about other students' work and is tuned in to student presentations.	Does not participate in discussions about other students' work and is not yet tuned in to student presentations.

From Striving to Thriving Writers copyright © 2018 by Sara Holbrook, Michael Salinger, and Stephanie Harvey. Published by Scholastic Inc.

Part III: Using Language to Learn About Self

Language is personal. Children become readers and writers when they fall in love with text they read or text they create themselves—text that opens their minds and hearts to new possibilities and empowers them to share. And, of course, there is no more alluring way to draw them into text than by exploring their favorite topic—themselves!

 scholastic.com/ThriveResources

My Official List: Likes and Dislikes, Just Because

TIME: about 45 minutes	GRADE LEVEL: 1–5

MATERIALS:

- Slides 1–2*
- My Official List GO Sheet*
- Notebooks, computers, or tablets

*Available online at scholastic.com/ThrivingWriterResources

WHY TEACH THIS?

1. To look at ourselves in terms of what we feel positively about and what we feel negatively about.

2. To learn about your students' personal likes and dislikes.

CONTENT AREA CONNECTIONS: Literature

Persuasive	Descriptive	Narrative	Procedural	Research	Vocabulary	Figurative Language
	X					

STEPH REFLECTS ON FRAMEWORK 20

Who doesn't like to think about what they like and what they don't like? Whenever kids are given a chance to write about things that matter to them, they will write better than when forced to write about things they don't care about. This is not rocket science! Personal likes and dislikes are a "top ten" for kids when it comes to choosing a topic.

This is a fabulous writing framework for getting to know your students. Good for the beginning of the year or to tie into a lesson on the difference between fact and opinion.

Sara: Some of my dislikes in the mentor text are obvious—mosquito bites, slimy hands, and sniffling sneezes are pretty universally hated. Others are more personal. Brussels sprouts, for instance.

Michael: I don't get what you have against the color aqua.

Sara: Not my favorite color. Just because.

The key to making this list work is simply listing facts—nouns and verbs. What do not appear are opinion words—no words like *horrible*, *beautiful*, or *awesome*. For instance, if a writer lists *awesome donuts* as a like, guide that writer to say *chocolate donuts* or something more specific. It's a good way to start the year, as vague adjectives aren't going to have a place in our writing going forward.

To avoid any bad feelings, writers may not list individual names as either likes or dislikes. No putting *Melissa* in the LIKE column and *Brady* in the DISLIKE column.

Michael: What about LeBron James?

Sara: One celebrity figure would be fine, but we want variety in the list, so no listing the entire team.

Have fun with this and see the Lesson Extension Ideas section for ways to take students' work public.

1. Introduce the Framework

- Project Slide 1, read it aloud, and explain to students that they are going to describe themselves in terms of their likes and dislikes, or personal preferences. Everyone has foods they like, types of literature they like, types of entertainment they like, and so on—and ones they don't.

Slide 1

- Tell students that together you will cocreate a list of preferences for the entire class and then they will have an opportunity to write about their own preferences.

2. Discuss Mentor Text

- Project Slide 2, read it aloud, and reread it, clarifying any unknown words. Note, the text can be read two ways: column 1 followed by column 2, or line by line, left to right.

Slide 2

- Divide the class in half and have one half read column 1 and the other read column 2.

- Note that the lists contain facts and not opinions. The kite was not *wonderful* or *beautiful*; it was *soaring*. Ask: *How does that make a difference to the reader?*

3. Co-construct Version 1

- Display the GO Sheet. (See below.)

- With your students, brainstorm subjects that a person might have preferences for, such as food, literary genres, sports, entertainment, games, celebrities, and animals, etc.

- Create a list from this outside of the GO Sheet to be used as reference.

- Let students know that the list is not exhaustive; it's just to get them thinking.

- Ask them to offer a few likes based on the brainstormed list and write them in the Yes column. Then have them offer a few dislikes and write them in the No column.

- Remind them that we are looking for facts, not opinions. So, no words like *cool*, *sweet*, or *horrible*.

4. Hand Out the GO Sheet

5. Have Students Write Their Version 1

- Ask students to discuss their likes and dislikes with a partner, using your co-constructed Version 1 and its accompanying list of subjects as a guide.

My Official List GO Sheet

- Have students list six to eight ideas of things they have opinions about (food, music, sports, animals, modes of travel, book genres, etc.). Have them complete the GO Sheet by selecting ideas and indicating their likes in the Yes column and their dislikes in the No column (Yes: *soccer*, No: *golf*, for instance), writing six to eight likes and dislikes in the appropriate columns.

- Ask students to read their Version 1 aloud at the same time.

6. Co-construct Version 2

- Return to your Version 1 co-construct and entertain ideas on how items on the lists might be rearranged. The first line and last line of any piece of writing are important. So, you might ask: *Which of the likes would be a great first line? How about a strong last line?*

- Ask: *Can any of the items be strengthened by adding a detail? There's a big difference between kites in a tree and kites soaring in the air. Make at least one change.*

- When you're finished, have the class read the co-constructed Version 2 aloud.

7. Have Students Write Their Version 2

- Direct students to continue working on their GO Sheets or transition to a notebook, computer, or tablet.

- Ask them to do some rearranging of items, looking for a strong beginning and ending, and add detail to at least three items.

8. Share!

- Ask students to share their work with a classmate.

- Ask for volunteers to start, but take time for every student to share. These go quickly. As you respond to each student, note anything new you learn about him or her from the writing.

Lesson Extension Ideas

- Have younger students illustrate their lists. Laminate their work and turn it into a placemat.

- Have older students turn their work into a slide show presentation or a video with visual images, props, and perhaps a favorite song in the background.

  Note: As students proceed to character development, this writing framework is an effective strategy for analyzing or developing fictional characters.

My Official List: Assessment Checkpoint

SKILL	3	2	1
Format	Demonstrates an understanding of how bullets work and the difference between facts and opinions.	Mostly demonstrates an understanding of how bullets work and the difference between facts and opinions.	Doesn't yet demonstrate an understanding of how bullets work or the difference between facts and opinions.
Revision	Demonstrates an ability to rearrange details for maximum effect, editing out opinions and adding relevant details.	Inconsistently demonstrates an ability to rearrange details for maximum effect. May have included an opinion or lacks additional relevant details.	Does not yet demonstrate an ability to rearrange details for maximum effect. Does not yet distinguish between facts and opinions and is not yet able to add relevant details.
Sharing	Uses creativity in showcasing work, including illustrations, hand motions, or photos that add to the theme.	Uses limited creativity in showcasing work, including illustrations, hand motions, or photos that add to the theme.	Doesn't yet demonstrate creativity in showcasing work, including illustrations, hand motions, or photos that add to the theme.
Speaking Skills	Is willing to share aloud and consistently demonstrates effective presentation skills using good voice projection, inflection, pacing, eye contact, and stance.	Is often willing to share and partially demonstrates effective presentation skills using good voice projection, inflection, pacing, eye contact, and stance.	Is not yet willing to share and/or does not yet demonstrate effective presentation skills using good voice projection, inflection, pacing, eye contact, and stance.
Listening Skills	Actively participates in discussions about other students' work and is tuned in to student presentations.	Occasionally participates in discussions about other students' work and is tuned in to student presentations.	Does not participate in discussions about other students' work and is not yet tuned in to student presentations.

PART III: USING LANGUAGE TO LEARN ABOUT SELF

From Striving to Thriving Writers copyright © 2018 by Sara Holbrook, Michael Salinger, and Stephanie Harvey. Published by Scholastic Inc.

Memoir: A Story to Tell

TIME: about 60 minutes	**GRADE LEVEL:** 4 and up

MATERIALS:

- Slide 1*
- Memoir GO Sheet*
- Notebooks, computers, or tablets

*Available online at scholastic.com/ThrivingWriterResources

WHY TEACH THIS?

1. To let students know that a memoir is one way we get to know one another. We tell readers our stories and we read or listen to theirs.

2. To focus on the importance of a strong lead. It's easier to become interested in a memoir if it begins with a bang!

CONTENT AREA CONNECTIONS: ELA

Persuasive	Descriptive	Narrative	Procedural	Research	Vocabulary	Figurative Language
	X	X				X

STEPH REFLECTS ON FRAMEWORK 21

As Sara and Michael say, "Everyone has a story to tell. In fact, everyone has a closet full of stories to tell." But to get readers to dive in and rummage around that closet, stories need compelling leads. My essay in Scholastic's *Open a World of Possible* (2014) focused on first lines. "I'm not great at hanging out with a book for 50 pages to get into it. I like being roped in right out of the gate. The opening lines from my early life seem to have influenced my outer life. The opening lines from my later reading seem to have shaped my inner life. Leads matter!"

"As Gregor Samsa awoke one morning from uneasy dreams he found himself transformed in his bed into a monstrous vermin." —Franz Kafka's *Metamorphosis* (1915)

One of the greatest opening lines in literature: Does it give the story away or does it compel you to keep reading?

Sara: It creeps me out a little, but I want to know more. So I'd say it compels me to keep reading.

Michael: One of the goals of this framework is to nudge students into using an engaging lead in their stories. We are going to enlist the ear of a friend to help us find that line.

Sara: And man, we've heard some doozies from kids:

My brother walked in with a butcher knife in his thigh.
A squirrel jumped out of the glovebox.
Chainsaws are not toys.

Don't you want to just add the word *and* to each of those opening lines and hear what comes next?

Everyone has a story to tell. In fact, everyone has a closet full of stories to tell. The hard part is getting them down on the page in a manner that is both readable and interesting in order for those stories to be heard. How do we take a personal memory and turn it into something that is just as enjoyable to read as it is to tell a friend?

This framework is a great way to introduce personal narrative. First, writers will tell their stories to partners who help them find their lead. Then writers use a GO Sheet to create a list of strong details relative to setting and characterization. Finally, we use this information to craft our memoir. It can also be used to craft a scene in a longer work.

This framework mirrors a memory and models how a robust prewrite makes our job as storytellers easier. It doesn't precisely follow our usual lesson process, but as the great storyteller Mark Twain might say, *it rhymes with it.*

1. Introduce the Framework

- Project Slide 1, read it aloud, and ask: *Does this cat look like he has a story to tell? P.S. The cat's name is Trashcan.*

- Let students know that this cat has nothing on them. They *all* have stories to tell!

A Story to Tell:
Mapping Memoir

What are we going to learn today?
1. We are going to write a personal memoir story.
2. We are going to organize a prewrite for setting and characterization.
3. We are going to discover a strong lead for our story.

Slide 1

2. Build Background Knowledge

- Discuss the term *memoir*. Explain that it is the retelling of a memory—a first-person account of a significant episode in the writer's life. It is the memoirist's job to re-create the episode to the best of her or his abilities—but very few of them have a photographic memory.

- If a nonessential detail—a detail that doesn't change the overall truth of the story—is fuzzy, it's okay to use a plausible stand-in. For example, the color of a T-shirt most likely will not affect the truth of a story as much as the location will. So, messing with the former is fine, but not the latter.

3. Discuss Mentor Text

- Read aloud the following memoir by Michael from his ignoble youth (also available for projecting in the Framework 21 slideshow). Another option is to substitute it with your own memoir, which will undoubtedly have more impact on your students. The memoir should be a little recollection, the kind of story that is told among friends and family at the holiday table and should take no more than five minutes to read.

- Notice that Michael's memoir does not have a strong lead. This is by intention because one of this lesson's goals is for students to create a strong lead. If you create your own memoir, be sure the lead is less than perfect.

- Before you begin reading, ask students to listen for an AHA line.

- After reading the memoir, ask students for the AHA line. When we've read Michael's memoir to students, they've chosen "your mother is in the office," "she had the face of a gargoyle," and "your cocoons hatched." Take several suggestions and write one on the board.

MICHAEL'S MEMOIR MENTOR TEXT

Behind our house, as my siblings and I grew up in semi-rural northeast Ohio, was a large open field with a hill where we sledded in the winter. During the warm months, that field seemed endlessly vast, crammed with goldenrod and milkweed, grasshoppers, katydids, garter snakes, toads as big as crows, and other creepy crawlies. I'm convinced I grew up strong playing in the dirt, chewing on sassafras twigs, eating stolen peaches without washing them, and digging many, many holes from sunup until the distant bell on our back porch rang at 5 p.m. for dinner.

My mother believed boys should be raised like wild wolves. She'd shove us out the door after breakfast every morning in the summer. After a few hours, she'd ring a bell and we'd come in for lunch. Then she'd throw us out again, and we'd have all afternoon to explore until that bell rang again at five. Mostly, we liked to dig holes. My younger brother and I, along with our friends Tom and Jay, built forts by digging into the sandy soil until the holes were deeper than we were tall. Then we would lay branches across the opening followed by a layer of leaves, then another tier of soil. We hoped to trap an animal, but we never did. These forts were damp and smelled of the wet clay that lay below the layer of sand. We'd swipe candles to light the holes or fill a coffee can three-quarters full of gasoline, light it and place it in a niche carved into the wall. No one had ever told us that we could have set ourselves on fire or about asphyxiation. I'm certain this lack of knowledge and dumb luck is what kept us alive. I'm not going to tell you about the time we burned down the garage, that's another story.

The summer before I entered second grade, my brother and I collected a bunch of cocoons from the field below the hill. The golf ball-sized cocoons were attached to milkweed stems, which we snapped off with the crack of a broken pencil. We collected hundreds of them, loading up our arms as if we were gathering kindling, and we snuck them all into our bedroom envisioning the day when we would wake up with thousands of butterflies flittering around like some scene from a Disney movie.

A few days later, school started. At St. Gabriel's Elementary School, they required mothers to volunteer in the lunchroom as monitors, or a mom could pay five dollars and another mom would cover for them. What do you think my mother did? She paid the five dollars. My mother never came to school.

I had entered second grade in my little clip-on bowtie with the enthusiasm of a soldier slogging mud-caked boots uphill during a downpour. One afternoon, the principal, Sister Mary Imelda, came into class. Sister Mary Imelda was a nun like we don't have any more. In my mind, she was huge and very scary in her black habit. HUGE, meaning she was four feet tall and four feet wide. She entered the class, looking like a grizzly bear, crucifix swinging from her neck.

"Mr. Salinger, your mother is in the office," she growled.

I froze. My mother never came to the school. I gulped and followed the sister to the office to find my brother and mother already there.

"Your cocoons hatched," my mother announced, looking down at me with the face of a gargoyle.

It seems our cocoons had indeed hatched—but instead of a glorious display of winged, fluttering wonderfulness, we had a room infested by what looked like the type of mold that grows on an old orange peel.

Except this stuff was moving.

The cocoons were full of praying mantis, literally millions of the little buggers, each about the size of a grain of rice. We filled a Shop-Vac three times vacuuming them up, dumping them into the field where we had swiped the cocoons.

That was decades ago—but I bet if I went to my old room at my parent's house, I could find tiny dried exoskeletons still resting in the cracks of our hardwood floor.

4. Hand Out the GO Sheet

5. Have Students Prewrite

- Explain to students that they will use the GO Sheet to prewrite their own memoir. Then ask them to pair up, sit knees to knees, and take turns telling a personal story of their own to one another.

- Tell them that the partner who's listening has an important job: to listen for an AHA line—something that makes the person laugh, gasp, or sit up straight. A line that she or he thinks is *really* important.

- After all students have had a chance to tell their story, call on a few students to relate the AHA lines they heard. Comment and guide as needed.

- Ask each student to write the important AHA line that her or his partner identified at the top of the GO Sheet. WARNING! Be sure students write at the top of the sheet the line *their partner identified*, and not the one they identified for their partner.

Memoir GO Sheet

Here students liked the framework so much, they were taking pictures. Kids love GO Sheets!

6. Have Students Construct Their Memoir Maps

- Instruct students to take three minutes to draw a picture, a map, or any other type of graphic representation of their story in the Map section of their GO Sheets. Be sure they work for the duration of the three minutes, adding details to their creations. No stopping early.

Setting Prompts: Write the following prompts on the board, one at a time, calling them out as you go. We like to write them out so students can check back if needed. No need for them to write down the prompts, only their answers in the Setting section of their GO Sheets. Move quickly. Take only about 10 seconds for students to respond to each prompt. Remind students that if they can't remember a detail, they should use a plausible substitution. And let them know they will have time later to revisit the prompts, if they miss one or two.

- Where did the story take place?

- Time of year?

- Time of day?

- How much time elapsed in the story?

- What was the light source (e.g., sun, table lamp, cell phone)?

- What was under their feet (grass, tile, carpet, etc.)?

- What was the weather or temperature?

- What were the background noises?

- What were the odors or aromas?

- What did not happen that could have?

- What might have happened around the same time whether it pertains to the story or not?

- Who (or what) else witnessed this event? A sibling? A lamp? A dog?

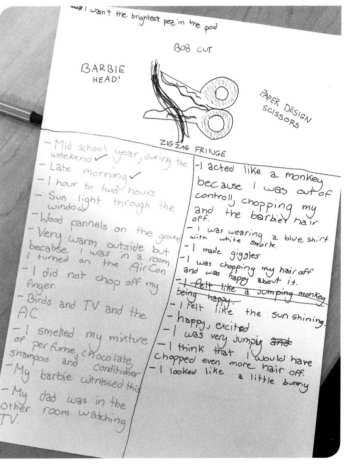

Character Prompts: Tell students that, next, they are going to move to the Character section on the GO Sheet. List the following prompts on the board as you go. Inform students that they should be focused on the main character. Since this is a memoir, that character will be themselves, the writer/narrator. But they may also want to think about other people in the story.

- What was the character wearing? Color? A hat? Details are important.

- If you were to compare the character's actions to an animal, what would it be?

- Compare the character's internal feelings to a force of nature.

- List three words that would describe that force of nature.

- What sound(s) did the character make?

- What did the character do with his or her hands? Feet?

- What did this character do that was a surprise?

- List two strong verbs that describe how the character moved. Did he or she spring or explode rather than walk or run?

- Compare this character's face to something else (a stop sign, a gargoyle).

- What might this character have done differently?

- What did the character not do, but could have?

- After you have finished delivering the prompts, give the students a few minutes to go back and respond to any they missed. Encourage them to discuss their responses with a writing partner. Tell them it's their job to make sure their partner has a response to every prompt. Offer assistance as needed.

7. **Have Students Write Their Version 1**

- In their notebooks or on a computer or tablet, have students begin their Version 1, keeping their Memoir GO Sheets face up and handy for reference.

- Remember that AHA line at the top of the page? Inform students that their Version 1 must begin with it. They may reword it slightly, but place it nowhere but at the beginning. Walk about and double check that this instruction is followed.

- Tell students also that they are to include each and every detail listed on their GO Sheets and at least a couple that are in their illustration, but that may not be articulated in the setting and character sections. These might include flowers in the garden or skid marks on the driveway. The order in which they are used doesn't matter, but every single detail must be included.

- Set a time limit for students to complete their Version 1. Usually 10 to 15 minutes suffice.

- When they're finished, invite them to read their pieces aloud at the same time and think about how the text is working for them. Then ask them to read it to a classmate other than their writing partner or person they first told their story to.

- Encourage several read-alouds—to a classmate, to the whole class, into the air. Remind students that Version 1 is a work in progress.

- Note how using that AHA line created a strong lead and entices the reader to continue reading.

8. Have Students Write Their Version 2

- Have students revise their Version 1 for fluency and voice, rereading for what "sounds" right, to create their Version 2.

- If you like, add one or two challenges by asking students to include a line or two of dialogue with proper punctuation or perhaps a simile (if they don't already have one).

9. Share!

- Give everyone a chance to tell their stories. This is great for community building because students learn about each other as individuals.

- Publish students' memoirs to create a lively, personal classroom anthology.

Lesson Extension Ideas

- Use this framework for any writing that requires a setting and characterization. We have used it to block out scenes in longer pieces and in fiction as well.

- Use it to help students visualize a scene in history or the site of a scientific discovery.

Sample Stages

This framework is a growing document, beginning with lists of observations and developing into written text. The better and more precise the detail in the lists, the better the outcome in Version 1 and beyond.

Here a sixth-grade student begins to compose his text. Note how he is keeping his notes and sketch close as he begins to incorporate the details into his Version 1. When students have access to computers, we usually suggest transitioning to them at this juncture in the writing process.

Memoir: Assessment Checkpoint

SKILL	3	2	1
Prewrite Organization and Implementation	Demonstrates an understanding of how a list of details and the relative importance of each leads to a logical outcome or conclusion. Takes a prewrite checklist and crafts it into a compelling narrative.	Partially demonstrates an understanding of how a list of details and the relative importance of each leads to a logical outcome or conclusion. May have trouble incorporating all of the details or some may seem "tacked on" rather than fluent.	Does not yet demonstrate an understanding of how a list of details and the relative importance of each leads to a logical outcome or conclusion. Cannot make meaning by connecting these details to a narrative pattern of writing.
Structure and Organization	Demonstrates the ability to recognize and create a strong lead, which impels the reader's interest in the text.	Partially demonstrates the ability to recognize and create a strong lead, which impels the reader's interest in the text. May have trouble selecting a compelling lead sentence—or may bury the lead later in the first paragraph.	Does not yet demonstrate the ability to recognize and create a strong lead, which impels the reader's interest in the text.
Informative Explanatory Texts	Creates a piece of writing that demonstrates understanding of the genre, including pertinent facts, appropriate weighting of details, and logical sequence.	Creates a piece of writing that demonstrates partial understanding of the genre. Some facts may be misrepresented or the weight of their importance may be skewed.	Does not yet create a piece of writing that demonstrates understanding of the genre. Writing shows no use of prewrite facts. Sequence is not logical. Piece is incomplete.
Speaking Skills	Is willing to share aloud and consistently demonstrates effective presentation skills using good voice projection, inflection, pacing, eye contact, and stance.	Is often willing to share and partially demonstrates effective presentation skills using good voice projection, inflection, pacing, eye contact, and stance.	Is not yet willing to share and/or does not yet demonstrate effective presentation skills using good voice projection, inflection, pacing, eye contact, and stance.
Listening Skills	Actively participates in discussions about other students' work and is tuned in to student presentations.	Occasionally participates in discussions about other students' work and is tuned in to student presentations.	Does not participate in discussions about other students' work and is not yet tuned in to student presentations.

In My Opinion: Clarifying Opinions With Senses

TIME: about 45 minutes	**GRADE LEVEL:** 1 and up

MATERIALS:

- Slides 1–5*
- In My Opinion GO Sheet*
- Notebooks, computers, or tablets

*Available online at scholastic.com/ThrivingWriterResources

WHY TEACH THIS?

To lead students to describe opinion words (e.g., *good*, *bad*, *wonderful*, *terrible*) in sensory terms.

CONTENT AREA CONNECTIONS: ELA

Persuasive	Descriptive	Narrative	Procedural	Research	Vocabulary	Figurative Language
	X	X			X	X

STEPH REFLECTS ON FRAMEWORK 22

I discussed visualizing and showing, not telling, in my commentary for Framework 4. But reading is even more robust when the reader goes beyond visualizing to sensory imaging that encompasses all of the senses in order to engage in text and read expansively. This framework teaches writers how to use hearing, touching, smelling, and tasting (as well as seeing) to write in a way that captures readers and carries them away. And Janet Angelillo (2010) reminds us that strivers, especially, benefit when we invite them to use alternative ways into writing.

It was all so wonderful. Amazing. Just fabulous.

These are words that might make us feel good but say very little—words we often see posted in classrooms beside the international prohibition sign—🚫—the universal No. Opinion words clutter up our writing and provide very little detail to engage our readers. We have another word for opinion words—we call them first-draft words. Opinion words (subjective terms) are among the first things we look for when revising our own writing, seeking to clarify them with sensory observations (objective terms).

This framework is designed to help students recognize subjective terms (opinion words) when they see them. Rather than looking at words such as *horrible* and *awesome* as words to edit out of writing, we can look at them as invitations to add descriptive language to support our opinions.

Michael:	Which is not to say that I would clarify every subjective word in a given piece of text with all of my senses.
Sara:	No, usually one or two will do.
Michael:	But it's fun to stretch our imaginations a bit.
Sara:	And when we use our sensory descriptions in a short creative writing text, the random nature of the descriptions encourages experimentation.

The short text the writers produce can grow into a mini story or a character description. Although this lesson is meant for language arts, it will also help students refine their writing in other content areas by leading them to recognize when opinions need to be supported by evidence.

1. Introduce the Framework

Project Slide 1 and read it aloud.

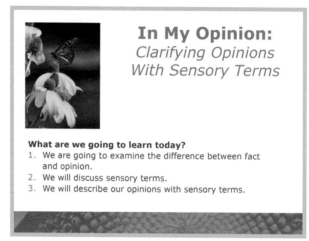

Slide 1

2. Build Background Knowledge

- Project Slide 2 and ask students which of the descriptors are fact and which are opinion. P.S. The puppy's name is Lili. A word such as *tiny* is an opinion unless it is defined. There's a big difference between a *tiny* elephant and a *tiny* puppy! Project Slide 3 to see another image of *tiny*.

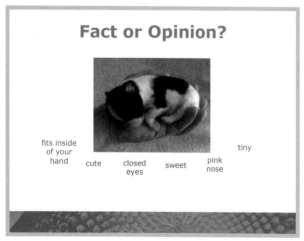

Slide 2

Slide 3

- Draw a crude image of a butterfly on the board, or project Slide 4, and note that it is an image of a butterfly, not a real butterfly. (We've been told it also looks like a cello, so be prepared for pushback.)

From Striving to Thriving Writers copyright © 2018 by Sara Holbrook, Michael Salinger, and Stephanie Harvey. Published by Scholastic Inc.

- Ask students if it's a good image or a bad image. Some of them may say it's a good image because butterflies are pretty, don't bite, don't carry disease. Good image, indeed. Others may say, "That's the worst picture of a butterfly I've ever seen." Bad image. Ask: *Who is right?* (Both!)

- Tell students that *good* and *bad* are opinion words and then brainstorm synonyms for both of them. See note on next page. Come up with and write down about five synonyms for each word and save the list for later.

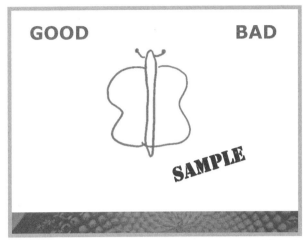

Slide 4

3. Discuss Mentor Text

- Project Slide 5 and read it aloud, clarifying the meaning of any unknown words.

- Ask: *What words and phrases in this mini-story say* comfy *to you? Can you identify any sensory terms—terms related to what something feels like, smells like, looks like, and so forth?*

- Project Slide 6 and tell students the author began this piece by compiling a list of sensory terms that describe the opinion word *comfy*. As is true of all opinion words, *comfy* means different things to different people.

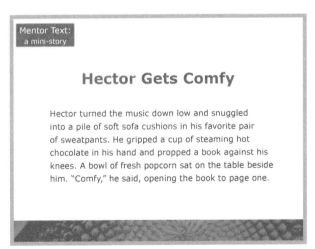

Slide 5

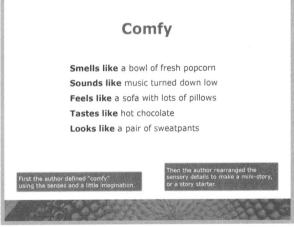

Slide 6

From Striving to Thriving Writers copyright © 2018 by Sara Holbrook, Michael Salinger, and Stephanie Harvey. Published by Scholastic Inc.

213

PART III: USING LANGUAGE TO LEARN ABOUT SELF

4. Co-construct Version 1

- Ask students to vote on whether they want to write about the opinion word *good* or *bad*.

- Work with students to write a list of sensory terms, similar to the ones on Slide 7. Push them for specifics. *Bad*, for example, isn't just the smell of garbage. It's the smell of yesterday's fish in the garbage. Warning! Stay out of the bathroom. Too easy. But know that this discussion could take you to some wacky places, like the armpit of a football player. Have fun, while remaining appropriate.

- Once your list is constructed, have everyone read it aloud together.

5. Hand Out the GO Sheet

6. Have Students Write Their Version 1

- Instruct students to fold their GO Sheets in half.

- Have students pair up with a writing partner and ask them to choose an opinion word from your brainstormed list to write about. With primary students, we sometimes put the words on slips of paper and have them randomly choose one to speed up this process. Have students write the opinion word they chose at the top of their GO Sheets.

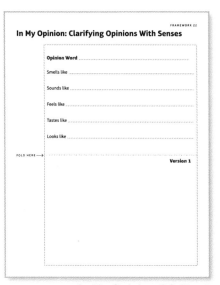

In My Opinion GO Sheet

- Walk them through writing their observations, one sense at a time, stressing the importance of being specific.

- Discourage students from defining one opinion with another. It's not good to say *horrible* tastes like a *terrible* sandwich, for instance. Better would be, *horrible* tastes like a mustard and jelly sandwich. Again, you are pushing students for specifics.

- When they're finished, asked students to read their completed sensory observations aloud at the same time. Let giggles ensue!

7. Co-construct Version 2

- Return to your co-constructed Version 1 and make a simple edit: Eliminate the sensory prompts—Sounds like, Smells like, etc.—so that all that is left is a list of images. Read them aloud.

- Ask: *What could we do with these images if we rearranged them? Could we make them into a mini-story by putting the images into sentences? Yes, it's kind of random, but maybe?*

- Begin the process of weaving your images into a narrative. Stop after a couple of lines and ask students to return to their own Version 1.

8. Have Students Write Their Version 2

- Ask students to edit out of their Version 1 the sensory prompts by drawing a line through them. Then invite them to read aloud the images that remain.

- Below the fold on their GO Sheets or in their notebooks or on a computer or tablet, have students create a mini story using all of their images. They may wish to continue with their partners or separate and work on their own.

- Encourage repeated read-alouds to see how the text is working for them.

9. Share!

- Ask students to share their work with a classmate other than their writing partner.

- Ask volunteers to share with the whole class.

- Encourage students to adjust their voices to reflect the topic of their writing. A reader of a text describing *horrible* should sound different from one reading a text describing *lovely*.

Lesson Extension Ideas

- Have students use their Version 2 as character descriptions for longer pieces of writing.

- Retitle a version titled "Horrible" to something like "Weekend Nightmare," and develop it with more detail.

- Ask students to pare down their texts to create free-verse poems.

From Striving to Thriving Writers copyright © 2018 by Sara Holbrook, Michael Salinger, and Stephanie Harvey. Published by Scholastic Inc.

Sample Stages

This framework facilitates a lot of discussion about the difference between subjective and objective language. Be sure to allow time to clarify that defining one opinion (subjective term) with another, as in attempting to define *beautiful* as *gorgeous,* is not an accurate description. This framework will adapt to the language sophistication of the students and can be used at all grade levels.

In this photo, Sara is discussing word choices with a first grader at the United World College of Southeast Asia in Singapore. He is asking if it's okay to use a word that was not on the board (YES!). His word choice was *dreadful.* Well, he actually told Sara that was his mother's word, but through his writing, it became clear that he understood his mom.

Second graders at The American School of Chennai, India, discuss and work together to complete their GO Sheets, then work independently to turn their sensory observations into a piece of short text.

Bad   Version 1

Looks like   a dog that was rolling in
                                         mud
Sounds like   Shattering glass
Smells like   Cigarette smoke
Feels like   a bear trap on the ankle
Tastes like   Sour milk

Version 2 Bad

A dog that was
rolling in sour milk
who shattered glass
after smoking a
cigarette and stepped
in a bear trap.

Version 3   Defeat

I felt like a soggy dog
who had rolled in sour milk
Ego Shattered like glass
trying to find my way out
of a cloud of cigarette smoke
and stepping in a bear trap.

In Scott Riley's class at Singapore American School, here is the progression through co-constructed Versions 1, 2, and 3. Note that on Version 3, at the suggestion of a sixth-grade student athlete, we changed the title from "Bad" to "Defeat."

Wonderful

Is a moon that melts like a lemon lozenge in a liquorice sky and is like nice cold ice cream dipped in the most beautiful, rich, silky chocolate syrup on a hot summer's day. Like the sound of warm laughter of a group of people and feels like the warm beams from the sun on your face on a cold winter's morning with the smell of freshly made cinnamon doughnuts.

Ever have a student surprise the heck out of you? Then you can imagine the look on the face of this sixth-grade boy's teacher when she read his description of *wonderful*.

Current version: 3

Evil Is

Evil is a corrupting whisper wearing a mask of shouts,
  Evil is footsteps in the night sneaking with a *tip, tap, tip, tap* that you realize too late are your own.
Evil is a big black scar from the past, slowly but surely cutting its way into the future,
  Evil is a growing stain on a tattered white shirt.
Evil is a muddy mound of trash that snares your ankle and pulls you down into the depths,
  Evil is a toothy mouth that entices you to step in-- then *snap*
Evil is a sweet elixir that tantalizes your tongue but in your throat it hurts and in your stomach it burns,
  Evil is a long sip of milk turning slowly sour.
Evil is the opaque smoke of burning hope and love, leaving only the ash of hate and pain,
  Evil is a gasp for breath in a world without air.

This student sample is from a sixth-grade boy who was a gamer and a lover of fantasy. We discussed that his observations could be woven into his own fantasy fiction, probably not all in one place, but scattered throughout.

PART III: USING LANGUAGE TO LEARN ABOUT SELF

In My Opinion: Assessment Checkpoint

SKILL	3	2	I
Fact vs. Opinion	Demonstrates an understanding of the difference between objective facts and subjective (opinion) words.	Partially demonstrates an understanding of the difference between objective facts and subjective (opinion) words and is able to make adjustments when prompted.	Does not yet demonstrate an understanding of the difference between objective facts and subjective (opinion) words and is yet unable to make adjustments when prompted.
Structure and Organization	Is able to create a story out of a list of observations, using logic in supporting opinions with sensory terms.	Is mostly able to create a story out of a list of observations, most times using logic in supporting opinions with sensory terms.	Is not yet able to create a story out of a list of observations, and is not yet able to consistently use logic in supporting opinions with sensory terms.
Speaking Skills	Is willing to share and consistently demonstrates effective presentation skills using good voice projection, inflection, pacing, eye contact, and stance.	Is often willing to share and partially demonstrates effective presentation skills using good voice projection, inflection, pacing, eye contact, and stance.	Is not yet willing to share and/ or does not yet demonstrate effective presentation skills using good voice projection, inflection, pacing, eye contact, and stance.
Listening Skills	Actively participates in discussions about other students' work and is tuned in to student presentations.	Occasionally participates in discussions about other students' work and is tuned in to student presentations.	Does not participate in discussions about other students' work and is not yet tuned in to student presentations.

Simile of Me: Just Like What?

TIME: about 45 minutes

GRADE LEVEL: 1–6

MATERIALS:

- Slides 1–3*
- Simile of Me GO Sheet*
- Notebooks, computers, or tablets

*Available online at scholastic.com/ThrivingWriterResources

WHY TEACH THIS?

To inform students that comparisons enrich writing with vivid, visual language.

CONTENT AREA CONNECTIONS: ELA primarily, but you may see other connections.

Persuasive	Descriptive	Narrative	Procedural	Research	Vocabulary	Figurative Language
	X	X			X	X

From Striving to Thriving Writers copyright © 2018 by Sara Holbrook, Michael Salinger, and Stephanie Harvey. Published by Scholastic Inc.

STEPH REFLECTS ON FRAMEWORK 23

How many of you remember being taught similes? They were easy to identify because they began with *like* or *as,* such as *eat like a pig* or *busy as a bee.* But they were also easy to overuse and suddenly, if we weren't careful, rather than creating language that was fresh and fun, we had captured a phrase that was old and stale—a cliché. Sara and Michael help students craft similes that sing like songbirds.

Like this? Or like that?

In this writing framework, we will examine what makes a good simile work. You can use this as an introduction or a refresher. Whether we are writing a love poem or describing an industrial accident, similes connect writers to their readers through common images. A well-placed simile can be the difference between an adequate report and really hitting it out of the park.

First, we will examine a text that is (basically) a stack of similes and discuss how they work to support the theme and tone. Describing something to be *quick like a hummingbird in the lilies* provides the reader with one image and tone while *quick like a purse snatcher on the sidewalk* paints a different picture. Of course, the depth with which you teach these nuances will be mitigated by the writers' ages and sophistication.

This is one lesson where students will write their Version 1 solo because writers are going to use themselves as the theme of their writing. In no way does that mean to suggest that students are to work quietly. We always encourage exchanging ideas and call for periodic read-alouds to see how the text is working.

We can also use this framework to gain a deeper understanding of clichés. We want to emphasize to students that while a cliché may be based on some truth, it is a good writer's job to provide the truth to their readers along with a little surprise.

After a professional development session at a school, the principal (kudos to him for attending the PD session!) noted that he could see how all of our writing frameworks would work with content area subjects, "Except that simile one, that one would only work in ELA." Since we love a good challenge, we wrote new text that weekend straight out of a science class. (See Slide 3, some amazing similes for *bats.*)

1. Introduce the Framework

Project Slide 1, read it aloud, and introduce or, if your students are familiar with it, review the word *simile*: a comparison using the word *like* or *as*. Clarify for students that a sentence such as *I like candy* is not a simile. No comparison. *Candy is like a dream to me* is!

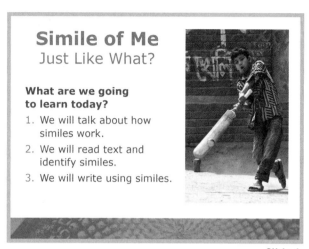

Slide 1

2. Discuss Mentor Text

Project Slide 2, read it aloud, and ask volunteers to read it again. Ask: *What is this piece about? What is its theme?* (Bicycling!) *Which lines in the text are similes, which are not? Why do those similes "go with" bicycle riding? How is the last line different from the other lines?* (It is a statement of fact and it reveals the theme of the text.)

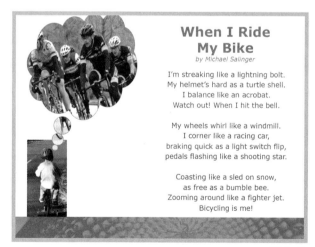

Slide 2

PART III: USING LANGUAGE TO LEARN ABOUT SELF

3. Co-construct Version 1

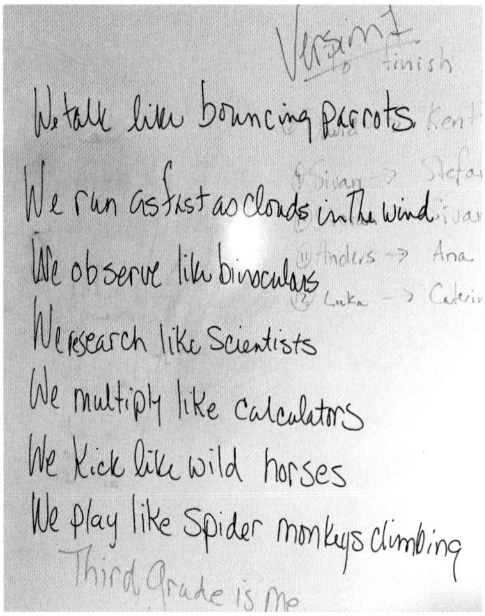

- Suggest "our class" as the theme for your co-constructed Version 1. Brainstorm ideas for the last line: *Third grade is us, Room 105 is us, We are Ms. McMahon's class*, etc. Vote on your favorite and write it at the bottom of your writing space.

- Brainstorm with students eight to 10 action verbs related to your theme and list them in the left-hand column. These are things your class does: *read, research, write, chat, run, laugh*, etc. Encourage discussion.

- Encourage students to give details as they suggest actions. For example, if they offer a word such as *learn*, ask: *What do you learn?* Math. *What do you learn to do in math?* To subtract. *Include* To subtract *in the list.* Leading students to specific actions like this leads to better similes. Read through the list with your students. Are there any important action verbs missing? Add one or two more.

- Ask the class to choose one of the verbs to create the first simile. Take several suggestions for the simile, steering the students toward one that is fitting yet not a cliché. (See box re: clichés.) Continue until you have about six.

- Announce to the students that it is time to write the last simile for Version 1, and they must pick the most important action verb still left. This again reminds students that as writers we are constantly prioritizing information.

- Read the piece aloud together several times. Applause! The crowd will go wild.

Handwritten notes:
Version 1
to finish
We talk like bouncing parrots
We run as fast as clouds in the wind
We observe like binoculars
We research like scientists
We multiply like calculators
We kick like wild horses
We play like spider monkeys climbing
Third Grade is me

CLICHÉ FREE!

The best similes are a little bit surprising. *Eat like a pig, fast as a cheetah, like nails on a chalkboard* may be true enough, but they are so overused—so cliché—that readers are apt to ignore them. The ideal simile is original and, therefore, connects the reader to the text, leading him or her from the unknown to the known.

Students can even use the internet to do a cliché check. Just type the first part, *like nails on a...*, into your search engine, and if it finishes it for you, *chalkboard*, it's a cliché.

4. Hand Out the GO Sheet

5. Have Students Write Their Version 1

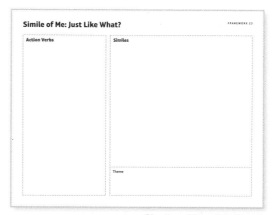

Simile of Me GO Sheet

- Ask students to come up with a theme for their Simile of Me Version 1—such as *Football is me, Dance is me, Minecraft is me, Reading is me, Artistic is me,* even *Silly is me*—and write it at the bottom of their GO Sheets. Explain that, just for fun, we will be writing from the bottom up instead of the top down.

- Ask them to come up with eight or more actions that relate to their theme. Urge them to use precise verbs in their list and to think a little beneath the surface. For example, if a student chooses soccer as her theme and lists *play* as an action verb, you might prod her to think of actions that are part of playing, kicking, running, defending, etc. This will afford more dynamic options for similes: *kick like a kangaroo, run like a skipping stone, defend like a castle moat,* for instance.

- Instruct students to begin creating their similes on their GO Sheets. Give them a goal number. This number should be less than the number of actions they have compiled in order to encourage some prioritizing of the best ideas.

- Occasionally invite a student to share one of his or her similes aloud during the writing process. Provide guidance, if necessary.

- When they're finished, have students read their Version 1 aloud at the same time, and then ask them to share with a classmate. Finally, invite volunteers to read to the class.

6. Co-construct Version 2

- Return to your co-constructed Version 1 and do a cliché check.

- Remind students that a comparison is a cliché if most people already have heard it before. We want similes that stop readers and encourage them to envision the images we wish to convey.

- Look over your list of similes and ask students if they can see a way to make one or two stronger.

PART III: USING LANGUAGE TO LEARN ABOUT SELF

7. Have Students Write Their Version 2

- Ask students to revisit their Version 1 and do a cliché check with their writing partner. Circulate the room. Have fun with this! Remind students that there is no right or wrong. Writing similes is a process, a treasure hunt to find the best comparison.

- Push students to use clichés as a stepping stone toward a more precise comparison. If a student has used *eats like a pig* as a simile, coach that student in Version 2 to come up with something more original. Ask: *What is it about the way that pigs eat that is important?* Students might respond: Pigs eat a lot. Ask: *Well then, what else or who else eats a lot?* (Our favorite answer so far is a sumo wrestler!)

- Help writers clarify comparisons. If a student has written, *We eat like crazy!* Remind students that a simile is a comparison between two things that clarifies meaning for a reader. *Eat like crazy* is too general. *Eat like a sumo wrestler* is a winner!

- Depending on the ages of the students, ask them to revise one or more of their similes to form a metaphor. They can start by removing *like* or *as*.

- Intersperse some read-alouds.

8. Share!

- Ask students to share their work with a classmate.

- Ask volunteers to share with the whole class.

- These pieces make a nice addition to a student's portfolio.

Lesson Extension Ideas

- Ask writers to choose their favorite simile and use it as the basis for a monologue, a paragraph, or a poem.

- Encourage students to rearrange their lines and stir in some hyperbole and creativity.

- Have them choose one simile and revise it to form a metaphor. (*I eat chips like a vacuum* might morph into *I am a vacuum sucking down chips*.) Briefly discuss the difference between a simile and metaphor.

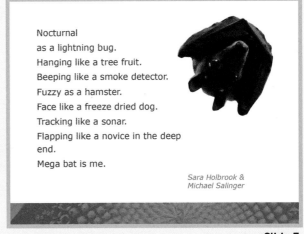

Nocturnal
as a lightning bug.
Hanging like a tree fruit.
Beeping like a smoke detector.
Fuzzy as a hamster.
Face like a freeze dried dog.
Tracking like a sonar.
Flapping like a novice in the deep end.
Mega bat is me.

*Sara Holbrook &
Michael Salinger*

Slide 3

- Take this framework into your content area unit. See Slide 3 for a sample of how to write about a creature. Use the simile framework to write about weather, community, the solar system, and so forth.

Sample Stages

Searching for just the right simile is not always an easy reach. We like to start young and use this framework at many grade levels, guiding students to think in more unique and surprising ways. Think of this as a mini lesson in creativity, pushing students to think beyond what they have heard before.

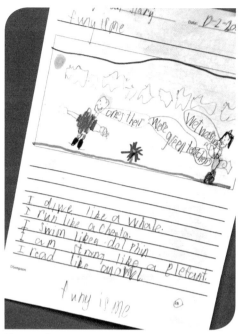

Here a first grader attempts his first similes. While they are not exactly unique, they are logical, and his illustration is terrific.

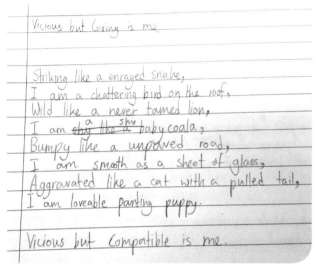

This sixth grader took her piece in a different direction (hooray!) and described herself as both vicious and caring. Too bad we weren't able to attain a parent permission in time for publication to show you the face of "vicious." She has the sweetest smile you've ever seen.

Building and crafting like architects, we hang out like bees in a hive.
We are vacuums sucking food
into a black hole and then cycle, legs moving like waterwheels. Watch out! We shoot basketballs like rocket launchers then pose like movie stars taking selfies.
We play table tennis like an
Octopus then crash like hibernating bears on weekends,
Sixth grade rocks!

(above) This co-construct from Scott Riley's sixth-grade class at Singapore American School is in the process of being revised into Version 2. See how line three has already been converted to a metaphor.

(left) At this point, we transitioned to a computer to continue revising. See Version 3—still not finished but getting better. At this point, it's time for some cutting. If we were really interested in refining this, we would prioritize and begin editing.

PART III: USING LANGUAGE TO LEARN ABOUT SELF

Simile of Me: Assessment Checkpoint

SKILL	3	2	1
Careful Reading	Demonstrates an understanding of the importance of using comparisons to clarify writing. Knows the difference between simile and metaphor. Is able to articulate meaning beyond the literal.	Partially demonstrates an understanding of the importance of using comparisons to clarify writing. May occasionally misidentify similes as comparisons other than those that use the word *like*.	Does not yet demonstrate an understanding of the importance of using comparisons to clarify writing. Cannot recognize simile in text.
Structure and Organization	Demonstrates the ability to recognize and re-create a writing structure that includes simile comparisons. Similes created are insightful, nuanced, and contain strong detail.	Partially demonstrates the ability to recognize and re-create a writing structure that includes simile comparisons. Some similes may be clichéd or lack supporting detail.	Does not yet demonstrate the ability to recognize and re-create a writing structure that includes simile comparisons. Assessed work contains no similes.
Connotative Word Meaning	Demonstrates an understanding of connotative word meanings by making comparisons while using visual language. Uses simile creatively and effectively.	Occasionally demonstrates an understanding of connotative word meanings by making comparisons while using visual language. Similes don't necessarily clarify the meaning of the piece and/or may be cliché.	Does not yet demonstrate an understanding of connotative word meanings by making comparisons while using visual language. Writing is void of simile.
Speaking Skills	Is willing to share and consistently demonstrates effective presentation skills using good voice projection, inflection, pacing, eye contact, and stance.	Is often willing to share and partially demonstrates effective presentation skills using good voice projection, inflection, pacing, eye contact, and stance.	Is not yet willing to share and/or does not yet demonstrate effective presentation skills using good voice projection, inflection, pacing, eye contact, and stance.
Listening Skills	Actively participates in discussions about other students' work and is tuned in to student presentations.	Occasionally participates in discussions about other students' work and is tuned in to student presentations.	Does not participate in discussions about other students' work and is not yet tuned in to student presentations.

Mentoring Metaphor: Metaphor With Mentor Text

TIME: about 45 minutes | **GRADE LEVEL:** 3 and up

MATERIALS:

- Slides 1–8*
- Mentoring Metaphor GO Sheets for primary and intermediate students*
- Notebooks, computers, or tablets

*Available online at scholastic.com/ThrivingWriterResources

WHY TEACH THIS?

To help students understand and create metaphors to enrich their writing and make images in their writing crystal clear.

CONTENT AREA CONNECTIONS: ELA

Persuasive	Descriptive	Narrative	Procedural	Research	Vocabulary	Figurative Language
	X	X			X	X

STEPH REFLECTS ON FRAMEWORK 24

Yay! A lesson on metaphor. The truth is I never had a single lesson on how to write metaphorically in elementary school except for simile. Without a single word to signal metaphoric language such as *like* in a simile, teachers seemed to avoid metaphor like the plague. Now there's a cliché for you! But seriously, so great to see a lesson on metaphor that goes beyond simile.

We are cranky grizzlies before we have our morning coffee.

Okay, you know we are not literally standing on our hind legs, roaring with claws extended. This metaphorical comparison just implies that we need morning caffeine before we interact with humans in the morning. Using metaphor in conversation and writing introduces imagery, which helps to clarify our message.

Finding the right metaphor takes some practice, which is what this writing framework is designed to do. We want to let students take some risks and not be terribly concerned that they are going to create an award-winning piece of prose or poetry. Students are putting on new ice skates and traveling around an unfamiliar rink a few times. Expect wobbles and falls and offer encouragement as writers test out new moves, tumble, pick themselves up, and try again.

This framework is designed to help students understand and write metaphors with the aid of mentor texts. In this lesson, students will work like artists, borrowing from prewritten text to lead them into expressing themselves. We have included three pieces of mentor text in this lesson, one for primary students ("My Brother"), one for intermediate students ("Disappointment"), and one for upper school ("911"). Choose from these based on your students' capabilities.

Sara: Keep in mind, this is a higher-order thinking skill. This lesson is designed to help students experiment with metaphor.

Michael: We are throwing them in a Petri dish of imagination.

Sara: A culture of creativity?

Michael: Almost as useful as penicillin.

Have fun building!

1. Introduce the Framework

Project Slide 1 and read it aloud. Let students know this will be an adventure in exploring metaphorical comparisons and that you will be giving their imaginations a little workout.

2. Build Background Knowledge

- Project Slide 2 and introduce or, if your students are familiar with it, review the word *metaphor*.

- Explain that metaphor is an older sibling to simile. Using it is a way of clarifying an idea in writing by comparing it to something else. In that way we connect the abstract (anger) and the concrete (a grizzly bear), creating sentences such as this: *The coach growled, claws extended as the hair on her back stood straight up.*

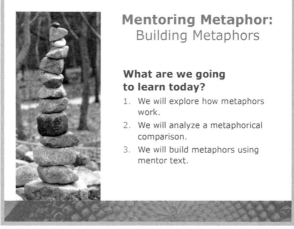

Slide 1

Slide 2

- Ask students to turn and talk about what the tower of rocks in the photograph might represent or symbolize. We have received answers ranging from instability to hope and diversity. Remember, there are no wrong answers as long as students can provide a logical explanation of their thinking.

PART III: USING LANGUAGE TO LEARN ABOUT SELF

3. Discuss Mentor Text

- Choose Slide 3 ("My Brother"), Slide 4 ("Disappointment"), or Slides 5, 6, and 7 ("911") and read aloud, clarifying any unknown words. Then ask students to read it aloud again, taking turns reading different lines.

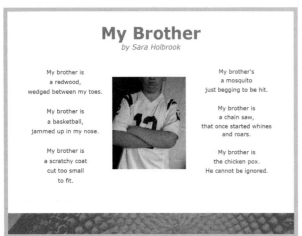

Slide 3

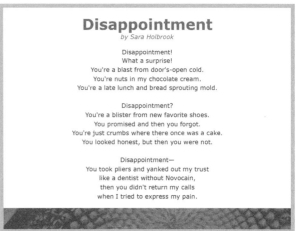

Slide 4

911
by Michael Salinger

hate is extremely flammable
its vapors may cause flash fire
hate is harmful if inhaled
keep hate away from heat, sparks and flame
do not breath the vapors of hate
wash thoroughly after using hate
if you accidentally swallow hate
get medical attention

Slide 5

- Ask students to identify one or more comparisons in the text. Ask: *What is the big idea of this text?* ("My Brother": he's annoying.) ("Disappointment": it's unpleasant.) ("911": hate is hazardous.)

4. Co-construct a Stanza

- Take one stanza of your chosen mentor text and rewrite it.

    My Brother
    My brother is a redwood, wedged between my toes.
    My brother is a basketball, jammed up in my nose.

- Take one stanza from "My Brother" and replace the subject with another important person, place, or thing, such as "my grandma." *My grandma is a teddy bear, who never runs out of hugs.* Other ideas: my sister, my backpack, my imagination, the library, etc.

- Invite many ideas and scribe them on the board.

- Urge students to use hyperbole. *My puppy is a mud pie, spilled on the kitchen floor.*

  Disappointment
  Disappointment, what a surprise, you're a blast from door's-open cold.
  You're nuts in my chocolate cream, you're a late lunch and bread
  sprouting mold.

- Take one stanza from "Disappointment" and replace the subject with a different emotion, such as *fear* (*Fear, what a shock, you're spiders crawling up my back*), or rewrite it using a content area vocabulary word (*Ludicrous, what a joke, you're a clown in giant red shoes. Fractions, what a divide, you're a pizza cut in eighths*).

- Invite many ideas and scribe them on the board.

- Urge students to connect words to images that are familiar to their audience.

  911
  hate *is extremely flammable*
  its vapors may cause flash fire
  hate is harmful if inhaled

- Take one stanza from "911" and replace the subject with a different word. Although the text should read like a warning label, it doesn't have to be negative. *Kindness is extremely contagious, its vapors may cause smiles. Kindness is transmittable if inhaled.* See Slides 5, 6, and 7 as examples.

- Invite many ideas and scribe them on the board.

- Follow the form of the mentor text, familiarizing students with the mentor texts' pattern and rhythm.

- Regardless of the mentor text you choose, read aloud your co-constructed stanzas with the class.

- Applaud yourselves. You're off to a good start.

911
by Michael Salinger

violence is harmful if absorbed through the skin
keep violence out of the reach of children
do not remain in enclosed areas
where violence is present
remove pets and birds from the vicinity of violence
cover aquariums to protect from violence
drift and run off from sites of violence
may be hazardous
this product is highly toxic
exposure to violence may cause
injury or death.

Slide 6

911
by Michael Salinger

prejudice is an eye and skin irritant
its vapors are harmful
do not get prejudice in eyes
or on clothing
prejudice is not recommended for use
by persons with heart conditions
if prejudice is swallowed induce vomiting
if prejudice comes in contact with skin
remove clothing and wash skin
if breathing is affected, get fresh air immediately

Slide 7

---

5. Hand Out the GO Sheets

Distribute the GO Sheet for "My Brother" or "Disappointment," depending on your grade level. (There is no GO Sheet for "911.")

6. Have Students Write Their Version 1

- Ask students of all grade levels to choose a topic for the three metaphorical comparisons they will write. If students seem stuck, take a couple of minutes and brainstorm some possibilities.

(top) "My Brother" GO Sheet
(bottom) "Disappointment" GO Sheet

Example: My cat		Example: Excitement
Is an: engine	that: idles on my bed	What a thrill
Is a: dandelion	that: drops fluff everywhere	You are: a roller coaster climbing into the sky
Is an: acrobat	that: does flips in the air	You are: a zip line racing through the trees
		You are: ping pong balls bouncing in my tummy

- Ask students to turn and talk to a writing partner about how they might create their comparisons.
- Circulate the room to support students as they complete their Version 1.
- When they're finished, have students read their Version 1 aloud at the same time.
- Ask them to read their texts to one another.
- Call on students to read their favorite comparison of the three they have written.
- Assign no Version 2, since the intention of this framework is to experiment with metaphor rather than replicate the mentor text.

7. Share!

- Use sharing time to reinforce learning, commenting on originality of metaphorical comparisons and strong word choices.

Lesson Extension Ideas

- Have students choose their strongest metaphorical comparison and grow it into a short paragraph, perhaps extending the metaphor (see Framework 25: "Extended Metaphor").
- Ask students to use their metaphorical comparison as the beginning of a poem.
- Ask students to illustrate through original art or photographs.
- Turn the comparison into a short video, choosing background music to match the tone of the comparison and a series of visual images.

Sample Stages

Metaphor is more than just dropping the *like* out of a comparison. At its best it is subtle and surprising. This is a writing element for students that takes lots of practice. We developed this framework to help students find success as they experiment with metaphor using a mentor text.

We wrote these with fifth graders in John Koski's class at Dostyk American School in Atyrau, Kazakhstan. Sounds far away? Most of these students were straight out of Houston. But wherever you are in the world, Friday afternoon "is a box filled with fun, waiting to be opened." Well, unless you are in the Middle East where they are on a Sunday through Thursday schedule.

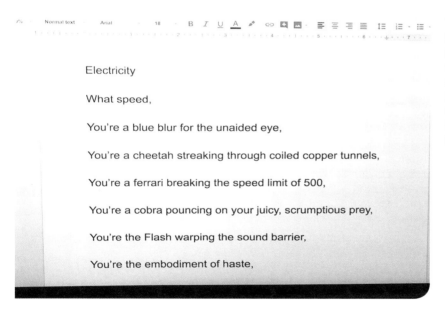

This fifth-grade student, also in John's class, asked if it was okay if he wrote about electricity since most of the other students were writing about emotions. We told him to go for it, and he sure did.

Mentoring Metaphor: Assessment Checkpoint

SKILL	3	2	1
Comparisons	Creates strong images through comparisons and demonstrates originality in choosing comparisons that are appropriate for the subject. Knows the difference between simile and metaphor.	Inconsistently creates strong images through comparisons and demonstrates accuracy in choosing comparisons that are appropriate for the subject. Knows the difference between simile and metaphor.	Does not yet create strong enough images through comparisons and is not yet able to demonstrate originality in choosing comparisons that are appropriate for the subject. May not understand the difference between simile and metaphor.
Structure and Organization	Demonstrates the ability to recognize and re-create a writing structure that includes metaphorical comparisons.	Partially demonstrates the ability to recognize and re-create a writing structure that includes metaphorical comparisons.	Does not yet demonstrate the ability to recognize and re-create a writing structure that includes metaphorical comparisons. Cannot move beyond literal meaning.
Connotative Word Meaning	Demonstrates an understanding of connotative word meanings by making comparisons while using visual language. Metaphor is used creatively and effectively.	Occasionally demonstrates an understanding of connotative word meanings by making comparisons while using visual language. Metaphors don't necessarily clarify the meaning of the text.	Does not yet demonstrate an understanding of connotative word meanings by making comparisons while using visual language.
Speaking Skills	Is willing to share and consistently demonstrates effective presentation skills using good voice projection, inflection, pacing, eye contact, and stance.	Is often willing to share and partially demonstrates effective presentation skills using good voice projection, inflection, pacing, eye contact, and stance.	Is not yet willing to share and/or does not yet demonstrate effective presentation skills using good voice projection, inflection, pacing, eye contact, and stance.
Listening Skills	Actively participates in discussions about other students' work and is tuned in to student presentations.	Occasionally participates in discussions about other students' work and is tuned in to student presentations.	Does not participate in discussions about other students' work and is not yet tuned in to student presentations.

Extended Metaphor: Illuminating Comparisons

TIME: about 45 minutes   **GRADE LEVEL:** 6 and up

MATERIALS:

- Slides 1–4*
- Extended Metaphor GO Sheet*
- Notebooks, computers, or tablets

*Available online at scholastic.com/ThrivingWriterResources

WHY TEACH THIS?

To help students understand extended metaphor by building one.

CONTENT AREA CONNECTIONS: ELA

Persuasive	Descriptive	Narrative	Procedural	Research	Vocabulary	Figurative Language
	X	X				X

PART III: USING LANGUAGE TO LEARN ABOUT SELF

If metaphor is the key in the ignition of deeper thinking, then extended metaphor is the GPS that guides our vehicle to its ultimate destination—clear communication.

Michael: Advertisers use metaphor all the time.

Sara: If I Photoshop a saltshaker to look like a grenade, that means I need less copy to explain that salt can be hazardous to your health. I connect more quickly with my audience.

Michael: Learning how to choose and manipulate metaphor is so much more than simply a poetical pursuit.

Comparison is the backbone of figurative language, and we would dare to say the foundation of communication. Used effectively, a metaphorical comparison gives the writer the power to introduce new subject matter to their reader by activating their reader's background knowledge, by comparing the new information to something the reader already understands. How often do we go into a new situation by asking another who has already experienced it, "What was it like?"

Metaphor is simile's older, more sophisticated sibling. Understanding equivalency is a higher-order thinking skill. When we say that something *is* the equivalent of another figuratively, we highlight the similarities while purposely setting the differences aside for the sake of explanation. We skip the signaling words of *like* or *as*, trusting our readers to identify and understand the comparison.

Metaphor is tricky. Taking a simile and booting the comparison words *like* or *as* technically transforms the phrase into a metaphor—but that's only a toe-dip into a possible river of meaning. By working with an extended metaphor, writers immerse themselves in the flow of comparison.

Sara: Did we just start out in a car and end up in a river? That could be dangerous.

Michael: Yep. Mixed metaphors are a water hazard, all right. We'll get to that in this lesson, as well.

1. Introduce the Framework

Project Slide 1 and read it aloud. If students show any apprehension, tell them to relax. This is going to be fun.

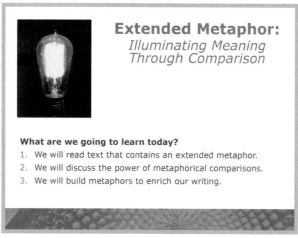

Slide 1

2. Discuss Mentor Text, Version 1

- Project Slide 2 and read it aloud.

- Ask: *What is being compared here?* (an idea and a light bulb) *Does this comparison work? Why? How is this comparison extended throughout the piece?* Ask students to identify the words that relate to a light bulb.

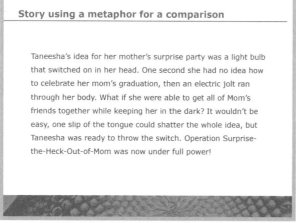

Slide 2

From Striving to Thriving Writers copyright © 2018 by Sara Holbrook, Michael Salinger, and Stephanie Harvey. Published by Scholastic Inc.

3. Build Background Knowledge

- Project Slide 3. As you read aloud the passage this time, encourage students to join in reading the orange words.

- Note that the author of the Taneesha story made a list of things a light bulb does. Conversely, he also listed a couple of things a light bulb does not do. A light bulb suggests illumination; the opposite would be darkness.

How to Build a Metaphor:	Comparison: Light bulb = idea
Comparison Details light filament glass globe electricity switch threaded base fragile shatter **Opposite** darkness shade	Taneesha's idea for her mother's surprise party was a **light bulb** that **switched on** in her head. One second she had no idea how to celebrate her mom's graduation, then an **electric** jolt ran through her body. What if she were able to get all of Mom's friends together while keeping her in the **dark**? It wouldn't be easy, one slip of the tongue could **shatter** the whole idea, but Taneesha was ready to **throw the switch**. Operation Surprise the Heck Out of Mom was now under full **power**!

Slide 3

- Notice that a few of these attributes appeared in the Taneesha story. Not all, just a few. The author brainstormed a broad list of traits and then selected the ones he needed when composing his text.

4. Co-construct Version 1

This is a two-step process. First, we brainstorm some words about a thunderstorm. Second, we brainstorm words to describe a short presentation we orchestrate with a couple of enthusiastic volunteers from the class. Both the thunderstorm and the short presentation illustrate a form of conflict. The thunderstorm is a conflict between a warm and a cold front. The presentation stages an altercation between our two participants. Ultimately, we will use the thunderstorm words to describe the altercation. We will be comparing a conflict between two people by using words that describe a conflict in nature—the thunderstorm. It's an age-old technique. But shh… don't tell the students yet. Check out the sample below (Slide 4) and divide your writing space accordingly.

Thunderstorm Words, Column 1

- Ask students to imagine there is a thunderstorm coming and brainstorm about a dozen words to describe the sky, wind, rain, sounds, and the causes of thunder and lightning, including some verbs (see sample).

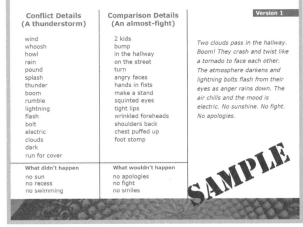

Slide 4

- Include two or three things that do not happen in a storm (sunshine, baseball games, etc.).

- Proceed to column 2.

Event Words, Column 2

- Stage an altercation, an *almost* fight, between two students (see box on page 238 for instructions).

- Ask students exactly what happened before, during, and after the almost fight. Start like a reporter, asking "who, what, when, where" questions. Where were the students' feet? Hands? Shoulders? What were their facial expressions? Collect students' responses in column 2 (see sample).

- Ask what did *not* happen. Jot down two or three responses.

Every good story contains a conflict of some kind. In order to craft our metaphor, we are going to create a conflict for students to write about. A simple scene that will ring familiar. Begin by asking for two volunteers and take them out of earshot of the other students to explain their roles in acting out the scene. Explain that they are to walk toward one another, pass, and lightly brush elbows. Then they are to turn and face off as if they are angry about being bumped. They should barely touch, just a light brush of the elbows. The whole point is that they are going to overreact to what was really no big deal.

No words are needed, just menacing stares and posturing. No chest bumping or other contact, but encourage them to puff up, take a stance, and get in a ready position. They can even raise fists and swirl them in the air, cartoon style. No contact beyond the elbow brush. That's all there is to it and when it is over yell, "Cut!" Applause.

Meantime, ready the rest of the class to observe the scene. Instruct them to watch as if they were reporters and that they are to be very conscious of what they do and do not see happening.

Co-construct, Column 3

- Ask if students could write about a thunderstorm using the words in column 1. Could they write about the almost fight using the words in column 2? Now ask if they could describe the almost fight using the thunderstorm words. Have them turn and talk about some possibilities.

- If necessary, prompt students to get them started. Was there lightning in the conflict? Winds? Rain? Who was involved (dark clouds)? Were there rumblings? Use the words in column 1 as prompts.

- Based on their responses, work with students to craft four or five sentences in column 3, pushing them to use the thunderstorm words as nouns and verbs.

- Use both lists to create one or two lines capturing what did *not* happen.

- When you're finished, read Version 1 aloud, and be prepared to be amazed. Ask students to read it aloud again.

- Explain that this is extended metaphor because thunderstorm words permeate the piece—they start at the beginning and don't stop until the end.

- Point out that the reason the extended metaphor works is because both lists are about a conflict. A thunderstorm is a conflict in nature, and a fight is a conflict between two people.

- Inform students that they will be writing about a personal conflict from their own lives.

- Slide 4 is just an example of the sort of piece this co-construct will create. You will be writing this in real time with your students. What you create will be similar but each time you run this framework, it will vary.

5. Hand Out the GO Sheet

6. Have Students Prewrite

- Instruct students to turn and talk to a neighbor about a conflict in their lives, either recent or from long ago.

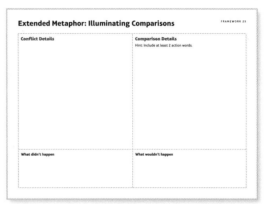

Extended Metaphor GO Sheet

- Remind them that Taneesha's conflict was an internal one, what to do for her mother's graduation. Other conflicts might be more external, such as what to do if your bike gets a flat tire, if your computer crashes, if your basketball coach is unfair, or if you lose the big game. Conflicts between siblings and friends are popular topics. If kids seem stuck, brainstorm ideas. The conflict doesn't need to be epic. We had a kid who wrote a great piece about a conflict with a lawn mower that refused to turn over.

Column 1

- We're going to switch up the order we use to collect our details. In our co-construct we started with the thunderstorm, the well from which we collected our descriptors to become our extended metaphor when we described our altercation (the human conflict). This time we are going to start by describing the human conflict and after that collect our descriptors. We've had success with this flipping—it helps for the students to have their conflict sketched out before we ask them to work more abstractly.

- Walk students through the "who, what, when, where" of their personal conflict by reading the following prompts, one by one, and having them list their responses on the GO Sheet in the column labeled "Conflict Details."

PROMPT LIST

- Who or what was in conflict? Another person? A pickle jar? A doorknob? A computer?

- What was the conflict about? A remote control? Lost Internet connection? Stuck door?

- When was this? Time of day? Time of year? Was it a weekend? Before school?

- Where did it happen? Be specific. Not just "at home." Were you in the kitchen? On the playing field? In the hallway?

- What was on the floor or under the writer's feet? Grass? Hot sand? Stairs?

- What was the light source? Blazing sun? Just the red light from the phone charger? A flickering screen?

- Were there any background noises? Traffic? Children laughing? Music? Screeching tires?

- Were there any odors or fragrances? Popcorn? Sea breeze? Exhaust? Urge them to steer clear of phrases like "smell of fear." Instead, what did that fear smell like?

- What was the temperature? Note: These are the external details.

- Move on to internals: What did you do with your hands? Our actors put their hands in fists. Ask: *Did you jam your hands in your pockets? Fold your arms? Wag a finger?*

- What did you do with your feet? The actors stood their ground. Did you stomp away? Kick a door?

- What happened to your face? Eyes? Mouth?

- Did your stomach tighten? Head hurt? Heart pound?

- Finally ask: *What did not happen? Did you not throw the computer or brother out the window?* (good choice) *Did you not get to go out because you were grounded? Did you not finish your dinner because the table collapsed?*

Column 2

- This is where we build our collection of descriptors that will become our breeding ground for an extended metaphor.

- Ask: *What was this conflict like? Was it fast, like a runaway train? Annoying like a mosquito? Slow like slogging through mud? Or was it like a natural disaster, a wildfire, volcano, earthquake, hurricane?* Tell students to turn, talk, and help one another find a comparison. Finally, ask what would not happen (e.g., a runaway train would not stop, a wildfire would not be quiet).

- Ask them to list eight to 10 words—nouns and verbs—in column 2 that detail the attributes of their comparison idea. Then have them add at least two things that would not happen during the conflict—for instance, recess during a thunderstorm, driving during a flood, sleeping in a room full of mosquitoes.

Storm | thunder
dark | crash
clouds | crackle
wind | growl
howl | rumble
whoosh | barking
blows | lightning
colder | flash
rain | strike
torrent | zigzag
spitting | no sun
balls | no vibrance
pours | no games
panic

2 guys | faced
hood | off
safeway | glare
hallway | sprint
school | jaw
street | clenched
walk | no smiles
toward | no hugs
collide | no words
smirk | no apologies
clenched | no deal
fists
sideways stance
fists up

Darkness glooms as
Two storms approaching
They clash, a low growl of
Belligerence
A flash of menace
Lightning from
Their hearts
Fists clenched into
Weapons about to strike
A crackle of tension
No weapons
No sun
No apologies

7. Have Students Write Their Version 1

- Invite students to spend about 10 minutes drafting a Version 1, using items from columns 1 and 2. They'll likely be ready and anxious to write at this point, brimming with ideas. They may wish to draft in a notebook or on a computer or tablet. Whatever they choose, be sure they keep their GO Sheets at hand for reference.

- Circulate the room offering support to students who need it and reminding them to use details from column 2, their comparison details.

- When they're finished, ask students to read their texts aloud at the same time.

8. Discuss Mentor Text, Version 2

- Project Slide 5 and read it aloud as an example of what writers *shouldn't* do: mix metaphors.

- Ask students to turn and talk about the comparisons in the piece.

- Guide students to understanding that an extended metaphor is more effective than a mixed metaphor.

🚫 Mixed Metaphor

Taneesha's idea for her mother's surprise party went off like a bomb in her head. One second she didn't know what she was going to do to celebrate Mom's graduation and the next her brain flashed a green light. What if she were able to blindfold her mom to the plan? It wouldn't be easy, but Taneesha was ready to jump into the pool. Operation Surprise-the-Heck-Out-of-Mom was an unfolding map.

Slide 5

9. Co-construct Version 2

- Return to the co-constructed Version 1 and have students examine it for any mixed metaphors: comparisons that don't fit the extended metaphor.

- Ask students to offer a couple suggestions for details to add, such as colors, sizes, sound, or other sensory terms. Weave in a couple of their suggestions and relabel the text "Version 2." No need to do a complete revision.

10. Have Students Write Their Version 2

- Instruct the students to go back to their Version 1 and revise it to create their Version 2. Have them start by checking for mixed metaphors unrelated to the extended metaphor. Then have them add details to enrich the text. They should make at least three changes overall.

- Ask them to do a read-aloud periodically to check the fluency of their writing.

11. Share!

- Invite students to share their work with a classmate.

- Ask for volunteers to share with the whole class.

- Understand that students are often writing about intensely personal conflicts; sometimes it may involve a conflict with a student in the room. For this reason, we let students choose if they want to share.

Lesson Extension Ideas

- Have students describe a literary character or a famous person in metaphorical terms. Was the Industrial Revolution like a steamroller? Was Mao's Cultural Revolution like a wildfire? No? What was it like? These discussions lead to deeper insights as writers list details.

- Use the conflict pieces as discussion starters to examine how things could have turned out differently.

- Have students expand their extended metaphors into essays, weave them into a longer work, or pare them down into poems.

PART III: USING LANGUAGE TO LEARN ABOUT SELF

Sample Stages

An extended metaphor is reaching for understanding with a tender filament. Most often when we do this framework with students, they write intensely personal pieces, reflections on conflicts that they may feel they could have handled differently, tough learning experiences, or grave disappointments. We are always a little gentler with these pieces when it comes to sharing.

Misunderstood

A storm driving through
   the door
A bolt of lightning
Spirals in the room
Cycloning Thanes into its arms
Bones snap like broken tree
   branches
He grumbles as Thanes howl
Gusts of bad breath
Booming thunder
All destruction, no peace
Calm,
No malice.

(above) This piece actually came about by writing an extended metaphor about the monster Grendel from *Beowulf*. We used the extended metaphor framework, only this time we did it with a fictional character and conflict.

A gift,
That I was too nervous to open,
Unsure of what would be hidden inside.
I couldn't help but wonder if we'd match up,
Or be forced to say goodbye

Our first encounter,
Just an average day,
Shimmering sunlight,
children chattering,
And teachers twittering,
The whole way.

Making friends is easier than I'd thought,
It's not so hard to talk to people.
As long as I stay content and hopeful,
I am sure that this present will give me,
much more than I ever aspired to be.

(left) An eighth-grade student used the framework to write about arriving at a new school. She beautifully portrays the opportunity of friendship as a gift she was nervous to open.

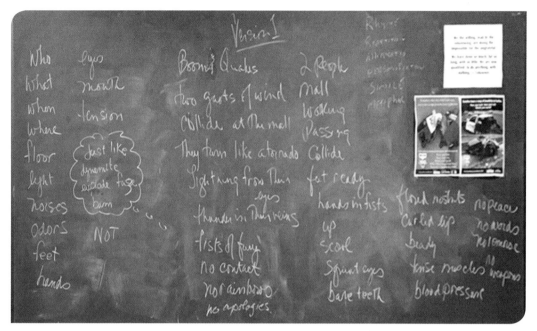

(above) Here is the thunderstorm exercise displayed old school blackboard style.

(right) An extended metaphor Version 2 by an eighth grader at Jakarta Intercultural School. In this tender retelling of the death of her grandmother, the writer compares the impact of the news to drowning. We had suggested that students boldface their metaphorical references to help them strengthen the comparison.

Version 3 of Grandma

Running downstairs, I see my family huddled
Balled up, cocoons of remorse. **Grey.**
No...
Sweat, sobs, searing. The pain is **crushing**
Not letting me breathe. Racked with tears
Helpless. **Can't fight, drowning** in my own breath
Warm arms around mine, binding
And soothing. I am gone, so is she.
Gone
      Gone
            Gone
The **blackness**, the end of the world, **devastation**
Pounding.
Birds outside chirping, light **flooding** the room
Happy.
Everything we are not.

PART III: USING LANGUAGE TO LEARN ABOUT SELF

Extended Metaphor: Assessment Checkpoint

SKILL	3	2	1
Careful Reading	Demonstrates an understanding of the importance of using comparisons to clarify writing. Recognizes extended metaphor and is able to explain why it is appropriate to the subject.	Partially demonstrates an understanding of the importance of using comparisons to clarify writing. May recognize metaphor but cannot discuss how it is extended throughout the text.	Does not yet demonstrate an understanding of the importance of using comparisons to clarify writing. Cannot recognize extended metaphor in text.
Structure and Organization	Demonstrates the ability to recognize and re-create a writing structure that includes metaphorical comparisons. Uses extended metaphor effectively in the piece.	Partially demonstrates the ability to recognize and re-create a writing structure that includes metaphorical comparisons. May use metaphor but may not extend it throughout the piece or may mix metaphors.	Does not yet demonstrate the ability to recognize and re-create a writing structure that includes metaphorical comparisons. Cannot move beyond literal meaning.
Connotative Word Meaning	Demonstrates an understanding of connotative word meanings by making comparisons while using visual language. Extended metaphor is used creatively and effectively.	Occasionally demonstrates an understanding of connotative word meanings by making comparisons while using visual language. Metaphors don't necessarily clarify the meaning of the piece or may not be extended throughout the piece.	Does not yet demonstrate an understanding of connotative word meanings by making comparisons while using visual language. Writing is void of metaphor, extended or otherwise.
Speaking Skills	Is willing to share and consistently demonstrates effective presentation skills using good voice projection, inflection, pacing, eye contact, and stance.	Is often willing to share and partially demonstrates effective presentation skills using good voice projection, inflection, pacing, eye contact, and stance.	Is not yet willing to share and/or does not yet demonstrate effective presentation skills using good voice projection, inflection, pacing, eye contact, and stance.
Listening Skills	Actively participates in discussions about other students' work and is tuned in to student presentations.	Occasionally participates in discussions about other students' work and is tuned in to student presentations.	Does not participate in discussions about other students' work and is not yet tuned in to student presentations.

100% Me: Prioritizing Data

TIME: about 30–45 minutes

GRADE LEVEL: 1 and up

MATERIALS:

- Slides 1–3*
- Notebooks, computers, or tablets

*Available online at scholastic.com/ThrivingWriterResources

WHY TEACH THIS?

To provide an alternative to acrostics, in which everyone is either *excellent* or *awesome*. Students weigh details, prioritizing their importance and producing a much more varied text than an acrostic. We assign specific attributes according to rational importance.

CONTENT AREA CONNECTIONS: Literature, Social Studies, Science, Math

Persuasive	Descriptive	Narrative	Procedural	Research	Vocabulary	Figurative Language
	X			X	X	

PART III: USING LANGUAGE TO LEARN ABOUT SELF

STEPH REFLECTS ON FRAMEWORK 26

When it comes to striving learners, there is nothing more important than getting to know them inside and out so we know how best to respond to their needs and support them where they need it most. To this end, we continuously search for engaging ways for kids to share their thoughts and ideas. 100% Me is yet another exceptional way for kids to present who they are in ways that enable us to gain a deeper understanding and insight into both their strengths and challenges.

No matter what the gym teacher says, you cannot give 110 percent!

We love using this framework for getting to know students. Basically, it is a list of qualities prioritized with percentages. Kids can have fun with it, get out the crayons to illustrate, add a photo, or even convert into a pie chart. After students have mastered the framework, use it to analyze characters in literature, famous people, or even to define subjective terms such as *success* or *friendship*. For younger students, you may want to just co-construct a class text until they gain skills in percentages. For older students, challenge them to use numbers with a decimal point.

Michael: This scaffolds to the preciseness of the percentages.

Sara: As we work and rework the percentages, we are really weighing the importance of evidence.

Unlike the acrostic in which the writer is stuck with the letters of the acronym, in this framework we choose the attributes and then assign them percentages. This creates a more valid assessment of the nuances of a subject.

1. Introduce the Framework

Project Slide 1, read it aloud, and explain that we can describe the qualities of almost anything in terms of percentages. Tell students they are going to write about themselves and then about a person, concept, or object from their studies.

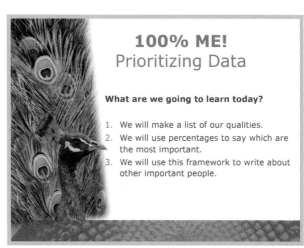

100% ME!
Prioritizing Data

What are we going to learn today?

1. We will make a list of our qualities.
2. We will use percentages to say which are the most important.
3. We will use this framework to write about other important people.

Slide 1

2. Build Background Knowledge

If necessary, review how percentages work and that a whole equals 100 percent.

3. Discuss Mentor Text, Version 1

- Project Slide 2 and read aloud, clarifying any unfamiliar words. Ask: *Which is more important in the author's view, the fact that she has eyebrows or that she has confidence?* Look over the percentages.

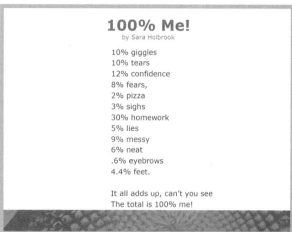

Slide 2

- Be sure students recognize that the last two lines break the language pattern and sum up the author's message, creating a strong conclusion, an important component in any writing we do.

4. Co-construct Version 1

- Ask students to take a good look at you and identify attributes they notice (brown sandals, red shirt, curly hair, big smile) and list three or four of them on the board. Or you can work with attributes of your entire class. (See sample from Katie Lufkin's classroom, below and page 250.)

- After the students have identified a few attributes that they could see, encourage research. Ask students to interview you (siblings? pets? children? favorite food? favorite sport? favorite vacation spots? birthplace?). Add two or three more answers to the list. Hint: About eight items total is plenty to get started.

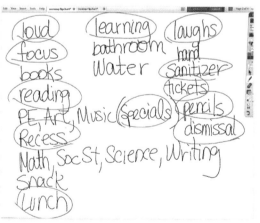

In Katie Lufkin's fourth-grade class, they co-constructed their text about the entire class.
1. They listed attributes of the class.
2. They co-constructed a Version 1.
3. They added a conclusion in Version 2.

From Striving to Thriving Writers copyright © 2018 by Sara Holbrook, Michael Salinger, and Stephanie Harvey. Published by Scholastic Inc.

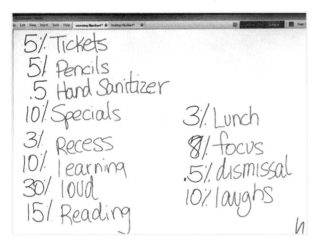

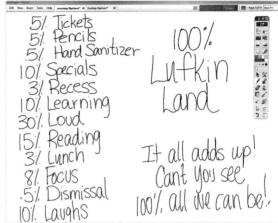

- Ask: *Which is more important, the fact that I like pizza or that I am a parent? What percentage should we give to each?* Limit the time you spend on this, just do a few to model the process. Tell students, in the end, the percentages need to add up to 100.

- Toss around some ideas for a conclusion. Entertain many. Choose one.

5. Have Students Write Their Version 1

- Ask students to turn and talk to a partner for a minute about their interests, facts about themselves, and their likes and dislikes.

- Ask students to label their papers "Version 1" and make a list of eight to 10 attributes about themselves.

- When their lists are complete, ask them to begin to assign percentages. Encourage them to use pencils because they'll undoubtedly need to make changes!

- Ask students to read aloud their Version 1 at the same time.

- Direct them to add a strong conclusion, one or two lines that break the language pattern. A strong "I" statement works: *I am creative, I'm not lazy,* and *I'm a little crazy.*

- Ask students to share their Version 1 with a classmate.

Katie Lufkin's grade 4 students list their attributes for Version 1.

Lufkin's students stand to share their Version 1 aloud.

6. Discuss Mentor Text, Version 2

- Project Slide 3 and read it aloud with the class. You should read the black words and students should read the red words, which have been added.

- Ask: *What do the added details do for the text? What other details might the author have added?*

7. Co-construct Version 2

- Return to your co-constructed Version 1 and, with students' help, add one or two attributes about you (your favorite color, your dog's name) and/or details to attributes already in place.

- Note that this co-construct is a work in progress, but that these revisions help.

8. Have Students Write Their Version 2

- Ask students to relabel their text "Version 2" and add attributes and/or details to the attributes in place.

- When they're finished, ask students to read their Version 2 at the same time. How does it sound? Does it need more work?

9. Share!

- Use as a getting-to-know-you writing lesson at the beginning of the year.

- Have students share with a partner, then share with another partner, and then take turns sharing before the class.

- Ask listeners: *What have we learned about Zoe?*

Lesson Extension Ideas

- Have students illustrate their personal characteristic lists with crayons or photos.

- Use this framework for character analysis or a study of important people and events.

- Ask students to present their information as a pie chart or graph for visual understanding.

- Post work in the hallways. Walls and halls teach!

100% Me!
by Sara Holbrook

10% all over giggles
10% quiet tears
12% confidence
8% shivering fears,
2% pizza
3% sighs
30% homework
5% lies
9% messy when it comes to my room
6% neat
.6% eyebrows
4.4% feet.

It all adds up, can't you see
The total is 100% me!

Slide 3

Content Area Extension Ideas

- See a mentor text below that Michael wrote about a firefighter (Slides 4 and 5). Students could create a percentage list about a person or event related to your unit of study. If your unit of study is, for instance, community helpers, you may wish to have students each choose a different community helper to research and write about.

- If you are reading a shared piece of literature or students are reading in book clubs, have students complete the framework about main characters.

- If you are studying an event such as the civil rights movement (see Slides 6 and 7 on Rosa Parks), renewable energy, or hurricanes, have students choose people or events related to your unit of study.

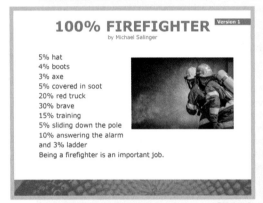

Slide 4

Slide 5

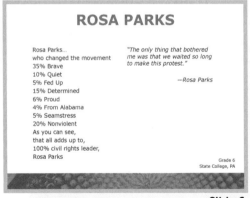

Slide 6

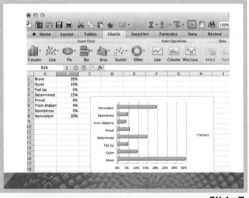

Slide 7

Bar chart based on the Rosa Parks Percentage text from State College, PA. Librarian: Dotty Delafield

Sample Stages

A student told us once that he was 100% skateboard. We've met kids who considered themselves 100% gaming, or music, or any number of passions. It isn't until we begin to talk it out that they begin to see themselves as a little bit pizza, a percentage of giggles, or 2.2 percent hiccups. Looking at any person (or thing) in terms of percentages gives us a more complete picture of the whole.

(above) A fourth grader from Katie Lufkin's class begins by making a list of her attributes.

(right) Students begin sharing with a partner.

Students learn about one another sharing in small groups.

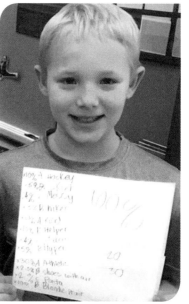

100% Me!

PART III: USING LANGUAGE TO LEARN ABOUT SELF

100% Me: Assessment Checkpoint

SKILL	3	2	1
Knowledge of Percentages	Demonstrates a working knowledge of how to apply percentages of a whole.	Partially demonstrates a working knowledge of how to apply percentages of a whole.	Is not yet able to apply percentages of a whole.
Character Traits	Demonstrates the ability to detail character traits including internal and external qualities that contribute to a character description.	Partially demonstrates the ability to detail character traits including internal and external qualities that contribute to a character description.	Is not yet able to identify character traits, either internal or external qualities that contribute to a character description.
Prioritizing Information	Demonstrates the ability to logically prioritize information according to importance as evidenced by assigned percentages.	Inconsistently demonstrates the ability to logically prioritize information according to importance as evidenced by assigned percentages.	Is not yet able to demonstrate an ability to logically prioritize information according to importance as evidenced by assigned percentages.
Speaking Skills	Is willing to share and consistently demonstrates effective presentation skills using good voice projection, inflection, pacing, eye contact, and stance.	Is often willing to share and partially demonstrates effective presentation skills using good voice projection, inflection, pacing, eye contact, and stance.	Is not yet willing to share and/or does not yet demonstrate effective presentation skills using good voice projection, inflection, pacing, eye contact, and stance.
Listening Skills	Actively participates in discussions about other students' work and is tuned in to student presentations.	Occasionally participates in discussions about other students' work and is tuned in to student presentations.	Does not participate in discussions about other students' work and is not yet tuned in to student presentations.

From Striving to Thriving Writers copyright © 2018 by Sara Holbrook, Michael Salinger, and Stephanie Harvey. Published by Scholastic Inc.

Scaffolding Into Sharing

TIME: about 45 minutes

GRADE LEVEL: K and up

MATERIALS:

- Slides 1–7*
- A piece of practice text on paper that students can use for repeated reading, ideally something he or she has written

*Available online at scholastic.com/ThrivingWriterResources

WHY TEACH THIS?

1. To strengthen students' abilities to speak with confidence and conviction.

2. To build their public speaking skills, whether they're speaking to an audience of one or hundreds.

CONTENT AREA CONNECTIONS: ELA or any subject where oral presentation skills can use bolstering.

Persuasive	Descriptive	Narrative	Procedural	Research	Vocabulary	Figurative Language
X					X	

Public speaking has been cited in many studies as being the number one fear of mankind—a ranking more terrifying than death.

Sara: This leads to an old Jerry Seinfeld joke.

Michael: Right. Most people would rather be in the box than delivering the eulogy.

Sara: A bit grim, but apparently true. The fear even has a name: *glossophobia*.

We define public speaking as anything said aloud to an audience of one or more. One leg of our three-legged stool of communication—reading, writing, and speaking—this invaluable skill is, unfortunately, often given short shrift in classrooms. Too often it is relegated to the back of the school year, after the tests.

Public speaking can't be graded by a bubble reader, and since it is not part of statewide assessments, too often it is dropped from the curriculum entirely. Beyond that, it is often viewed as difficult to assess in general. That fact is compounded by the reality that it's hard to entice reluctant speakers out of their shells, especially if their hesitancy has already been rewarded by years of sincere if unproductive empathy.

Too often oral presentation is tacked onto a lesson as an afterthought—or the more panic-inducing final component of a research project requiring the student to stand in front of his or her peers shuffling index cards.

Good news! Fear of public speaking *and* fear of teaching public speaking can both be overcome.

We want our students to be able to look someone in the eye and speak with conviction. What better place than the safe space of our classroom to provide the practice for our kids to find their voices?

This is why every framework includes spoken elements. We scaffold kids from everyone reading aloud at the same time—getting used to the sounds of their own voices—to sharing with partners, to sharing in front of the class. We always like to have the kids stand when reading aloud. This adds just a tiny bit of formality to the act—a bit of ritual denoting some importance. Just as the writing frameworks are designed to be short texts that later can be combined or grown into more complex works, their presentation offers opportunities for mini performances. Typically, 10 to 30 seconds and the reader is done. We're building stamina for longer renditions by practicing sprints.

We are building a culture of thoughtful conversation.

The following framework, while not guaranteed to chase away all the butterflies, will quantify the main components of successful public speaking into five easy-to-assess features. Students should all have a text in front of them with which to practice. They each need to have different texts—something they have recently written themselves is a good choice but not mandatory. We just don't want them all having the same script—otherwise it becomes a choral reading rather than an exercise in individual speaking.

1. Introduce the Framework

- Project Slide 1 and discuss the importance of being able to speak with conviction.

- Have each student make two fists, raise them, and shout, "Conviction!" Do this a couple of times.

- Ask: *When might a person need to speak with conviction?* (Talking with adults, asking for a favor from Mom or Dad, during an oral presentation, while lobbying for an extended curfew.)

2. Build Background Knowledge

- Project Slide 2, introduce the acronym PIPES, and have students write it down for future reference. Tell them you will go through the letters and words one at a time: **P**rojection, **I**nflection, **P**acing, **E**ye contact, and **S**tance. These are the skills public speakers require to speak well.

- Explain that public speaking is not acting because the speaker generally does not assume a dramatic role— the speaker is speaking for and as him- or herself.

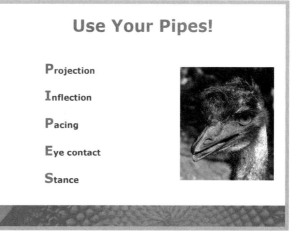

Slide 1

Slide 2

3. Discuss Projection: Speaking at the Right Volume

- Project Slide 3 and explain that there is no quicker way to public-speaking disaster than not being heard. One common complaint we hear from students is, "No one listens to me." Kids, like the rest of us, want to be heard, and the first step in accomplishing that, of course, is speaking loudly enough.

Projection

1. Stand tall and smile.

2. Remember: Projecting is not screaming.

3. Practice: *I can't take it anymore.*

4. Remember: The audience *wants* to hear you.

Hint: It is impossible to project your voice and be slumped over like this koala.

Slide 3

- Select two enthusiastic volunteers, but keep in mind, enthusiasm is relative. Generally we find our best "volunteers" for this drill are those who don't make eye contact. Because we want to show that anyone can learn to project, a couple of soft-spoken participants usually do nicely.

- Ask your two participants to stand facing one another about three feet apart, as if engaged in conversation.

- Instruct each one to take turns saying, "I can't take it anymore" loud enough for the listener to hear him or her, but not so loud that it's uncomfortable to the listener.

- Ask them to take two big steps back from one another and repeat the phrases— a bit louder this time, but not louder than necessary.

- Continue this process until the two participants are across the room from one another. Be sure to monitor them so that they are projecting and not yelling.

- Explain to the whole class that the participants found just the right volume to project to the entire room.

- Ask all students to pair up with a partner and do the same exercise, all at once. Again, monitor that pairs are projecting, not yelling.

- Once everyone is all the way across the room from one another, get them to stop and stay in place. Warning: Not always easy!

- Call on each pair to perform the lines. If you are satisfied with their projection, if they're loud enough to be heard but not yelling, ask them to return to their seats.

- Instruct students to turn to their text, sit up straight, and read it aloud with good projection, all at the same time. This will be quite cacophonous! Bathe in the dulcet tones of your students' voices.

- Ask students to remember the physical feeling of projecting—how it resonates within them.

- Reinforce that as much as speakers want to be heard, listeners want to be able to hear.

4. Discuss Inflection: Speaking With Expression

- Project Slide 4 and explain that inflection is the tone of voice one gives to his or her spoken words, and the extent to which he or she emphasizes those words. When we are asked to read with more emotion or feeling, we are being asked to use inflection.

- Write or project on the board a sentence for students to use to practice inflection. We have had good luck with the sentence, "I really like your sister," which invariably elicits chuckles.

Slide 4

- Ask students to repeat the sentence in unison.

- Ask them to repeat it, but this time emphasize the word *I* a bit. *I* really like your sister.

- Follow by having them repeat the sentence, this time emphasizing the word *really*. I *really* like your sister.

- Next, *your*. I really like *your* sister.

- Lastly, change the period to a question mark. I really like your sister?

- Discuss how changing inflection changes the way our listeners interpret what we are saying. We influence our audience not only with the words we choose to say, but also with the way we say those words.

- Instruct students to look at their practice text and to select a few words to emphasize in the first couple of lines.

- Have them read aloud their lines in unison with good projection, adding the inflection to their chosen words.

- Ask students to repeat this a couple of times, but select different words each time.

- End by pointing out how inflection makes public speaking more interesting because speakers emphasize passages that they believe will be most important to their audience.

5. **Discuss Pacing: Speaking at the Correct Speed**

- Project Slide 5 and explain that *pacing* is the cadence we use when we speak—the speed, the pauses, and the articulation we use. Tell students that one of the common mistakes newcomers to public speaking make is talking too fast. The sooner they get over it, the better.

Pacing

1. Slow down!

2. Practice reading fast and slow, then choose the right speed.

3. Speak no faster than you can say the word **articulate.**

Hint: Don't speed up at the end in order to get it over with. Slow and steady wins the race!

Slide 5

- Inform students that the larger our audience, the slower our pace should be.

- Ask students to repeat crisply the word *articulate* a few times to get the juices flowing. Then assure them that speaking at the correct pace may feel a little unnatural at first, but it becomes more natural with practice.

- Say: *This is the correct speed for an audience this size* at a deliberate pace. Then invite students to say it with you at the same pace, in unison. Repeat three or four times.

- Ask students to read their rehearsal texts silently and then read them aloud in unison, with good projection and inflection, but as quickly as they can.

- Ask students to read their texts again, again with good projection and inflection, but this time in slow motion.

- Remind them of the "This is the correct speed for an audience of this size" pace and instruct them to read their texts at that speed.

- Ask students to build a few deliberate pauses into their readings. We like to say, "The important thing about a pause is…" and then stop and wait until every eye in the room is on us. Then we continue, "…it gets everyone's attention."

- Discuss how a few pauses give the audience time to digest the words and break up our cadence so it doesn't become monotonous.

- Instruct students to read their texts again at a good pace, this time building in a few opportunities to pause. They may want to annotate their text with a slash to indicate where the pauses are inserted.

6. **Discuss Eye Contact: Connecting With Your Audience**

- Project Slide 6 and explain that our eyes are powerful. Where the speaker's eyes go, the audience's eyes follow. Therefore, we don't want to throw that power away by looking at our toes, the ceiling, or the most disastrous place of all, over the heads of audience members.

- Explain that our eyes are the laser pointer for our voices. Our voices will point in the same direction as our eyes.

- Note that making eye contact as we speak signals immediacy and importance to our audience. It signals that we are interested in them and therefore deserving of their interest in return. Instead of staring at our page ignoring our audience, we look them in the eye creating a human bond.

- Tell students that the easiest way to make eye contact is to have memorized whatever we are presenting, but this is not always practical. So, some strategies for reading from the page can be useful.

  - Always work from a clean copy. We often format our texts specifically for performance. We use word-processed copy, rather than handwritten copy, in a large font size.

  - Formatting the copy into two columns, rather than paragraphs stretching across a whole page, is another tip that makes reading from the page easier.

  - Following along with a thumb helps us return to the correct spot if our eyes depart from the page.

  - Treat the page as if it were a plate, and the words are loose upon it. We do not hold it in front of our faces like mirror.

  - A deliberate pace also helps in making eye contact—speed kills.

- Have students stand with their texts and practice making eye contact with you as they read. Instruct them to memorize one phrase that they're confident they can deliver while looking you in the eye, no matter where you are in the room. Then have them deliver it.

- Move about the room as students read and encourage them to notice your location in order to make eye contact.

Eye Contact

1. Your eyes are powerful.
2. Connect with individuals in your audience.
3. Look up from the page frequently. If you can't look up, slow down!

Hint: The audience will follow your eyes left, right, up, or down. Use them wisely!

Slide 6

7. Discuss Stance: Positioning Yourself for Speaking

- Project Slide 7 and explain that stance is what we do with our bodies in front of an audience.

- Newcomers to public speaking need to be aware of distracting body movements.

- Ask students what nervous habits they have noticed in people speaking publicly (shifting from foot to foot, twirling their hair, playing with their clothes, tapping their feet).

Stance

1. Plant your feet shoulder-width apart.
2. Use natural gestures that help explain your message.
3. Don't fidget or flap your papers around.

Hint: Avoid movements that draw focus away from your message.

Slide 7

PART III: USING LANGUAGE TO LEARN ABOUT SELF

- Instruct students to stand with their feet shoulder-width apart, and have them make sure they don't lock their knees. The knees are the body's natural shock absorbers, so locking them increases the tension the body and can lead to noticeable shaking in the rest of the body.

- Instruct students to perform their practice text with a solid but relaxed stance. The first time through, ask them to keep their entire body still, remembering to use good projection, inflection, pacing, and eye contact. The next time through, let them free up one arm to help convey meaning. Remember, when we are starting out with public speaking, we want to control any unproductive movement.

8. Allow Time to Rehearse

- Ask a volunteer to read his or her practice text to the class.

- Ask the rest of the class to pay attention to the speaker's PIPES.

- After the speaker has read his or her piece for 30 seconds to a minute, stop him or her and ask the class to state which skill was executed best: projection, inflection, pacing, eye contact, or stance? No matter how new someone is to public speaking, he or she will exhibit one of those skills better than the others. We assure you.

- After deciding which PIPES skill the speaker did best, ask the class to decide which of the remaining skills could use the most improvement. Then ask the speaker to read again, paying special attention to that skill.

- Have students partner up and stand four feet apart to practice reading their texts and then assessing one another, as modeled. Which skill is on track, which could use more attention?

- Inform them that they can use PIPES as a rubric when self-assessing and helping one another prepare for presentations.

Lesson Extension Ideas

- Integrate PIPES as a continual part of your classroom conversation.

- Let students introduce visiting speakers.

- Choose students to read school-wide announcements from the office.

- Bring a milk carton to class and invite students to take turns "spouting off." It's a proud American tradition!

- Plan a poetry reading or coffeehouse. Invite parents, and ask them to bring in one of their favorite poems to read.

Scaffolding Into Sharing: Assessment Checkpoint

SKILL	3	2	1
Projection	Demonstrates the ability to speak with proper projection for the audience. Is not too loud or too soft. All words are heard by all audience members.	Partially demonstrates the ability to speak with proper projection for the audience. May trail off at the end of lines or may be too loud once or twice during recitation.	Is either too quiet to be heard or too loud to be understood.
Inflection	Demonstrates the ability to use pitch and dynamics in a way that enhances the audience's understanding of the text being spoken.	Partially demonstrates the ability to use pitch and dynamics while reciting a piece. May fall into a sing-song or inappropriately emphasize a word.	Does not demonstrate the ability to use pitch and dynamics while reciting a piece. Reading is monotone or full of inappropriately emphasized words.
Pacing	Demonstrates the ability to control pace, using pauses effectively and articulating all words to enhance the audience's understanding of the text being spoken.	Partially demonstrates the ability to control pacing, pauses, and articulation. May perform portions of text either too fast or too slow. May miss an opportunity to use a pause for dramatic effect.	Is unable to demonstrate the ability to control pacing, pauses, or articulation. Speed reads through text or loses place several times when reading from the page.
Eye Contact	Demonstrates the ability to make eye contact across the whole audience and to create a feeling of conversation with listeners.	Occasionally demonstrates the ability to make eye contact with the audience. May only occasionally look up from text.	Does not demonstrate the ability to make eye contact with audience. Never looks up from the page, or stares off into space.
Stance	Consistently demonstrates effective stance. Does not display any distracting movements and adds to the audience's understanding of the piece by using appropriate body language.	Partially demonstrates effective stance. May display a distracting or cliché movement or two.	Does not demonstrate effective stance. Movements during recitation are distracting or disconnected from text being spoken.

Use Your Voice

BY SARA HOLBROOK AND MICHAEL SALINGER

Are you in fear of retribution
from a boss or institution?
Need a stay of execution?
Use your voice!

Have you had it up to here?
Don't choke up on fear.
Take a piece out of an ear—
Use your voice!

Have you been misunderstood?
Mumbling does no good.
You know that you should—
Use your voice!

Your vocal chords aren't broken,
Time to be outspoken.
Don't anticipate rejection.
Use inflection and projection.
Pontificate!
Articulate!

Be loud.
Be proud.
Stand tall.
Speak clear.
So everyone can hear.
There's no need to fear.
It's all up to you,
It's your choice.

To be forgot or got.
Use your voice.

Closing Thought

It's a long path that students are on to find their voices, but it doesn't have to be a lonely one. Writing with purpose is to compose and speak with conviction—the conviction that writers know their subject and can manage the intricacies and rhythm of English language to express their understanding. And then, too, that they can develop their ideas through conversation and collaboration, turning knowledge into well-articulated text and speech. We want students to use the framework strategies described in this book to support their diverse academic, personal, and professional communication needs as they step out to speak for themselves.

ACKNOWLEDGMENTS

Thank you to Steph Harvey, for your friendship, your wise guidance, and for being an enthusiastic partner throughout this project and over the years. We are beyond grateful for your support. Our editor, Lois Bridges, took a proposal in the form of an infographic and sold the idea to Scholastic. Your confidence and depth of knowledge have no bounds. Many thanks. Thank you, Kylene Beers, for generously talking at length to guide us to the term "writing frameworks." We feel smarter just being around you people. Thank you to Stevie Quate, Laura Lynn Benson, and Nancy Johnson for answering panicked and/or pedagogical questions no matter the time zone.

Thank you to our teacher friends who generously invited us into their classrooms and supplied samples to share in order to help other educators discover new ways to teach writing. Particularly, thank you to Katie Lufkin and Dawn Neely-Randall for collecting all those permissions and for your invaluable input. Thank you to Libbie Royko for the many times we invited ourselves into your class to test out new lessons. To all of our friends abroad, to Karen McDowell, Scott Riley, and Scott Townley at Singapore American School, to our go-to grammar queen, Rebecca Clark, and Betsy Hall, whose wisdom is also embedded in these pages. To Lee Ann Spillane, wherever you are in the world. To Bick McSwiney and the library staff at Shanghai American School, Barbara and Tim Boyer, Kimbra Powers, Kathy Lynch, Beth Rohrbeck, and Marie Slaby for inviting us for long stays where we could have repeated visits with the same classes. Thank you to Laura Fishman for sharing classroom artifacts from Shanghai and Abu Dhabi, and to Bridget Suvansri and all the sixth-grade ELA teachers at Eastern Middle School in Connecticut for having us return to try new strategies with your students. Thank you to our friends at Kirtland Elementary School in our own backyard and to Richard and Colleen Boerner and Heather Pillar and Tom Pado for inviting us to Korea, Bangladesh, and Brazil. Thank you to Terry Maguire and Dana Olson for late night talks on theory in Lusaka, Zambia. Much gratitude to Seamus and Theresa Marriott of Shanghai, China; Cairo, Egypt; Balikpapan, Indonesia; and Atyrau, Kazakhstan. Fair to say, we would follow you anywhere. Thank you to Lisa Levi at the American School of Chennai and to Jeremy Willette for extending the invitation. Thank you to Larry Dane Brimner for lending us your words from *Four Days in May,* and to Rita, Lyle, and Jordan Moltzan for the photo of Jordan and for all the good memories from Sumatra and Nigeria. Thank you to Catherine Hodgson of Jakarta Intercultural School as well as Jenn Hopp and Chris Rose, who helped keep this book current 'til the final edit, and to Dianne and John Salminen of Jakarta, Abu Dhabi, and Nansha, China, for turning your libraries into a classroom on repeated visits. Add to this list the many teachers and librarians who have welcomed us into their classrooms at home and abroad. Thank you.

We can't say enough about the Scholastic staff: Ray Coutu, your insightful editorial guidance shaped this book, and we are so grateful. Thank you to Sarah Longhi, Danny Miller, Molly Bradley, Shelley Griffin, Brian LaRossa, and Maria Lilja for lending your talents to this book.

This is a compilation of our greatest hits from previous books along with all-new applications and many new ideas. Thank you to Boyds Mills Press, Calkins Creek Press, Red Giant Press, and Heinemann.

Thank you to our children, Franklin Salinger and Taylor Miller, for keeping our home safe, and to Kelly Weist and Max Salinger for helping us feel closer to home when we're far away.

REFERENCES

Afflerbach, P., Pearson, D., & Paris, S. G. (2008). Clarifying differences between reading skills and reading strategies. *The Reading Teacher, 61*(5), 364–373.

Allington, R. L., & Gabriel, R. E. (2012). Every child, every day. *Educational Leadership, 69*(6), 10–15.

Allington, R. L. (2002). What I've learned about effective reading instruction from a decade of studying exemplary elementary classroom teachers. *Phi Delta Kappan, 83*(10).

Atwell, N. (2016). *The reading zone: How to help kids become passionate, skilled, habitual, critical readers* (2nd ed.). New York: Scholastic.

Beck, I. L., McKeown, M. G., & Kucan, L. (2013). *Bringing words to life: Robust vocabulary instruction* (2nd ed). New York: Guilford Press.

Borrero, N. & Bird, S. (2009). *Closing the achievement gap: How to pinpoint student strengths to differentiate instruction and help your striving readers succeed.* New York: Scholastic.

Brimmer, L. D. (2016). *Four days in May.* Honesdale, PA: Calkins Creek Press, A Highlights Company.

Chapman University Survey of American Fears (2017). https://www.chapman.edu/wilkinson/research-centers/babbie-center/survey-american-fears.aspx

Chouinard, M.; Harris, P.; & Maratsos, M. (2007). Children's questions: A mechanism for cognitive development. *Monographs of the society for research in child development, 72*(1). i, v, vii-ix, 1–129.

Daniels, H. S. A., & Daniels, E. (2013). *The best-kept teaching secret: How written conversations engage kids, activate learning, grow fluent writers. . . K–12.* Thousand Oaks, CA: SAGE Publications.

Dickinson, D. K., & Smith, M. W. (1994). Long-term effects of preschool teachers' book readings on low-income children's vocabulary and story comprehension. *Reading Research Quarterly, 29*(2).

Dorfman, L. (2013). Reading, writing, and mentor texts: Imagining possibilities. *National Writing Project.* Retrieved from https://www.nwp.org/cs/public/print/resource/4090?x-print_friends

Duke, N. K., & Cartwright, K. B. (2018). The DRIVE model of reading: Deploying reading in varied environments. To appear in D. E. Alvermann, N. Unrau, & M. Sailors (Eds.). *Theoretical models and processes of reading* (7th ed.). Abingdon, UK: Routledge.

Duke, N. (2018, March 24). Response: "A powerful purpose propels effective student collaboration" [Blog post]. EdWeek. Retrieved from http://blogs.edweek.org/teachers/classroom_qa_with_larry_ferlazzo/2018/03/response_a_powerful_purpose_propels_effective_student_collaboration.html

Duke, N., Pearson, D., Strachan, S., & Billman, A. (2011). Essential elements of fostering and teaching reading comprehension. In J. Samuels & A. Farstrup (Eds.), *What research has to say about reading instruction* (4th ed.). Newark, DE: International Reading Association.

Dweck, C. (2014). The power of believing that you can improve. TED Talks. Retrieved from https://www.ted.com/talks/carol_dweck_the_power_of_believing_that_you_can_improve

Echevarria, J., and Goldenberg, C. (2017). *Second language learners' vocabulary and oral language development.* International Literacy Association.

Fletcher, R. (2017). *The writing teacher's companion: Embracing choice, voice, purpose, and play.* New York: Scholastic.

García, E. (2010). *Education and achievement: A focus on Latino "immigrant" children.* New York: The Urban Institute.

Halliday, M. A. K. (2004). Three aspects of children's language development: Learning language, learning through language, learning about language. In J. Webster (Ed.). *The language of early childhood, 4 (Collected works of MAK Halliday).* New York: Continuum, 308–366.

Harvey, S. (2014). First lines and the power of books. In L. Bridges (Ed.). *Open a world of possible: The joy and pleasure of reading*. New York: Scholastic.

Harvey, S., & Goudvis, A. (2013). Comprehension at the core. *The Reading Teacher, 66*(6), 432–439.

Harvey, S., & Ward, A. (2017). *From striving to thriving: How to grow confident, capable readers*. New York: Scholastic.

Holbrook, S. (1997). Poet as patriot? *The Journal of Children's Literature, 23*(2), 42–46.

Holbrook, S. (2000). *Wham! It's a poetry jam.* Honesdale, PA: Boyds Mills Press.

Holbrook, S. (2016, April 3). Involve hesitant writers in co-creating text. *MiddleWeb*. Retrieved from https://www.middleweb.com/29063/involve-hesitant-writers-in-co-creating-text/

Holbrook, S. (2017). *The Enemy: Detroit, 1954*. Honesdale, PA: Calkins Creek Press, A Highlights Company.

Holbrook, S., & Salinger, M. (2006). *Outspoken! How to improve writing and speaking skills through poetry performance*. Portsmouth, NH: Heinemann.

Holbrook, S., & Salinger, M. (2010). *High definition: Unforgettable vocabulary-building strategies across genres and subjects*. Portsmouth, NH: Heinemann.

Hurlow, M. (2014, February 25). The wrong way to teach grammar. *The Atlantic*. Retrieved from https://www.theatlantic.com/education/archive/2014/02/the-wrong-way-to-teach-grammar/284014/

Isaacson, I. (2017). *Leonardo da Vinci*. New York: Simon & Schuster.

Johnston, P. H. (2004). *Choice words: How our language affects children's learning*. Portland, ME: Stenhouse.

Johnston, P. H. (2012). *Opening minds: Using language to change lives*. Portland, ME: Stenhouse Publishers.

King, S. (2010). *On writing: A memoir of the craft*. New York: Scribner.

Klein, A. F., & Afflerbach, P. (2018). *Whole-group reading instruction*. New Rochelle, NY: Benchmark Education Company.

Koch, K. (1974). *Wishes, lies, and dreams; Teaching children to write poetry*. Spoken Arts, SAC 6107–6108.

Lewison, M., Leland, C., and Harste, J. (2015). *Creating critical classrooms: Reading and writing with an edge*. New York: Routledge.

Ohanian, S. (2012). Against obedience. *Critical Education, 3*(9). Retrieved from https://www.scribd.com/document/156591152/Critical-Education-Against-Obedience-Susan-Ohanian

O'Hara, C. (2014, July 30). How to tell a great story. *Harvard Business Review*. Retrieved from https://hbr.org/2014/07/how-to-tell-a-great-story

Pearson, P. D., & Gallagher, M. C. (1983). The instruction of reading comprehension. *Contemporary Educational Psychology, 8*(3), 327–324.

Rasinski, T. (2018). *The megabook of fluency: Strategies and texts to engage all readers*. New York, NY: Scholastic.

Robinson, K. (2006). Do schools kill creativity? TED Talks. Retrieved from ted.com/talks/ken_robinson_says_schools_kill_creativity

Salinger, M. (2009). *Well defined: Vocabulary in rhyme*. Honesdale, PA: Wordsong.

Salinger, M. (2016, April 15). Why you should teach public speaking. *Corwin Connect*. Retrieved from http://corwin-connect.com/2016/04/teach-public-speaking/

Salinger, M. (2016, July 13). How we use writing to make learning visible. *Corwin Connect*. Retrieved from http://corwin-connect.com/2016/07/use-writing-make-learning-visible/

Serafini, F., & Gee, E. (2017). *Remixing multiliteracies: Theory and practice from New London to new times*. New York, NY: Teachers College Press.

Su, T. (Ed.). (2009, January 1). CU-Boulder researchers show why peer discussion improves student performance on 'Clicker' questions. *Colorado University Boulder Today*. Retrieved from https://www.colorado.edu/today/2009/01/01/cu-boulder-researchers-show-why-peer-discussion-improves-student-performance-clicker

Vezzali, L., Stathi, S., Giovannini, D., Capozza, D., & Trifiletti, E. (2014). The greatest magic of Harry Potter: Reducing prejudice. *Journal of Applied Social Psychology, 45*(2), 105–121.

Family Literacy Workshop

Ever say, "That was so good, we should have written that down?" Here's an idea! Buy a blank book (it doesn't have to be anything fancy) and begin by jotting down some notes. What's more important than the story of your family? Add a photo, or better yet, a couple of the kids' drawings. It's as easy as that. Here are three ideas using three of the frameworks to get you started.

1. **Using Framework 3: Picture This,** make a word picture about a time, place, or thing. This can be about a trip to the zoo, the beach, grandma's house, or whatever you want to write about. Use the framework as a guide, and remember, use facts, not opinions. Don't say, "The weather was yucky," say, "It rained all day." This will help preserve the memory. Here is a page from Sara's family journal, which she made with her girls when they were young. You can approximate their ages from their artwork. It is a poem, but it began with a simple list of observations.

2. **Refer to Framework 4: Pinpointing Vocabulary** to examine words. Begin again with lists, this time a list of what is and what is not true about a word such as *family*. Here is an example that we wrote recently with parents at Jakarta Intercultural School. Use all of your senses. Does family taste like grandma's chicken? Does it sound like Uncle Ned's laugh? Don't stop there, try other words such as *hope*, *happiness*, and *resilience*.

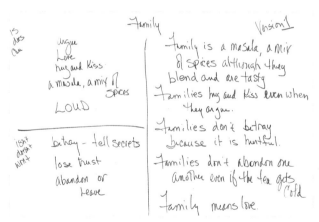

3. **Using Framework 13: Wonder of Wonders,** make a list of your kids' questions (and throw in some of your own). Kids love to ask questions, and here you can record some of their doozies. Read Michael's poem, "Where Does the Sky Begin?" as a guide. You can list questions about an upcoming move, a trip to the science museum, the first day of school, and so on. Have kids illustrate with drawings rather than photos. It will give you a window into their thinking.

INDEX